GERMAN POLICE

GERMAN POLICE

Ideals and Reality in the Post-War Years

By

ERIKA S. FAIRCHILD

*Department of Political Science
and Public Administration
North Carolina State University
Raleigh, North Carolina*

CHARLES C THOMAS · PUBLISHER
Springfield · Illinois · U.S.A.

Published and Distributed Throughout the World by

CHARLES C THOMAS • PUBLISHER

2600 South First Street

Springfield, Illinois 62794-9265

© *1988 by* CHARLES C THOMAS • PUBLISHER

ISBN 0-398-05437-1

Library of Congress Catalog Card Number: 87-31217

With THOMAS BOOKS *careful attention is given to all details of manufacturing
and design. It is the Publisher's desire to present books that are satisfactory as to their
physical qualities and artistic possibilities and appropriate for their particular use.*
THOMAS BOOKS *will be true to those laws of quality that assure a good name
and good will.*

Printed in the United States of America
Q-R-3

Library of Congress Cataloging in Publication Data

Fairchild, Erika.
    German police: ideals and reality in the post-war
years/by Erika S. Fairchild.
        p.   cm.
    Bibliography: p.
    Includes index.
    ISBN 0-398-05437-1
    1. Police — Germany (West) — History. I. Title.
HV8207.F35   1988   87-31217
363.2'0943 — dc19   CIP

To David, Karen, and Laura

INTRODUCTION

THIS BOOK is about the organization, history, and problems of police in the Federal Republic of Germany. The focus is on the postwar police although within the perspective of the totality of Twentieth Century German police history.

Among Americans the German police is stereotyped in two ways. Popularly, and reinforced by countless films, television shows, and written accounts, this organization is still identified in many minds with the police apparatus of the Third Reich, which has become a symbol of evil for our times. Within police circles, however, the German police has built a reputation for excellence, professionalism, scrupulousness, and cooperation. In this book I attempt to describe and analyze the Federal Republic's contemporary police development as it has actually occurred since 1945.

Police research that is not of a purely technical nature is generally hampered by a certain suspicion of outsiders that seems to be endemic in police organizations, and Germany's police forces are no different from others in this respect. Nevertheless, my research was aided immeasurably by a month spent in residence in the fall of 1982 at the national Police Leadership Academy in Münster-Hiltrup. In addition to numerous interviews with police leaders at the Academy, I was able to discuss problems informally with many of the students, who were themselves leaders within the various state police organizations. I was also given free access to the two Academy libraries, one a collection of historical materials, and the other the comprehensive police library used by the students and staff of the Academy. The library personnel were unfailingly courteous and helpful.

I also spent one week in one of the two police departments in Stuttgart, interviewing the police chief and going through historical materials. I visited two training installations, a Bereitschaftspolizei installation in North Rhine-Westphalia and the State Police School for middle-level police supervisors at Maria Tan in Baden-Württemberg.

The bulk of the research, however was done in various libraries in Tübingen, Freiburg, and Stuttgart. In Stuttgart the personnel of the state archives and the state library were particularly helpful. I was a guest for one month at the Institute of Criminology of the University of Tübingen and I spent the spring semester, 1987, as a visiting scholar at the Max Planck Institute for Comparative and International Criminal Law in Freiburg.

Much of my reading was done in police journals and police reports. These included the official police journal *Die Polizei*, various union journals, the journal of the Bereitschaftspolizei, the yearbook of the Police Leadership Academy, and several others. Most of the articles in these journals are written by police officials. They reveal the contemporary concerns and policies of police at various periods in their history. Both the volume and the nature of articles at different times give us information about police concerns: traffic and community relations in the 1950's; civil unrest, data-gathering technology, and the environment in the 1980's.

Archival materials provided me with details about the early post-war efforts to reconstruct a police organization. I have also gone through most of the accounts of research on German police done by German sociologists in the past twenty years, and through most of the police histories generated by police historians. Finally, I have read many of the critical analyses of German police by hostile commentators, both within and outside academic circles. Despite an atmosphere that is often charged with a good deal of emotion, I have used every opportunity available to discuss police with German professors, justice system officials, graduate students, and other citizens in order to test my own perceptions or to develop new insights.

The resulting methodology might be called historical/analytical in that I am combining a good bit of historical narrative with my own and others' perceptions of its significance. Although I much admire the kind of police research that is done at the street level in analyzing the behavior of individual police officers, and although such analysis would have strengthened the research for this book, the predominant themes, which have to do with organizational change, historical influences, and control of civil unrest, have allowed a fairly comprehensive, if less intimate, analysis.

A few explanations about the text are in order. For purposes of textual simplicity I generally use the terms "German" and "Germany" when I am actually talking about the Federal Republic of Germany, or West

Germany. The German Democratic Republic, or East Germany, is not included in the analysis. Since I am not comparing the two German nations, I hope that my use of these words will not prove confusing to the reader. Also, for reasons of clarity, at least to the American reader, I use the terminology "state" and "federal" in talking about the basic divisions of the Federal Republic. In Germany these divisions are known as "Land" and "Bund." Because both the states and the federal government have autonomous police there is danger in generalizing across the entire nation when speaking of the "German police." I have tried to explain the different degrees of diversity and uniformity that exist in German police operations and have tried to be explicit when talking about operations that exist only in one or a few states, but inevitably generalizations will be made that do not apply in every instance. For example, although West Berlin is equivalent to the other city-states — i.e., Bremen and Hamburg — with respect to most aspects of police organization, training, and operations, this city still is under Allied control, and some matters, such as police deployment in other states, are affected by this peculiar status.

In translating from the German, I have attempted to stay close to the original, even if the resulting English may suffer from occasional awkward phraseology. The two languages are so different in sentence structure, however, that it has been necessary to take some liberties in order to provide a coherent and logical presentation of the material in English. All translations are my own.

The research was supported by grants from the German Academic Exchange Service, the American Philosophical Society, and North Carolina State University. In addition, North Carolina State University provided me with research leave during the fall semester, 1982 and the spring semester, 1987. I am sincerely grateful for all this support.

Among the many individuals to whom I am indebted I would like to mention especially Günther Kratz and Konrad Paitz at the Police Leadership Academy in Münster-Hiltrup; Albin Eser and Günther Kaiser, Directors of the Max Planck Institute for Comparative and International Criminal Law; Hans Kurzinger, head librarian at the Institute; Sylvia Tellenbach of the Institute; Thomas Weigand of the University of Cologne; Hans Göppinger, former Director of the Institute of Criminology in Tübingen; and Hans-Peter Sturm, Polizeipräsident of Landespolizeidirektion I in Stuttgart. I am especially grateful to my colleague Eva Rubin, who read the entire manuscript and made invaluable suggestions for improvement. Needless to say, I am solely responsible for the resulting product.

CONTENTS

Page

Introduction vii

Chapter

One.   The Uses of the Police   3

Two.   The Legacy of the Past 21

Three.   Demilitarization: The Grand Ideal 57

Four.   Decentralization and Recentralization 95

Five.   Democratization 125

Six.   Policing a Democratic Social Order 159

Seven.   Conclusion: Police Power and Public Accountability 187

References 209

Index 221

GERMAN POLICE

CHAPTER ONE

THE USES OF THE POLICE

I am reasonably certain that in the next ten years we will see many failures of institutions and leadership — that is, people will try, painfully and ever less successfully, to continue in the same old patterns. We will become ever more deeply involved in the problems of inflation, unemployment, reduced growth, protectionism, helplessness, inability to keep social promises, and the like. Those in power will explain to all that they can do nothing, that they are the victims of conflicting forces and that therefore power is only an optical illusion. The powerless perceive that they as individuals also cannot achieve change. And they will then seek to lay responsibility on those in power. And since they will not be able to do this, in the end the police must bear the brunt of the criticism. In other words, in the end the police will become the symbol of power, and the entire struggle, with great violence in the streets, will be maintained, not against those in power, but against the police.

Ralf Dahrendorf (in a speech to the Police Union of Baden-Württemberg, October 29, 1981)

RALF DAHRENDORF, in his statement quoted above, captured much of the sense of frustration that is experienced by professional police authorities in a time of social unrest or national crisis. For a democracy, the problem is this: How does a police force, in the face of serious social order problems and provocation, remain responsive, responsible, objective, or even law-abiding? Whom do the police serve in a democratic society? The law? The people? A ruling elite?

This book deals with one modern police force, that of the Federal Republic of Germany. It details the efforts, starting in 1945, to build a new police on the ruins of the notorious Nazi police apparatus. The situation in 1945 provided a rare opportunity to design and implement an ideal organization. The major goals of the post-war reconstruction of police were demilitarization, decentralization, and democratization. Although this organization was imposed upon the conquered by the conquerors, and one of the prime goals of these conquerors was to insure that the German police apparatus would not become once again a powerful para-military force, it was also meant to be an organization that would be structurally, ideologically, and operationally fit to serve the needs of a fragile new democracy. The evolution of these structures, ideologies, and operations for the past forty years is therefore instructive for those who are concerned with policing a democracy.

The book details also the problems faced by the German police in the face of the crises of social order that have erupted again and again in recent years in West Germany. The exercise of police power becomes particularly difficult in times of social stress and protest against government. Thus this book presents a case study of organizational response to environmental stress.

Contemporary German police forces, like police forces elsewhere, reflect historical, political, and social circumstances that often go back for hundreds of years. In Germany, however, two major Twentieth Century traumas have had particularly intense effects on police operations. In considering the course of German police history since 1945 it becomes apparent that the crisis in civil order control that triggered the end of the Weimar Republic, as well as the dark history of the Third Reich, in which the German police were so much implicated, continue to influence modern police operations, coloring police response to social order emergencies as well as public response to police in these same situations. Police behavior that would fall within the scope of the normal in other nations often becomes a source of controversy and suspicion in Germany. Furthermore, major changes in police structure, imposed by the Allies in the name of responsiveness and democratization, were seen by the Germans, with some justice, as efforts that at heart were designed to cripple the police apparatus. Thus there was little effort to block the rapid return to comfortable and familiar bureaucratic structures and organizational culture as soon as the occasion allowed.

These two themes, the need to overcome the past on the one hand and, on the other hand, persistence of historical organizational culture, constitute a dialectic that pervades contemporary German police history. In this book these themes will be explored and analyzed at the same time that today's police organization is described.

THE TASKS OF POLICING

Most societies expect their public police forces, however constituted, to perform two functions. The first is to secure an orderly, predictable, and safe commerce of individuals within the social order. This function may be called the *deviance control function* and encompasses the duties of crime prevention and control that are normally associated with police operations. It includes also the duties of conventional order maintenance: traffic control, nuisance abatement, and general service activities.

Corollary to the deviance control function is the duty, assumed more or less consciously by police authorities in various systems, to educate or socialize the public into the prevailing social values. Although this duty hardly provides a rationale for the existence of police, it cannot be divorced from the police mission in general and especially from the deviance control function. A population that consents to, and believes in, the wisdom of the laws by which it is governed obviously is less likely to break those laws or to undermine the polity. Thus public education furthers the goal of lawful behavior.

The second function of police is to preserve public order through the monitoring and control of manifestations of civil unrest. This second function may be called the *civil order control function*. Inevitably civil order control takes on political connotations and is much more problematic with respect to police behavior, police loyalty, and acceptance of police power than is deviance control.

At various times and in various cultures one or the other of these functions assumes dominance. Nevertheless, both failure to inhibit the actions of criminal predators and failure to preserve a relative degree of civil order lead to increasing tension, insecurity, and social breakdown. In other words, under optimal conditions both functions of police serve to preserve a peaceful, orderly society in which citizens are free to engage in private pursuits unhampered by excessive fears or insecurities.

Each of the two major police functions has its own imperatives of organization, action, and accountability. The execution of each function has the possibility of both benign and pathological development. It is the balance, not only between functions, but also between pathological and salutary manifestations of these functions, that is of concern to those who are involved in developing a police force for a democratic society.

Deviance Control

At its best, the deviance control function of police makes them guarantors of community values. Their mission is to protect citizens against predators and those whose actions impede the relatively smooth operation of society. They help to reinforce a sense of predictability in everyday life and in social relations, a sense that people will live according to the rules that have been established in order to facilitate and improve communal life. As such, the police are a benign force for protection of citizens. In addition to reacting to calls for help and dealing with incidences of crime, they perform a didactic service in instructing citizens about protective strategies and about the law in general. Carried to a further extreme, this aspect of policing is typified by publicity campaigns emphasizing a friendly police, by the use of police sports, concerts, and clubs to humanize the police in the eyes of the public, and by police social service activities, such as police athletic leagues. Such activities are meant to foster favorable attitudes toward, and cooperation with, police. The impression is conveyed that only "bad elements" — criminals, delinquents, deviants — need fear the police.

In exercising the deviance control function, however, police may also engage in behaviors that are violative of the very rules they seek to enforce when it comes to other citizens. The most obvious of such behaviors is quite simply venal corruption, the abuse of the police office for monetary gain. Such corruption may assume alarming proportions in departments in which it is the norm and in which it destroys the possibility for honest action by virtually any of the members. In addition, such wholesale corruption breeds contempt for the police as well as resentment by those otherwise honest citizens who are forced to pay bribes in order to conduct their businesses. Entrepreneurs in illegal trades such as gambling and prostitution benefit greatly from this form of police corruption.

Another form of violative behavior by police who are practicing a deviance control function is abuse of police coercive or manipulative power with respect to suspects, arrestees, and minority groups. Because of the vast amount of street-level discretion that police officers normally have, and because of the ignorance or fear of many of those who are most closely monitored by the police, this aspect of police behavior is one that must be of concern to all professional departments.

With increasing technological sophistication, another form of police corruption, one that may be particularly insidious, is excessive and unwarranted data-gathering and dissemination by police about citizens who are not suspected of deviant actions, but rather of political dissent. In Germany, with its history of totalitarian control, especially through the Gestapo, the possibility of police lawlessness in data-gathering is one of the most sensitive areas of concern about police power.

Opinion polls in the United States as well as in other industrialized countries generally show a high approval rating by the public for police operations. Nevertheless, police efforts to project themselves as protectors of public life and property through suppression of crime and criminals and, more extremely, as benign and friendly agents for public services may be a luxury of good times. In Germany, for example, both the Weimar Republic and the Federal Republic had times in which a positive public image was actively courted by the police and accepted by the public. These were the periods 1922-1929 and 1950-1965, periods in which the post-war upheavals had subsided and major new economic and social problems had not yet developed.

In each of these periods police leadership made great efforts to portray the police as "friend and helper" and to encourage cooperation between citizens and police. In the Weimar Republic, says Liang, (1970: 10) " . . . the police leaders . . . had decided to shed the pompous image of the prewar constable . . . for the benevolent motto 'The Police, Your Friend and Assistant.' " The police were encouraged by Prussian Interior Minister Carl Severing to think in terms of developing good relations with the public. In 1926 the Great Police Exhibition was held in Berlin and attracted 50,000 visitors. According to Liang, the success of the campaign of rapprochement between police and public was evidenced by the fact that in 1926 dolls dressed in police uniforms were sold in the Berlin toy stores (Ibid.: 79). In the 1950's the motto "The Police, Your Friend and Helper" again achieved popularity. At that time zealous concern for good community relations made the German police an international example of a police that works closely with citizens and places great emphasis on public service.

More recently the "friend and helper" motto has been rejected and even ridiculed in German police circles (Hunold, 1968: 63). As one police official explained, being a friend is not an appropriate mission for a police officer—it is rather to be impartial and a guardian of the law. The bad repute into which this slogan has fallen both among police and among their critics in today's Germany is evidence of how far at least the public relations efforts of the police have come since the halcyon post-war times when it seemed that the major task of the police was to regulate the ever-increasing motor traffic engendered by the ever-increasing prosperity of the German people.

To be sure, the slogan "The Police: Your Friend and Helper" can be seen as merely that — a slogan. In fact, this slogan has a rather grim echo in a publication of the centralized police of the Third Reich (Englisch et al., 1936). Entitled *Die Polizei — Dein Freund — Dein Helfer* (the Police — Your Friend — Your Helper) this book was published to celebrate Police Understanding Week and was directed specifically at German youth. In addition to explaining the work of the police in various fields such as traffic (with emphasis on bicycle traffic and rules for riding street cars), criminal investigation, and border patrols, the book is full of advice to young people on how to cooperate with the police by reporting suspicious people, and by helping in cases of air attacks and similar occasions.

Even in 1936 National Socialist Germany, however, the effort to bring the police closer to the people and to picture the police as servants of the public good characterized a phase in which the regime had consolidated its hold on the public, was relatively secure, and was progressing rapidly in industrial development and achievement of full employment. Although the conditions at that time can be compared only tenuously to those in the 1920's and 1950's, this situation tends to support the claim that a service emphasis and a "police as friend" emphasis are most likely to blossom in noncontroversial times or in areas where social stress is minimal.

Civil Order Control

Activities designed to control civil unrest are on a different level of complexity and intensity than are those designed to control deviance. In many countries a separate division of police exists that specializes in dealing with social order control. In some situations, to be sure, control of civil unrest is an extension of deviance control work. "Rioting for fun and profit" (Banfield, 1968) threatens the values and well-being of the large majority of the population, that naturally wishes for an effective police deterrent or counterforce to such activities. Nevertheless, even relatively minor disturbances have a political component, in that they are expressions of anger and discontent, usually by the socially dispossessed, and are often engaged in by those who are not otherwise involved in criminal activities (Fogelson, 1968).

As social disorder escalates, the position of the police becomes more and more difficult. Gradually the escalation of force and resistance to force feed on each other and the confrontation between police and citizens assumes the nature of a military operation, with police in the role of the enemy. This is the situation which Chalmers Johnson (1966) describes as "power deflation." As the legitimacy of the regime decreases, political life becomes characterized by increasing levels of coercion, and violence against citizens becomes normal. A confrontational mentality on the part of police and of citizens develops and the breach between police and public widens.

In such a situation the problem for the police organization, even in a democratic society, is that the police is in danger of developing a life of its own, rather than reflecting the values of the citizens. Police personnel move from trying to be part of the conventional society to the grim and tense relationship of adversaries. Inevitably the brutalization, not only of the public by the police, but of the police itself becomes more intense. At some point a line is crossed and the police can become the agents of an increasingly desperate social class that sees its power slipping away in a revolutionary situation.

We are talking about the changes that a general peace-maintaining police force undergoes in a time of social unrest, and not about the specially chosen and specially privileged police who often are hired by dictators to suppress dissidents and to stifle public expressions of discontent. These latter police are frankly ruthless agents of the controlling powers and have no pretensions to popular support. As such, they are of little academic interest to those who are concerned with the role of police in democracies. The question for a police force in a democracy, however, is: "What is the nature of the drive toward corruption of power that exists in times of social unrest? Is there a problem of delinquency or delinquent personalities within the force that only becomes evident in such times of crisis?"

Comfort (1970) discusses the concept of delinquency on the part of those in power. Comfort claims that there are "rogue" personalities — people who are violent and predatory — who will insinuate themselves into positions of power, including the armed forces and police, in order to act out their pathologies in a quasi-legitimate manner. In normal times, organizational controls and mores tend to inhibit the active expression of these tendencies. In times of crisis, such as war and social unrest, on the other hand, such pathologies become unleashed and threaten to characterize the entire organization.

Comfort's claim that delinquent personalities in situations of power have the opportunity to express their delinquency overtly in times of

crisis is in some ways a reassuring one, because it suggests that the problem is one of particular personalities rather than one that is determined
by the nature of the situation and the nature of the organizational imperatives that this situation creates. As a problem of personalities, it is
amenable to personal solutions: more effective screening of personnel,
recognition of stress factors associated with the work, and therapeutic
opportunities.

We have little evidence to suggest, however, that individual personalities are predominant causative factors in police pathologies in times of
stress. The police profession in general has attracted working-class individuals who are drawn by the salaries, benefits, and pensions associated
with the work rather than individuals who are hoping for adventure,
power, or moral entrepreneurship. Studies of German as well as American police recruits confirm the conventional motives that attract individuals to police work (see., e.g., Murck, 1976). Rather, the conflict
between police and disturbers of civil order may be "preprogrammed," as
one German official says (Maikranz, 1986: 434): "Violent acts, denun-
ciaton of police, stress, overtime work, uncomfortable lodgings far from
one's normal base, lead to aggression, and not only by our young inexperienced officers."

If it is organizational need or inherent organizational pathology that
informs police action in stressful times, we are faced with a different
problem, one that involves a search for new organizational forms and
styles of operation, ones that are geared specifically to the exigencies of
such stressful periods. In the post-World War II era, there have been
major attempts in the German police to deal with this problem of preventing the development of organizational hysteria or mass organizational pathology within the police. This was to be done through new
organizational forms, training of recruits, training of leaders, emphasis
on cooperative work with citizens, and special training in the law and
constitutional rights of citizens.

Probably it is too simplistic, however, to conceive of the civil-order-
related problems of police as purely a function either of individual personalities in the organization or of organizational hysteria. There is a
host of variables that are involved in the dynamics of police action in relation both to civil unrest and to internal peace maintenance. These variables include the nature of the opposition (e.g., terrorism, social-class
unhappiness), the tenor of public sympathy, and the degree of public involvement in the actual incidences of unrest. Depending on the degree
and kind of civil unrest that is occurring, however, conscientious police

leaders as well as individual police officers are faced with two dilemmas about appropriate goals and actions. These dilemmas concern organizational imperatives and obedience. Both of these dilemmas need to be explained in some detail.

Organizational Imperatives in Civil Order Control

Isaac Balbus (1977) has explained the conflicting forces that are at work in a situation of civil unrest. These are *formal rationality,* the *need for order,* and *need for maintenance* of the organizations that are involved. At the highest level and in the long run, the legitimacy of the state in a liberal democracy is dependent upon the maintenance of the formal rationality (i.e., procedural justice rules) that characterizes such a state. At the same time, the state cannot afford to have maintenance of formal rationality take absolute precedence over the immediate imperative of keeping the social order from collapsing. Although the drive for order takes precedence over the drive toward formal rationality in times of stress, there must be some acknowledgment, even if symbolic, of this legitimacy constraint. There is also the immediate need of the involved organization to serve its internal goal of organizational survival. These three forces, then, must be balanced in a time of crisis, and none of them must be allowed to be totally submerged if both the enforcing organization and the social order are to survive.

In the short run, it is the drive toward formal rationality that would appear to be the weakest force of the three involved in times of intense crisis. Nevertheless, neglect of this imperative can lead to further disorder as well as a crisis of legitimacy. The difficult question is: "How and to what extent can we maintain formal rationality when under seige and attack or when threatened in other ways by dissident groups or disgruntled citizens?"

The German police today are aware of this conflict and this dilemma. Efficiency ("Zweckmässigkeit") as opposed to upholding law and justice ("Rechtmässigkeit") have become subjects for discussion (see, e.g., Kiskalt, 1964). Thus, for example, a peculiar compromise between the need for order and the need for formal rationality has been worked out by the leaders of one state's Bereitschaftspolizei (the general civil order control police in the Federal Republic). During demonstrations a particular squad of police officers is delegated the task of handling arrests and booking of demonstrators who break the law. In order to be more mobile and to be able to catch the young and often fleet-footed offenders, this commando also wears tennis shoes and dispenses with the shields and helmets usually used to protect riot police. When a demonstrator is arrested, the police officer has the obligation to stay with the individual until a photograph of the officer and the demonstrator are taken, the officer describes the circumstances of the arrest to a detective, and preliminary statements are taken by the detective force. In this way the possibility of making arrests that are illegal or that cannot be substantiated in a court of law is minimized. Other states use "arrest troops" that specialize in obtaining evidence and maintaining some semblance of formal rationality in crowd control situations. Alhough a smaller number of individuals is arrested through this provision for procedural care, the requirements of formal rationality in the cases that are processed is met, and the prosecutions that follow these demonstrations have a greater possibility of coming to a resolution that is satisfactory for the police authorities. At the same time, the need for preservation of the social order is being met by concentrating on crowd control and emergency measures. These procedures were instituted as a substitute for the random, confusing, and wholesale arrest of individuals against whom it was later impossible to produce sufficient evidence for prosecution. Despite these efforts, however, or perhaps because of them, one of the major criticisms that has been leveled against police handling of civil unrest has been the small number of arrests that have occurred.

As with so many other problems that have faced the German police since the end of World War II, the concern for formal rationality was evident also in the turbulent days of the Weimar Republic. The Prussian Police Administration Law of 1931 (Preussisches Staatsministerium, 1931) describes the responsibilities of the officer to deal only with the person who is responsible for disturbing the peace (Para. 19) and allows for exceptional police action in crisis situations. At the time a commentator on this law (Troitzsche, 1933: 34) said that when "the normal political struggle becomes abnormal (as now in Germany), the necessary result is that the State cannot exercise its obligation to uphold security and order with the use of normal means." However, he explained the narrow limits within which this permission to bypass formal rationality must be exercised and he warned of the dangers of a too-liberal interpretation of this clause of the statute. In a further plea for formal rationality, he called for the gradual development of standards within which the exceptional use of police power can be exercised.

For the police, organizational survival and credibility is also related to action in social order situations. The use of military resources or a declaration of martial law are indicators that the police are not able to carry out their functions as prescribed. Again the Weimar Republic provides an example. In the early years of that regime, police were hard put to assert themselves as against the various pseudo-military organizations, such as the Freikorps and the Spartacusbund, that were also engaged in preserving order in the chaotic aftermath of the formation of the Republic. Respect for, and legitimacy of, the police as an organization depended upon the outcome of this struggle for control of the means of imposing public order. In that struggle, the police managed to assert themselves and become the dominant force in control of civil unrest, partially because of the capacities of the police and partially because of a natural lessening of tensions as time went on. Nevertheless, in those early years the primary function of police leadership was to assert the very fundamental premise that control over public order and security should be the province of the state rather than of private organizations (Liang, 1970; Schwarze, 1977).

In the final days of the Republic, when an exhausted police was still trying to cope with predations of the armed forces of both right and left, the imposition of martial law in Prussia and the takeover of the streets by army troops were the epitome of what the police had been trying to avoid for several years. In effect, the police attempt to balance the forces of formal legitimacy, social order, and organizational survival had failed, with ominous consequences for the Republic.

Obedience

Perhaps the most agonizing and difficult of the ethical problems that face police as an organization and individual police officers are those that concern individual responsibility as opposed to system responsibility for the actions that are taken in the name of the organization. Those who choose to pursue occupations, whether police or military, in which the ultimate reality is that force and violence must be employed against others, cannot escape the ultimate questions: What is my responsibility to my superiors? What is my responsibility to the state and its laws? What is my responsibility to the public or to humanity in general?

The German people have developed the reputation of being inordinately duty-bound. Immanuel Kant is the admired German philosopher who extols duty as a premier virtue (see, e.g., Kant, 1959). The hero of German novelist Siegfried Lenz' widely-read novel *Deutschstunde (The German Lesson)* is a young man in a reform school who is given the assignment to write an essay on "the joy of doing one's duty" ("die Freude der Pflicht"). As he writes, he remembers his father, a rural police officer in a northern coastal area. The father's narrowly-conceived and exaggerated sense of duty leads him to actions that in various ways destroy those who are closest to him, including both of his sons and an artist friend who had saved his life. Throughout the novel, the author contrasts the artist, with his tolerant outlook and passion for beauty, to the police officer, with his passion for making sure that strict legality is adhered to in all circumstances even when such legality is absurd, inhumane, and in the service of an evil regime.

Deutschstunde provides a bitter reflection on some vaunted German virtues. For individuals, however, and especially police officers, there are no easy answers to the questions raised by the dilemma of obedience. These questions become critical during times of civil unrest, when the nature of the "enemy" is not as clearcut as when the police are fighting conventional criminals. In the German context, the terrible history of the Nazi police also serves to make the debate over the matter of obedience particularly relevant and intense.

There are several elements in this debate. The argument on one side is that the police should be nonpolitical civil servants who carry out the orders of their superiors, and who do not question the policies of duly constituted authorities. Placed in the context of limiting discretionary or illegal behavior by police officers, this argument has great cogency. It is obvious that most people do not want an independent police that does not respond to the authority of the state in a democratic regime. The German experience during the Kapp Putsch of 1920, when many of the Prussian police sided with the right-wing insurgents rather than with their own Social Democratic government, is a well-remembered example of the dangers of independent action by the police (Liang, 1970: 46-48). This incident serves as a reminder that raising the specter of the desirability of disobediance by police forces is a two-edged sword that may be used in ways that are not foreseen by advocates of individual responsibility.

On the other side is the argument that individuals as human beings have an obligation to refuse to carry out orders that are morally repugnant. According to this argument, the individual must not commit atrocious crimes or crimes against humanity in the name of carrying out superior orders. Well known because of the prosecutions of war criminals in this century, this argument has particular cogency for our times. Nevertheless, as a standard of conduct it poses difficult problems. The behavior demanded of the individual is so extreme that only the exceptional person would have the moral courage to resist such orders.

The most obvious reason for compliance is fear for one's own safety. Furthermore, as the Milgram experiments have shown us (Milgram, 1974), authority itself commands a strong presumption of legitimacy and we have few structured ways to resist even a relatively benign authoritative command.

With the reestablishment of the new republic in 1949, the German police, in the course of trying to shed the image of a force that is "gehörsam," or obedient at all costs, struggled to develop, and in some cases to propagate through police training, concepts of legitimate behavior that could be reconciled with the desire for a disciplined and responsive police force. In reaction to the personal oaths to the Führer that were required of SS and other officials in the Nazi regime, there was emphasis on allegiance to law as opposed to allegiance to individuals as the basis for police behavior. Police training emphasized that police are political individuals who have a responsibility to uphold the democratic order. Special training in citizenship was used to supplement these assertions. The concept of "zivil Courage," or the courage to resist repugnant orders, was promoted as a substitute for the concept of gehörsam as a guiding maxim for police behavior. The concept of "innere Führung," or self-determination, also was offered as a substitute for blind obedience to authority (Grosser, 1971: 226). These efforts are discussed in detail in Chapter Five.

Not all these concepts or proposals to emphasize individual initiative in the face of superior orders were supported wholeheartedly by police authorities, or provided a basis for considered opposition to superior orders. In recent years, with the increasing threat of civil disorder, there has been great emphasis once again on the need for police recruits to follow through on their obligation, even if they find that in doing so, they must sacrifice their own feelings of sympathy for one or the other side in an argument.

One police training official described to the author how many of the very young recruits are influenced by the environmental movement and tend to sympathize with the many demonstrations against nuclear power plants, airport development, and missile deployment. Others, for historical reasons, do not wish to get involved in "political" police work, i.e., civil order control. According to this official, the recruits are told that they can join organizations or support causes in their spare time, but must agree to carry out police orders even when their erstwhile comrades are the targets of these orders. Impartial administration of the law is the prime value that is furthered, rather than legitimate police discretion in politically sensitive situations.

Does this mean that the concepts, slogans, or rhetoric devoted to the cause of making police more responsible as individuals are in the end just ideas and that what everyone truly wants is a neutral, nonpolitical civil servant who will carry out whatever orders are given him? Probably not, for the very fact of the debate should have the effect of raising the consciousness of the officers with respect to the problems that have occurred as the result of the past emphasis on obedience as the prime virtue in policing. Futhermore, as will be explained later in this book, there is a whole complex of changes in policing style and administration that affect the individual officer's attitudes and behavior and that have indirect influence on the resolution of the dilemma of obedience vs. individual responsibility.

In the final analysis, training and oratory cannot substitute for organizationally-approved channels for dissent within the police. It is obvious that the level of dissent in an organization will be a function of the sanctions that are attached to its exercise, the openness of communication that is fostered, and the general spirit of the organization. Organized channels of dissent, such as those provided by unions, are obviously the least threatening to the individual officer.

Exposing themselves to danger is a final concern the police have with respect to their civil order maintenance function. Police recruits know that they are entering an occupation in which there will be some danger and excitement. As explained, however, they generally enter police work because it provides upward mobility, reasonably good pay, steady employment, and the possibility of a generous retirement plan. Escalating the level of activity that is involved in civil order control for such a group of individuals can lead not only to overreactions in situations of crisis, but also to avoidance of responsibility in dangerous or revolutionary situations. Time and again history has given us examples of police forces that wavered on the edge in times of regime change, waiting to see who would be the new masters before a decision was made to get into action. The German police indecision in the wake of the announcement of the Republic in 1918 as well as the easy takeover of the police in 1933 are examples of this process. It would be naive to think that these hesitations are simply a function of the degree of right-wing sentiment within the police force. In fact, we have every indication that in Germany the Social Democrat influence was just as strong or stronger than the right-wing sentiment (Kohler, 1975). Rather it was unwillingness to become part of a revolutionary resistance or a minority pocket of resistance that seemed to be at work. Hired to preserve law and order, the individual police officer does not feel equipped or committed to engage in major political confrontations. In times of extreme crisis the level of commitment of the ordinary street police may indeed be problematical.

THE GERMAN POLICE TODAY: A FRAMEWORK FOR ANALYSIS

In the chapters that follow, a brief history of the police of the Federal Republic will be followed by an analysis of each of the major aspects of the plan for reorganization of the German police and a description of the developments that have come about with respect to these aspects since 1945. In the final chapter some conclusions are drawn about accountability, civil order control, and the nature of German police culture. Through this analysis we should arrive at a better understanding of the stresses and efforts to deal with them that mold the nature of police departments in an increasingly dangerous world. We should also be able to develop some greater ability to judge the viability or nonviability of particular approaches to police function in modern democracies.

In order to provide a framework for understanding German police I am including, with respect to the major post-war goals of demilitarization, decentralization, and democratization, some discussion of each of three elements of bureaucratic operation. These three elements are *structure, ethos,* and *leadership.* Description of structures provides the basic information that helps us to give shape to an organization and to understand its mission. However, by analyzing, as much as possible, the ethos and leadership elements involved in post-war police development, I am attempting to go beyond a simple discussion of the rules and units that define the boundaries of the organization and to give a more comprehensive picture of the complex of formal and informal realities that make an organization what it is. *Structure* refers to the formal skeleton of an organization: the rules, divisions, technologies, and procedures that identify the organization to outsiders and that are developed in order to create a rational framework for operations. Structures can be simple or complex, with many hierarchical levels, subdivisions, and rules of operation, or with few and informal ones. Although organizational structure seems to enclose an organization and to give it concrete reality in the minds both of members and nonmembers, it includes interdependencies and interrelationships with those outside the organization, and the structural arrangements often affect profoundly the nature of these relationships. This is especially so in the case of public service organizations like police. For example, the locus of control over police forces, i.e., the agents to whom the police is formally accountable, will affect the efficiency of those forces, especially during times of public order crises. It will also affect the efficiency of those forces in dealing with the public on a day-to-day basis in crime prevention and deviance control. In Germany, the postwar plan to create municipal police forces, as well as some aspects of the demilitarization plan, were designed not only to disempower the police, but also to change its character. Britain, with its combination of local police authorities and its national involvement with the police through the Home Office, has tried to combine the advantages of centralization and decentralization in its structural arrangements for police. The Japanese Koban, or "police box," that is found in every neighborhood, is a structure that allows for close surveillance over all aspects of neighborhood activity.

That the Koban assumes a benign rather than a malevolent form is a consequence of the organizational *ethos* within the Japanese police. The ethos of an organization is its spirit, its values, symbols, or internal culture. The conscious promotion of a particular organizational ethos may or may not be effective depending upon the degree of consensus on its values among the members. The value given to freedom from corruption (at least in its more venal form) was part of the ethos of the Federal Bureau of Investigation under J. Edgar Hoover. Police in France, despite efforts to soften their image in recent years, still operate under the legacy of Fouché, Napoleon's grim internal spymaster. In Germany, with its opportunity to re-create a police force in 1945, the matter of organizational ethos was of prime importance. Abandoning military symbols and emphasizing citizen-friendly operations were part of this reconstruction effort. Although describing the ethos of an organization is difficult for an outsider who has not actually experienced the organizational life, public and internal statements of values, the content of the training that is given to new employees, and analyses by organizational members can give important information about this rather formless element of organizational makeup.

Hoover's FBI also exemplifies the role of *leadership* as a third force in organizational development. A reformer who had a vision of a thoroughly professional law enforcement agency, Hoover created a force in which high standards of education, intelligence, and honesty created an image of professionalism that was worldwide. Hoover became immensely powerful, however, and used his power to further his own conception of the needs of the country, focusing major effort on internal security matters while neglecting more conventional crime control activities. In the end the FBI symbolized corruption of power rather than professionalism.

In a wider sense the history of the Prussian Schutzpolizei of the Weimar Republic is another example of the importance of leadership in determining the direction in which an organization may move at a crucial time in its development. According to Kohler (1975), it was the failure of the Social Democratic Party to purge the middle-level leadership of the Schutzpolizei that led to the half-hearted support that that leadership gave to the Republic. This was so despite the fact that the rank and file of police were generally behind the republican principles and were in opposition to their own leaders. On the other hand, the top leadership of the police, under Carl Severing, moved to bring about reforms and changes that have persisted to this day.

These organizational elements naturally are affected by historical/social circumstances. To take the true measure of an organization we need to understand the interplay between external forces and internal organizational development. In Germany the important question is: "To what extent do the imperatives of external circumstances, and especially social order control and crisis situations, determine the internal composition and spirit of the agency? To this question we must also pose its corollary: "To what extent can or should internal organizational forces counteract external pressures?" The search for answers to these questions is of particular interest in post-war German police history. Starting with a new blueprint for organization, new ideals, and new leadership, and passing through forty years of sometimes turbulent history, how has the German police fared as it has responded to shifts of opinion, crises, changes of government, and threats to social order? These are the questions that will be dealt with in the succeeding chapters.

CHAPTER TWO

THE LEGACY OF THE PAST

ACCORDING TO David Bayley, "The structures of public national police systems display remarkable permanence over time" (Bayley, 1985: 60). This does not mean that modifications and new structures have no part to play in police reform: rather that they tend to be incremental and to take place within the conventional framework of policing within particular countries. In Germany, today's police apparatus goes back in large degree to the nineteenth century. This historical organization, and its modification during the Weimar Republic, an earlier postwar era, is closely reflected in the present-day police organization of the Federal Republic despite the major efforts to change it during the period after the Second World War.

Police institutions whose memory has been suppressed, however, are those of the Third Reich. Within police circles there is understandable reticence to retell, recapitulate, or rethink the years 1933 to 1945, when the German police organization and personnel became so totally identified with the Nazi regime. There is little in German police training today which refers to that time; there are few documents available; memoirs and case histories of those involved are almost totally lacking. In histories of German police written by police historians this period is given short and often defensive mention, with the authors taking pains to point out that the regular police was taken over by outside elements and thus could hardly be blamed for the crimes of the organization (see, e.g., Raible, 1963; Riege, 1959). Indeed, in writing about the German police as a legitimate law enforcement and order-maintenance organization, the temptation is to close the book on that time and to say "enough."

Nevertheless, in order to place in perspective the search for a more democratic police ideal in post-World War II Germany, one cannot leave out the history of the Nazi period. Although an aberration, it still stands

21

as an example of the pathology of police that can develop in dictator-ships. Furthermore, and probably because it has not been truly di-gested, this history returns in insidious ways to plague the modern German police.

This chapter, then, presents a short history of the German police since the end of World War One. We will examine the main currents of police history during the Weimar Republic, the Third Reich, and the post-war reconstruction, thus providing the background necessary for a good understanding of the analysis to follow in the succeeding chapters. The chapter closes with some basic information about police makeup, strength, and training in the Federal Republic today, again providing the background for understanding the material to follow.

THE WEIMAR REPUBLIC

The crisis of the German social order that followed the defeat of Ger-many in the First World War was in some ways more intense than that which occurred after the Second. The shock waves engendered by the Weimar Constitution resulted in large part from the fact that Imperial Ger-many, which had such strong and able administrative structures, was weak in the political development that was essential to the establishment of a true constitutional democracy. Political involvement and political pragmatism, which are inherent in the very concept of a republic, were lacking. The Germans were unprepared, both psychologically and in terms of evolved institutions of participation, for democratic government. As Dahrendorf (1965: Ch. 3) tells us, Germany at the turn of the twentieth century was that peculiar anomaly: a feudal-capitalist state and an authoritarian welfare state. The Social Democratic Party, which came into power following the defeat of Germany and the abdication of the Emperor, was an organization that had been suppressed for so long that it was unaccustomed to the prob-lems associated with the actual exercise of power.

The difficulty of developing a democratic spirit was exacerbated in post-World War I Germany by two events that served to create further formidable obstacles to normal recovery (Bracher, 1975: Ch. 1). The first of these was the Versailles Treaty with its astronomic reparations demands backed up by French eagerness to incorporate the industrial sections of Germany in the Ruhr and Rhine valleys in case of failure to meet reparations payments. The second was the devastating inflation of 1923, that destroyed both the money supply and the confidence of the people in rational governmental processes. In a nation known for its thrifty lower middle classes, this latter misfortune was perhaps the most unnerving and shattering of the post-war developments.

By contrast, in the aftermath of the unconditional surrender to the Allies in 1945 German society suffered more severely from physical hardship, starvation, and breakdown of public order than it did from major problems of legitimacy. This is not to minimize the shocks, recriminations, and self-searching that the end of the Nazi era engendered. The Nazi regime, however, was the embodiment of an hysterical ideological mass movement, and lurched from crisis to crisis, becoming always more awesomely ruthless and suppressive of normal relationships in German society (Friedrich and Brezinski, 1956). Thus it cannot be compared to the German Empire which, despite its relatively recent founding (1871), had incorporated the German states without trying to destroy their particular traditions or even administrative organs, and had achieved a relative degree of stability and legitimacy within German society.

Three elements of police reform — demilitarization, democratization, and improvements in police-community relations — were major goals in both post-war periods. The additional goal of decentralization, that was a controversial but crucial aspect of the reform program in the 1940's, was not an issue in 1918, since the new Republic at that time took over the Empire tradition of having police forces based at the state level. Of the three goals, demilitarization was of the highest priority, and was closely monitored by the victorious Allies in both periods. In the Federal Republic, however, democratization of internal organizational operations, as well as creating a less threatening and more helpful image to the public, were prescribed by the occupying authorities whereas in the Weimar Republic they were more a function of the general democratic ideals of the new government. In this earlier era the German governments at both state and national level were strongly committed to reform of the police apparatus as an integral aspect of the effort to move away from the paternalistic and authoritarian climate of imperial Germany. This was especially so in the dominant state of Prussia, ruled by liberal Social Democrats, and containing 65 percent of the German territory and 60 percent of its population (Jacob, 1963:45).

Demilitarization

After each World War the victorious Allies, determined to prevent a resurgence of German war-making potential, directed particular efforts toward regulating both the military establishment and the police. Despite the strong endorsement by the Social Democrats of the plan to make the German police less militaristic, however, the chaotic conditions that prevailed in the 1920's resulted in two successive organizational efforts to strengthen the social order control capacities of the German police by creating barracked and highly armed police troops. The Sicherheitspolizei (Security Police) or Sipo, was the product of the first of these efforts. The second was the Bereitschaftspolizei (literally: Readiness Police) or Bepo (Liang, 1970).

The Sipo was a short-lived organization that was created in 1919 in various states to deal with the prevailing disorder that threatened to undermine the new republic. It was also meant to be a police counterpart to the paramilitary Freikorps groups, bands of ex-soldiers who had been encouraged to form as a civilian order-keeping auxiliary to the military. These Freikorps groups rapidly got out of hand and became in many cases independent marauding bands who took the law into their own hands and were not above pillaging, looting, and other forms of undesirable behavior.

Sipo troops were heavily armed, lived in barracks, and acted in large formations. As Jacob tells us (1963:88): "In December, 1919, the Bavarian state police consisted of 10,000 men with equipment that included 10 cannon, 15 mortars, 51 heavy machine guns, and numerous lighter arms. The Hamburg police had 5000 men with equally heavy equipment. Prussia's security police forces were similarly equipped." Shortly after its creation the Sipo was ordered to be disbanded by the Allied Control Commission on the grounds that it was a subterfuge for the kind of military buildup that was forbidden by the Versailles Treaty.

In 1920 a new force, the Bereitschaftspolizei, was set up in Prussia, and soon the other states, with financial help from the central government, also established such police units. The Bepo, like the Sipo, consisted of troops living in barracks and was established to help the authorities maintain order. The Bepo, however, was also designed to be the first step in the career ladder of the German police officer. It was impossible to get into the regular state police or into the regular municipal police without spending several years in this force (Raible, 1963). Much of the early time in the force was spent in training for conventional police duties. The central government provided arms, equipment, and uniforms for the Bepo. In exchange, it was authorized to use Bepo troops as it saw fit in emergencies. Attempts to exercise this latter power were met with determined resistance in the powerful state of Bavaria, however, and the central government never had the control over the Bepo that it wanted. Nevertheless, this peculiar institution, that has played so important a part in the history of the German police since the early 1920's, had its beginning in the efforts to preserve the German republic from the forces of both right and left that sought to destroy it in the early years of its existence.

Although the Bepo as constituted represented a new structure in German police, there had been an order-control militia during the Empire and before. This militia, called Gendarmerie in most states and Landjäger in Württemberg, handled order control demands and also acted as regular police for rural areas. Urban areas at that time had a communal police that handled peace keeping and minor crimes. Criminal investigations were coordinated at the state level. Thus the organization in Germany prior to the Weimar Republic bore some similarity to the French police today, with its Gendarmerie, affiliated with the military, assigned to handle rural areas and, in part, civil order control functions. The Bepo itself, as it was established in the Weimar Republic, was an institution that in its essence was familiar to Germans: a militarized, barracked social order militia.

The Bepo, despite the fact that it was organizationally completely separate from the military, was an easy target for early incorporation into the military by the war-eager Nazi regime. A police observer claims, in fact, that the Bereitschaften, or Bepo troops, proved to be some of the best-trained and most able troops in the army (Ibid.:Ch.2). It is not to be wondered, then, that the occupying powers in 1945 were thoroughly opposed to the re-creation of paramilitary units in the German police.

Democratization

In both of the post World War periods, there were plans to make the German police a more democratic organization, suitable to the policing of a democratic nation. The difference was that in occupied Germany, the prescriptions for police democracy came from the occupation authorities whereas in Weimar Germany the impetus for democracy came from the state governments, most notably the government of Prussia. In both eras the new police was made up chiefly of returning war veterans, which made the task of relaxing a traditionally highly hierarchical and rigid organization all the more difficult.

In the Weimar period, the changes were not as precipitate. The effort evolved gradually after some of the turbulence of the post-war period and the attempts to overthrow the new republic had subsided. Among several dedicated and able officials of that time the values, personality, and accomplishments of one individual, Carl Severing, stand out.

Although not himself police-trained, Severing spearheaded the German police reforms from his posts in the Interior Ministries, first of Prussia and then of the Republic. The son of a tobacco worker, Severing started his working life as a mechanic. After Bismarck's death and the lifting of the ban on activities of the Social Democrats, he soon devoted all of his time to union activities. He was editor of the Social Democratic newspaper *Volkswacht* and worked also on the journal *Sozialistiche Monatshefte* before entering parliament and devoting all his time to elective and appointive office (Kosch, 1976:1107).

Severing promoted acquiescence with the intentions of the Entente powers to make the police entirely a force for internal order. Further, he worked continually to combat the isolation from the public and the military-like behavior that police work tends to promote. The Prussian Police Administration Act of 1931 represents the culmination of his efforts to change the quality of policing in his state (Severing, 1950: Ch. 9; Liang, 1970: Ch. 3).

Attempts to democratize police in Weimar Germany were gradual, however, and were constantly hindered not only by the prevailing social, economic, and political disorder, but also by the tension within the police itself between right-wing nationalist elements and the defenders of the Republic. Nevertheless, the notion that the German police was riddled with right-wing factions who refused to support the Republic is not correct. Compared to other leading institutions such as the army, which refused to be involved in the effort to suppress the Kapp Putsch of 1921, and the judiciary, which was notorious for its prejudice on behalf of right-wing as opposed to left-wing revolutionaries, the police was a model of rectitude in its response to threats to the social order (Fowler, 1979: Ch. 2; Liang, 1970: Ch. 5).

Whether the loyalty of the police to the Republic can be ascribed to democratic sentiments or to the respect for the traditional duty of police to obey whatever authorities happen to be in command can be debated, however. It was never the official policy of the police to insure that recruits were committed to the Republic before they entered the police service. Severing's efforts to recruit urban working class youth were frustrated by the fact that these individuals were not attracted to police work whereas rural youth found police work an opportunity for social and economic advancement (Liang, 1970). Furthermore, the rather timid "wait and see who wins" attitude of the police leadership in 1919 and 1920 suggests rather that the police were not much concerned with politics but were concerned with maintaining their positions, no matter who was in charge.

Nevertheless, there were indicators that the endeavor to develop a democratic police force was not confined to the rhetoric of the Social Democratic Party leadership, but did penetrate to the level of organizational activities. The strong police unions in the Federal Republic today have their origins in the unions of the Weimar Republic. These unions were numerous and represented various shades of opinion as well as occupational groups such as officers, rank and file uniformed police, and detectives. The Association of Prussian Police Officers (also known as the Schrader-Verband after its chairman, Ernst Shräder) was the largest union and was affiliated with the national civil servant's union (Deutscher Beamtenbund). Because almost all police officers were union members, it was impossible for police leaders to ignore union demands and grievances. Although most union activity was centered on classic union concern with working conditions and renumeration, most unions also supported the Republican government. Political engagement by both right-wing and liberal unions became more intense as the republic itself became more fragile in the latter part of the 1920's (Ibid.).

Changing the organizational spirit of the police was an important part of the conscious effort to democratize the organization. Education in democracy and the republican constitution were stressed at the police academies; police were encouraged to become participants in the democratic process; officers were encouraged to deal with the rank and file courteously and without arrogance, while the rank and file were encouraged to act with pride and without servility (Ibid.: Ch. 3; Severing, 1950). One police newsletter put it this way: "The great division between Commanders and men must disappear by all means. That is the first step in developing a good spirit in our group . . . . Military arrogance and other harassments should no longer be able, as previously, to undermine the rights of the individual" (*Württembergischer Landjäger*, June 1, 1919). For a country that was famous for arrogance of officers and docility of the lower ranks in both military and police organizations, these efforts represented a major change of attitude. As the disorders increased, however, it became more and more difficult to provide a coherent education for the recruits, who were constantly being pulled out of the classroom in order to deal with civil order emergencies (von Harach, 1983).

The drive toward democratization culminated with the famous Prussian Police Administration Law of 1931 (Preussicher Staatsministerium, 1931). This law, that in large part undergirds modern German police practice (see, e.g., Scheer and Trubel, 1961) constituted a major codification, simplication, and reform of police operations in Germany. The law itself is a direct descendent of the Prussian Comprehensive Police Law of 1891, which itself was a major landmark in the process of realizing the German goal of a Rechtsstaat, or "law-state" — i.e., a state whose legitimacy is based on law rather than on arbitrary authority (Raible, 1963; *Die Polizei*, 1931).

To an American, the 1931 law does not appear to be unusual. It declares that police responsibility is restricted to necessary measures to protect public security and order against threatening dangers (Paragraph 14). The police must restrict themselves to dealing only with the people who have caused the public security and order to be endangered (Paragraph 19) and the measures that police can use in the fulfillment of their tasks are delineated (Paragraph 21). The issuance of police ordinances is carefully restricted (Paragraphs 24-39). A procedure is established according to which a citizen can proceed against police authorities when an abuse of power has taken place (Paragraphs 70-73). The law also provides for new responsibilities of police and new relationships with prosecutors in the case of petty misdemeanors. It is the third of three major laws dealing with police matters; the two earlier ones dealt with personnel and with financial arrangements between states and cities for paying the costs of policing (Klausener, Kerstiens, and Kemperer, 1932).

In post-imperial Germany, however, with its tradition of the wide-ranging if generally benevolent police state, in which police power encompassed by definition all state responsibilities with the exception of military, foreign affairs, and justice matters, the 1931 law was a bold venture in establishing new parameters for the nature and limitations of police work. As one commentary put it, "It comes down to this: that in a democracy, police power is to be restricted to necessary measures, and everything must be done to create out of the citizen a truly self-assured, individually responsible comrade (Volksgenosse)" (Ibid.: 8). All the more tragic, or perhaps significant, then, is the fact that this law was to be superceded so shortly after its passage by the administrative centralization mandated in the Third Reich.

The degree of success achieved in the attempt to democratize police organization is difficult to determine. In terms of external support for the Republic, certainly the police in Prussia acted conscientiously and against overwhelming odds to maintain a measure of order in the increasing chaos of the early Depression years (Liang, 1970). Likewise, in Bavaria the police struggled to maintain order while remaining neutral (Schwarze, 1977). Although there were right-wing union organizations among police groups their membership was small compared to the vast majority of police who belonged to the liberal unions. When the final takeover came, it was the army, during the chancellorship of von Papen, that took over the Prussian government and declared martial law in 1933. This action was taken on the grounds that the Prussian police could no longer maintain order.

Severing is sometimes criticized for allowing this takeover to take place without a shot being fired. It was his contention that the Prussian police had inadequate resources and that it would have been futile to sacrifice its personnel in the face of overwhelming military superiority. After the Second World War, when the desirability of rearming the police and establishing police troops came up he used the example of what he considered to be the weakness of the Weimar police as justification for developing a well-armed and powerful police force. "I believe," he said, "that . . . if each police officer had had a rifle, if machine guns would have been readily available and also heavy weapons, we would have had no Hitler putsch and no national uprising" (Severing, 1949, quoted in von Harach, 1983: 95).

Severing's claim that it would have served no purpose for the Prussian police to resist the military takeover seems a legitimate one. Nevertheless the Prussian police was oddly passive at an earlier and more questionable crisis known as the Kapp Putsch. The Kapp Putsch was an effort by a band of right-wing extremists, including military personnel, to take over the government of Germany in 1920. Both the police and the armed forces made little effort to become involved in the effort to stop this takeover attempt and it was thwarted largely as a result of a general strike called by the Social Democratic Party (Liang, 1970).

The passivity of the police in this crisis involved a certain amount of sympathy for the putschists. The circumstances suggest, however, that the desire not to shed police blood in combat with well-armed and disciplined military forces was also a consideration. It was as if the police leadership were waiting to see which side was going to prevail before they engaged their personnel. This "wait and see" attitude of the Prussian police in the Kapp Putsch was similar to that taken just a few years earlier, when the police refused to become embroiled in the conflicts leading to the establishment of the Republic. In fact, it appears that, faced with a critical civil order challenge involving armed combat, the Prussian police was willing to serve whichever side was the strongest, and did not operate as automatic protectors of the regime in power. This tendency within the Prussian police was much criticized by elements in the German military, despite the fact that the latter were themselves guilty of some obvious fence-sitting at times of threat to the established Constitution (see, for example, Severing, 1927: 132). Nevertheless, it seems obvious that these police forces, despite their paramilitary training and operations, were at a loss when faced with a true military confrontation.

Police and Public

The Weimar Republic lasted a mere fourteen years, with few "normal" times. The Federal Republic has been in existence for more than thirty-five years and, despite a large amount of civil unrest in recent years, shows no signs of developing the degree of internal chaos that destroyed the earlier government. Nevertheless, in both eras a period of initial upheaval, uncertainty, and organizational insecurity was followed by a period of good feeling, effective police operations, and public approbation of police. This period in turn was followed by the trauma of dealing with political dissidents of both the right and the left, an intensification of police activities directed against demonstrators as opposed to conventional criminals, and resulting disenchantment with police by large segments of the population, either because the police was not maintaining order effectively enough, or because the police was too eager in its efforts to suppress dissent.

The birth pangs of a new police in the Weimar Republic were directly associated with the tremendous psychological and social changes occasioned by the Revolution of 1919, which overthrew the Empire and put the formerly marginal Social Democratic Party in control. Although police forces were still in existence (in contrast to 1945) there was some fear that the new revolutionary government would carry through on its old threats to replace the entire state apparatus. In fact, although the police were at first disarmed by the revolutionary authorities, they were ordered to remain at their posts. Some of the difficulties of the police in 1919 seem amusing to an outsider. Liang, for example, says (1970: 34):

> (Police subordinates) hesitated among monarchism in the name of loyalty to the king, democracy in the name of loyalty to the nation,

sympathy for the right because of their affinity with soldiers, and political neutrality based on the ethics of public servants. In fact, even senior police officials seemed undecided.

The editors of *Die Polizei,* a weekly newspaper that generally reflected official police attitudes, entered the period of Germany's democratic experiment with a grand display of political evasiveness. In the first issue to come out under the rule of Emil Eichhorn (the newly-appointed Berlin police chief), six pages were taken up with the reprint of Immanuel Kant's *Metaphysical Principles of Jurisprudence,* Goethe's poem, "The State," and brief announcements of orders and decrees by the Council of People's Commissars. This was followed by an article on the reform of the law on licensed public houses and items of administrative news. Very much at the end came a curt notice to the effect that Emil Eichhorn had assumed command of all the police forces in Berlin.

In Weimar the period of relative stability, that lasted from 1923 to 1929, was somewhat like a shaky truce between major battles. Carl Severing's statement in 1927: "The ruins have been removed from our way; in the future a clear path beckons!" (Severing, 1927:9) echoes grimly over the soon-to-succeed disasters. Nevertheless, the completion of the currency reform and the gradual resignation to the claims made on German wealth and territory by the post-war treaties allowed for a period of consolidation and expansion, perhaps best typified by the hysterical gaiety, creativity, and dynamism of mid-twenties Berlin.

For the police, the slogan "your friend and helper" was advanced, and efforts were made not only to democratize police practice but also to create goodwill toward the police on the part of a public that had typically respected police power but had little liking for police. Severing (1950), in defending the concept of a barracked police to replace the banned Sipo, spoke of the advisability of putting the young recruits into these barracks and having the older police on the streets: "For independent police work (Einzeldienst) older, experienced, and less volatile civil servants would be used; in contrast, younger members of the organization who were perhaps in strength and bodily development more capable of withstanding resistance than their older comrades, but whose impetuousness needed to be tempered through training and through experience of professional responsibilities, were to be kept in barracks. The development of police schools in various provinces went hand in hand with these organizational arrangements. The schools pursued the objective of creating civil servants who, in their concourse with the public, could be trusted with all the requirements of their job, and in addition, who had character traits necessary for the elevated task of being a

friend and confidante rather than a bully and terror to the citizen"
(Ibid.: 315). Severing went on to explain his ideas about the development of a highly trained and capable officer corps that would be an example to the lower ranks: "The requirements that, it seemed to me, had
to be developed in police supervisors were much greater and more complex than had previously been expected of army officers." Police supervisors had to be familiar with and sympathetic to social and economic
conditions among all classes of people and had to be careful to avoid
everything which could lead to "a renewed alienation between police and
public. . . . The more a police leader became a businessman, a sociolo-
gist and, not least, a psychologist, the easier would become the fulfilling
of his responsibilities." Those leaders who saw the police as just another
form of military service had no room in the police and would have to
leave police service. "I am not claiming that the searching of the con-
science that many leaders at that time had to engage in resulted in a
clear understanding in each case. But gradually the Police Leadership
Academy was able to convince the police leadership, from whom the
archtype of the true police civil servant could be developed" (Ibid.: 316).

Severing's words highlight a point that needs to be made about German police leadership since the Weimar time. This is that the two national police academies, the one at Berlin-Charlottenberg in the Weimar
Republic and, in the Federal Republic, the one at Münster-Hiltrup,
provided the Germans with an important opportunity to influence police thought and action throughout the otherwise state-level police. The
present academy at Hiltrup, which trains the top leadership of all the
states, develops cohorts of elite officers who attend at similar stages of
their careers. These officers, through the living arrangements and emphasis on comradeship and national police needs, provide a strong uni-
fying link among the police of the various states.

The major good-will effort of the 1920's was the famous police exposition that was held in Berlin in 1926. According to Severing, the exhibition represented an effort to overcome the vestiges of old prejudices
against police as well as an effort to counteract new criticisms that the
police had been transformed into a guardian force for Marxist elements
in the population. The exhibition was to include "state of the art" exhibits on police technology and equipment as well as materials on the development of the new police organization. The theme of the exhibition,
"Please, step closer" ("Bitte, treten Sie Näher") was meant to counteract
the aloofness and arrogance with which previous police leaders had
treated the people (Ibid.: 83-84).

Although some of the police proclamations and actions designed to effect a rapprochement between police and public may be seen as chiefly public relations efforts, the top police leadership, at least in Prussia and in the central government, appears to have been genuinely devoted to democracy and to have been inspired in large part by the philosophy of the ruling Social Democratic party. In any case, these efforts were soon overtaken by events and the police found themselves more and more thrust into the thankless and increasingly hopeless task of trying to keep the peace between roving bands of armed right-wing and left-wing pseudo-armies. The takeover of the Prussian police in 1933 by the Reich military on the grounds that it could no longer keep order was the pathetic culmination of all the attempts to create a new and democratic police presence.

THE THIRD REICH

During the Third Reich the German police became for the first time in its history a centralized organization. In both Imperial and Weimar Germany, police forces were based within the Länder, or states. A state-based police force was part of the peculiar tradition of administration that was masterminded by Chancellor Otto von Bismarck after the creation of the German Empire in 1871. Legislative powers, military matters, and foreign affairs were handled by the central Reich government, while administration was left to the state governments. In this way, a dual administration was avoided, and the states, which were uneasy about giving up their powers to the central government, retained control over execution of the laws. Supervision of the police was given to the Landrat, who was the appointed county executive (Jacob, 1963). State police were thus in the position of administering legislation, and especially criminal law, that was passed by a central legislature, the Reichstag, for all of Germany. This arrangement persisted until the breakdown of the Weimar Republic. It was reinstituted in the Federal Republic.

Centralization of the police under the Nazis was part of the "Gleichschaltung" (roughly: "bringing into like-mindedness") of German society, in which the state governments in general lost their sovereignty and gave way to a centralized administration. In effect Bismarck's great compromise between nation and states was ended. Soon the concept of the German people as a single entity became not only a rationale for centralized control within the borders of Germany but also an excuse for predatory incursions into neighboring territory.

The destruction of the state-based police started in 1933, when German military forces under General Gert von Rundstedt entered Berlin, relieved the police leaders of their duties, and declared a state of martial law. This action was taken on the grounds that the police were no longer able to maintain order (Liang, 1970). Shortly thereafter, with the appointment of Hitler as Chancellor, Hermann Göring was made Prussian Minister of the Interior and thus head of Prussian police, and Heinrich Himmler was made head of the Bavarian police (Erdmann, 1980: 91). With these appointments, two of Hitler's most trusted followers were placed in crucial internal order positions in the two largest German states, the two states that were most likely to inhibit a smooth takeover of the entire country. In Prussia, the liberal Social Democratic majority was not congenial to the Nazis, while in Bavaria a strong tradition of independence mitigated against central control.

The new Reich Interior Ministry officials moved swiftly to suppress the varied and often contentious police unions of the Weimar Republic and to infuse a spirit of loyalty and centralism into their new police forces. Estimates vary about the number of police who were let go under the general Berufsbereinigungsgesetz, the law designed to "purify" the civil service by getting rid of subversive personnel. One author (Riege, 1959: 41) says that in Prussia, out of 85,000 police personnel, 2668, including 294 supervisory personnel, were dismissed. Another (Werkentin, 1984: 68) puts this number at 5000.

A new police journal, *Der Deutsche Polizeibeamte (The German Police Officer)*, was initiated, and the projected character of the new police was evidenced in its first edition. Interior Minister Frick deplored the "personal interest conflict" that characterized the police unions and declared that "the Chancellor himself and the men he has put in leadership positions are taking care of the interests of the compatriots entrusted to them, whether they are civil servants or in other occupations. The interests of the individual have succumbed, under the basic principle: 'common good goes before individual good,' to the interests of the community. The National Socialist state needs a police built on comradeship and discipline. Only a police with the spirit of our army and of our struggle for the National Socialist revolution can do the work that the new state demands of it . . . . may it be a goal of the new brotherhood of police officers that next to comradeship iron discipline holds it together. May each police officer act in the spirit of truly carrying out his duty, a fighter for

Adolf Hitler in creating a great and powerful German state" (*Deutscher Polizeibeamte*, 1933: 1).

In the same edition, Joseph Goebbels greeted the Reich police with a challenge to be strong and firm against internal enemies:

"Discipline and righteousness, protection against all societal weaknesses, ruthless struggle against all who would harm the people and the state . . . to dedicate oneself to this will be the rewarding task of the new police brotherhood . . . " (Ibid.: 2).

To these remarks, the new Prussian police chief, Daluege, added: "We have no more place in the Prussian police for the interest groups that furthered themselves in the parliamentary system . . . may our motto 'I serve' be written in the heart of each German police officer" (Ibid.).

The first major operational change that resulted from this takeover was the change in the character of the Bereitschaftspolizei, the units of recruits who, while in training for the regular street police, acted as disturbance-control forces. In the particular circumstances of the time, it can be seen that these Bereitschaft groups, living in barracks, and consisting of the youngest, most malleable, and most disciplined and organized elements of the police forces in each state, constituted an important resource for increasing the military potential of a regime that even then was thinking in terms of preparation for war (Erdmann, 1980). During the succeeding two years the policing duties of the Bereitschaftspolizei were increasingly de-emphasized and military maneuvers, training, and ways of thinking were stressed. This process culminated in the integration of the Bereitschaftspolizei into the military in March of 1936 (Raible, 1963). The regime justified this takeover by declaring that the newly-obedient German people no longer needed the numbers of police who had existed previous to the takeover (Riege, 1959). "Only the ruins of a police force were left," according to one police commentator (Dierski, undated: 8). This remark itself is enlightening in that it shows how essential a specialized disturbance control force seemed to the Germans. Nevertheless, since the Bereitschaftspolizei had, because of its training function, provided the personnel for the entire future police force, its appropriation by the military made for a serious deficiency in the police organization.

This thinning of the ranks was followed shortly thereafter, however, by a systematic integration into the police of the many unemployed SA troops who had paved the way to Hitler's accession to power. With their tradition of brutality and lawlessness, a new element was introduced into the German police, a police which, while never popular among the people, had generally been regarded as at least "correct" in demeanor. At the same time the *Kriminalpolizei* (criminal investigations, or detective, forces) assumed a new character, becoming chiefly concerned with internal subversion as opposed to investigation of crime. The *Gestapo* was then formed as a special unit within the *Kriminalpolizei* and soon begin to dominate its activities. Within the *Schutzpolizei* (the regular uniformed street police), the former SA troops became part of the SS after the Rohm assassination and the decline of the SA. These SS troops became military troops in the course of the war and were given the task of policing the occupied territories and running the death camps.

Police gradually took on quasi-judicial powers and thus were not only purveyors of order and security but also judges, executioners, and soldiers for the regime. In this way the degeneration of the German police was accomplished, with many of the most feared, most hated, and most brutal elements of the entire National Socialist movement clustered in this one organization, which has become a symbol for evil in modern history and thought. From a strength of 190,000 in 1931, the German police rose to a strength of 2,000,000 during the height of the war (Kemperer, 1953).

The ease with which the police were able to be changed to a military fighting force, the identification of the police with elite Nazi organs of terror—SS, Gestapo, SD—and the general determination of the victorious allies to prevent possible future incursions of German military forces into the rest of Europe led to a radical dismantling of this police apparatus at the end of the war. In addition, through a plan which had its origins at the Yalta Conference in 1945, the new German police organization was to become a *democratic* police force, or at least a police force that would be appropriate for policing a democratic society.

THE FEDERAL REPUBLIC OF GERMANY

Germany in 1945 was once again a defeated nation, subject to the victorious Allied powers. The conditions of that time—destruction of the cities, millions of homeless and hungry people, untold numbers of refugees—contributed to a massive wave of murder and lawlessness (Kosyra, 1980). The occupation by four different powers and the need for an entirely new police force also made the transition particularly difficult for law enforcement authorities.

Once again demilitarization, democratization, and changed police-community relations were major goals of police reform. These reforms, in addition to the various efforts to decentralize police, will be considered in detail in subsequent chapters. Two radical further changes were also mandated: reconceptualization of police functions in order to exclude general regulatory functions, and complete purification of police ranks in order to get rid of Nazi elements.

Reconceptualization of Police Functions

To understand what is involved in this projected change one needs some explanation of the concept of "police" in pre-1945 Germany. To an American, police are the forces whose mission is law enforcement and order maintenance. The concept of enforcement, or the power to use force to insure compliance is central to this concept of police role, and has been described as the distinguishing mark of police service, as opposed to any other kind of government service (Bittner, 1980). This is also the aspect of police service that makes it intensely important both that police activities be closely controlled and that recruitment and training of police be directed at the development of police officers who are able to accept this power without either shirking or abusing it (Muir, 1978).

In pre-1945 Germany, the law enforcement forces comparable to American police forces were known as Executive Police (Vollzugspolizei) and were distinguished from Administrative Police (Polizei Behörden). Administrative Police functions consisted of a large variety of regulatory work, including regulation of restaurants and other food outlets, housing regulations, citizen identification work, and passport controls. Thus large segments of German life were affected by agencies that were called police agencies. Within the government bureaucracy, however, the administrative police work was performed by separate units within the Interior Ministries.

There were historical reasons for this organization (Chapman, 1970). To the victorious allies in 1945, however, it seemed that one of the prime indicators that Germany was a police state through and through was this ubiquitous use of the word "police" to refer to what in other countries are nonpolice regulatory functions. The Allies ordered strict organizational separation between administrative and executive functions and the former was no longer to be known as police work. Executive police were to be called in to enforce the regulations only when regulatory officials found that compliance with rules could not be achieved without their help.

German police officials were not happy with this organizational separation. Their claim was that the organizational ties between these two types of agencies allowed greater flexibility and cooperation on important matters. For example, close cooperation between citizen registration units and detective units made law enforcement tasks easier. Also, having the administrative function tied to the executive function allowed for taking police officers off street duty and assigning them to administrative functions once they had reached their middle years and found the street work physically difficult. Nevertheless, this change was insisted upon and carried out, at least during the years of the Occupation.

Denazification

Purging of the ranks to get rid of Nazi elements was a first order of business for the post-war police. The first orders of the Allied High Command to German police officials illustrate the problems of this period (Militärregierung, 1945: 30-35):

"---You will no longer take orders from superior German police officials,

---You are to take over the Kriminalpolizei in your area,

---You will submit lists of police agency employees each month,

---You will submit lists of resisters, Jews, former trade union leaders in your district (within twenty-four hours and continuing thereafter),

---You will submit lists of National Socialist leaders in your district (within twenty-four hours),

---You will detain forthwith the following police officials found in your jurisdiction and release them to the Counterintelligence Branch of the United Nations:

(a) all police Presidents and Directors

(b) all members of the Gestapo and Sicherheitsdienst of the SS

(c) all administrative police who served with the Gestapo either in their headquarters or as special investigators

(d) all officers of the Ordnungspolizei or Kriminalpolizei above the rank of Lieutenant Colonel or equivalent

(e) all police who have had commissions as officers in the SS, SA, NSKK, or NSFK, or who have held office in the NSDAP with the rank of Ortgruppleiter or above, or in the Hitler Jugend with the rank of Bannführer or above."

It is not clear who was to carry out these orders. Gradually, however, some of the police leaders of the pre-Nazi period surfaced and were reinstated. In Hamburg, for example, police chief Donner, who had been removed by the Nazis after a dramatic refusal by the Hamburg Senate to sanction the efforts to replace him, was reappointed police chief in 1945. His tenure was short, however, since the British occupying authorities replaced him soon thereafter with one of his subordinates who was more fluent in English (Innenministerium Hamburg, 1964). The subsequent attempts to purge police ranks of the Nazi elements, to reorganize, to provide for training, and to carry out general police work were all monitored and even controlled by the Allied powers.

Success of the purging process is difficult to assess because of the post-war confusion, the number of documents that had been destroyed either in the bombing of German cities or by the police themselves, and the difficulty of obtaining records from the Russian-occupied eastern portion of the country. The records indicate, however, that decimation of those police forces remaining in 1945 was the result of early efforts to purge the Nazi elements. In the American zone, strength of police forces in the various communities and the reasons for dismissing officers show some of the results of this effort to create a new police force. The town of Heidenheim, for example, reported that of 53 police officers who were still in service at the end of the war (i.e., not missing or prisoners of war) 19 were let go for political reasons and 10 had resigned or retired. In Ludwigsburg 25 out of 42 officers were dismissed; in Heilbronn 35 out of 52. In Ulm a first wave of dismissals included 26 police officers, 15 civilian employees, and 19 reserve officers. Of the remaining 86 officers in service, 25 were suspended, retired, or resigned between July and December, 1945 (HS, EA 2/11, 137: #8-19).

The magnitude of the recruitment problem can be seen in Stuttgart, where, in July 1945, out of 2,844 sworn officers on the books, 2,680 had not reported back for duty. The authorities were unable to ascertain how many of these officers were missing, how many were prisoners of war, and how many failed to report back for political reasons (Ibid.: #28). In 1947 it was reported by the mayor that of 623 Schutzpolizei officers, 576 had to be let go after further investigation. The Kriminalpolizei was reduced from 104 to 98, and the administrative force lost 111 out of 154 (Ibid.: #19).

The picture became even more clouded as the denazification process cleared some people who had previously been dismissed; as returning prisoners of war claimed their right as former civil servants to reenter the police; and as partial amnesties in particular situations were declared. Some of the problems are evidenced in the 1949 annual report of the Stuttgart police, which complains that only 20 percent of those who apply for police positions can be hired and that not enough recruits can be found. Most important among the refusals to take on officers is their political background (HS, EA 2/11, 173: #260).

> At most 20 percent of those applying can be considered qualified for police work. The others must be rejected because of their performance on the entrance examination, inability to pass the physical examination, and previous criminal or political history. . . . Especially the question of political past imposes a particular obstacle to be overcome by applicants. Particularly high standards of political acceptability must be demanded of police officers. Those hired for police work represent a very carefully chosen group. A comparison of police with other administrative positions is not possible. The result is that, even when we are hiring previous police officers who have some political disadvantage (*die politisch belastet sind*) a different standard must be employed than with other administrative agencies. There is a difference between hiring a politically suspect (*belastet*) street police officer for the new democratic state or hiring him as bookkeeper for the credit union. The police is therefore not in a position to rehire politically suspect individuals. We have reached the outer limits on the hiring of such formerly banned individuals. Raising this limit cannot be justified in view of the particular situation and particular tasks of the police, even if it means that a large number of former civil servants cannot be hired.
>
> The law which frees former prisoners, combined with the civil service law and the returning prisoners' amnesty theoretically makes it possible to rehire, in their previous salary group, previous officers who are returning from prisoner of war status, without consideration of their political past. This solution to the personnel problem is not good in view of the attempt to build a democratic police force. It must be guaranteed that each rehired officer has the proper political qualifications. If he cannot meet these qualifications, another use should be found for his services. Another matter is that of the grade in which politically hindered individuals should be installed and what kind of work they would be doing. It is intolerable to conceive of having politically hindered officers placed before (literally: set before the noses of) politically acceptable officers who have now for years rendered service to the new state in the spirit in which the new state was conceived.

Despite the emphasis on political purity of the early post-war period, it is obvious that some adherents of the old order were able to become reinstated as police officers. In addition, the need for personnel resulted in a rather motley assortment of ill-trained, hastily-chosen police personnel, even including some with criminal histories (Bottscher and

Schäfer, 1949). This evidence does not suggest, however, that the police leadership was composed of ex-Nazis or that the leadership was at pains to protect or advance these individuals. One account says that, among those who had been forbidden to continue their work by the Nazis, and who now occupied leadership positions in the police, "one finds impressive individuals, with a highly-developed sense of public responsibility, a good inheritance that remains from the Weimar times" (Ibid.: 139).

In the development of a more democratic police, it was especially the large infusion of ex-soldiers with their habits of military obedience and military order who were likely to inhibit progress. One commentator with memories of that time says that in the confusion of the immediate post-war period, returning soldiers did not have many opportunities for employment and thus chose to apply for police work rather than for some of the less attractive opportunities such as coal mining.

Since almost all men between the age of 16 and 50 had been taken into the military by 1945 it would have been impossible to staff the police with other than ex-soldiers. Nevertheless, developing habits of self-reliance, tolerance of diversity, and greater openness in police organizations was not easy given this raw material, and it was not until the second post-war generation of police was hired that the police leadership was able to work in more desirable circumstances.

The post-war leadership itself seems to have been rather colorless. Perhaps because reform of police was imposed from the outside, one does not get the impression that attempts to democratize police were the result of strong and visionary leadership on the part of the Germans themselves. Rather, the impression one gets from the police journals of that time and from the records is that of a committee effort with many adherents but without the flavor of personal leadership that people like Severing, Heimannsberg, Weiss, and van den Berghe brought to the Weimar police. Severing, however, was trying to counter the authoritarian imperial tradition of policing and his attention was directed largely at the police leadership. The leadership of the post-1945 German police, on the other hand, were more likely to be heirs of the Weimar tradition and the 1931 police law than of the National Socialist period. Severing's effort was also more ideological and rhetorical in tone, and had the goal of fostering the ideals and the fortunes of the Social Democratic Party. By contrast, the post World War II police was both less partisan and more carefully controlled by outside forces. Furthermore, the burden of historical liability and disgrace probably mitigated against the rise of flamboyant or charismatic leaders. In effect the reforms were carried out faithfully by bureaucrats working in situations of extreme complexity and difficulty.

An exception to the generally faceless bureaucracy that was concerned with restructuring the German police after World War II was Herbert Kalicinski. Kalicinski was director of the Police Institute (Since 1972 known as the Police Leadership Academy, or Polizei-Führungsakademie) in Münster-Hiltrup, from 1950 to 1962. This academy is located administratively within the structures of the police of the state of North Rhine-Westphalia. It derives much of its support from federal government funds, and trains the top leadership of the police of all the states of the Federal Republic. It is essentially the successor of the police academy at Berlin-Charlottenberg, which was directed by Van den Berghe during the Weimar Republic.

Kalicinski himself was born in East Prussia in 1897. He followed the typical career route of many police of this time, moving from military service to border patrol service to police service. During his tenure as a police adjutant in Beuthen, he also studied political science and law at the University of Breslau. A man of drive, talent, and ambition, he gradually rose through the police hierarchy to a position of leadership in Upper Silesia. During these years Kalicinski was actively promoting improvements in police training and developing cooperative arrangements with police in other countries. During the National Socialist regime Kalicinski was gradually demoted and then separated from the police. After his separation he supported himself through manual labor (*Die Neue Polizei*, 1962).

After the war Kalicinski offered himself for police service once again and eventually was made the first director of the police academy. He is credited with building renewed ties to international policing, gradually restoring the German police to credibility among other national police forces, and with making Germany a center for police information and training in Europe. In 1961 he was elected president of the International Police Association (Ibid.; Kalicinski, 1960). Through his writing and his work at the Academy, Kalicinski is known for his emphasis on a more democratic style of policing, on good relations between supervisors and subordinates and between police and public.

The Era of Good Feeling

In 1949, with the passage of the Basic Law, or Constitution, of the Federal Republic, the occupation of Germany came to an end. The Allies, however, continued to have the power to control both military and police strength in the new republic. Ironically, as the pressures of the Cold War accelerated, it was the western powers that began to push for greater German military capacity. It was over the protests of many Germans that the Allied High Commission decided that the Bepo should be reconstituted in the western zones and that 20,000 men should be allocated to this barracked force. At the same time a 20,000 man border police, the Bundesgrenzschutz, or BGS, was authorized. Although it was shortly thereafter that Chancellor Adenauer convinced the allied authorities of the need for a regular military force in western Germany, both the BGS and the Bepo remained as part of the regular police apparatus. They continue to be a source of controversy to this day. The details of these developments are taken up in the next chapter.

With the end of the occupation, the German states also gave up the radically decentralized police forces that had been imposed in the British and American zones. In each of the four zones of occupation the locus of police power had been structured to reflect police structures in the home territory of the occupying power. Thus the Soviets had a single centralized police, the French had police centralized to the state level, and the Americans and British had forms of communal police.

From the German perspective, only the French plan represented a desirable structural arrangement for the police. This was no doubt because the organization in the French zone was the same as that which had existed in Germany prior to 1933. The American plan for radical communalization was especially distasteful to the Germans, who believed it would lead inevitably to politicization of a sensitive branch of the civil service. After the occupation ended the Germans returned with some haste to a state-based police force, although allowing for communal police forces to remain in the larger cities of the American zone. By 1975, when Munich gave up its communal police, the Germans had completed the reconstitution of the major structures they had had in 1931. Starting in 1950 and gradually thereafter all of the northern states readopted the 1931 Prussian police law almost in its entirety. The other states have adopted legislation that is heavily influenced by this legislation. In sum, given the chance to chose, the Germans decided to resume their police history from where it had been interrupted in 1933.

The period of the 1950's and early 1960's may be described as an era of good feeling in post-war German police history. Indeed, this period was generally one of relative tranquillity and domestic growth. It came to an end with the widespread citizen unrest that plagued not only Germany but much of the world in the late 1960's.

The slogan, "The police, your friend and helper" was resurrected as an important component of the image-building efforts of the 1950's, as it had been both during the Weimar Republic and during the National Socialist era. Speeches, journal articles, and books spoke of the development of a "citizen-friendly" (Bürgernahe) police. Police training courses stressed citizenship and constitutional rights of citizens. Touching examples of police concern for citizens were given wide circulation. In one such story (*Deutsche Polizei*, 1960) an old man is arrested by a Kripo officer for stealing an umbrella. The officer notices a simply-dressed old woman, who is crying while he is making this arrest. Upon his inquiry, she tells him that she is a war widow, that she and the arrested man, who is an ex-convict, have been friends since he was released from prison seven years earlier, that he has committed no crimes since that time, and that he took the umbrella in order to please her, since it had started to rain while they were on a shopping trip. With a warning from the officer, the two old people go away together. In the same article, the example is given of a young woman whose sports car, with a flat tire, is standing in the middle of the street. Two Schupo officers arrive on the scene, move her car to the side, and change her tire. A crowd of bystanders cheers. "Friend and helper is more than an advertising slogan," says the author of this article. "Rather it is also a duty and an obligation. However, the police cannot carry it out all by themselves. We must all help them with it" (Ibid.: 115).

Also during this era of the 1950's the leadership moved to end the pariah status of the German police and to reestablish ties and cooperative efforts with police in other European countries. Under the leadership of Herbert Kalicinski, the German police became a central force in the International Federation of Police Leaders (*Féderation Supérieure des Chefs Internationales de Police—FSCIP*). Gradually, close cooperation on law enforcement and internal security matters developed among the nations of Western Europe, with the Federal Republic of Germany as a center for activities such as seminars and training sessions.

Rapid industrial and commercial expansion of the Federal Republic's economy fueled the activities of the police in the 1950's. Even a superficial perusal of the police journals of that time shows a major preoccupation with traffic problems. Such concern put the police in the role of facilitators of the general prosperity and dynamism of West German society at that time. As Germany prosperity increased, the trend toward ever-increasing auto ownership intensified these concerns. Even today the Police Leadership Academy library subscribes to 16 journals and newsletters devoted to traffic problems and their solution.

With the major upheavals that started in the late 1960's and that have persisted to the present, the tone of the relationships between police and citizens changed. Although the triggering events for police-citizen conflict have changed in recent years, the problems remain. Student riots of the 1960's have been replaced by demonstrations against environmental depredations caused by nuclear power plants and new airport runways, as well as by protest against foreign, especially American, military initiatives on German soil. In addition, public insecurity has been heightened by a rising crime rate. As will be described in Chapter Three the police have provided a convenient target for airing of resentments and, in turn, a hardening of attitude toward the public has taken place.

A superficial comparison of these developments to those in the latter 1920's and the early 1930's might lead to the conclusion that the German police are now going through a similar losing battle to keep order in a dangerously volatile society. Such a conclusion, however, would fail to take into effect almost forty years of development in German society, forty years during which two generations have been born and grown to adulthood under a democratic constitution that is systematically invoked by all sides in the struggles of today. Habits of compromise, or pragmatism, or moderation, that seemed so alien to German thought, have become part of German political life. Thus, while the degree of public unrest and tension may be great, the danger of disintegration of the social order is in no way as imminent as it was during the entire life of the Weimar constitution. Furthermore, as will be described in detail in Chapters Five and Six, the police itself went through a major period of self-assessment and reform in the early 1970's. A new post-war generation of police officers and a central government that was particularly interested in police reform, were catalysts in this effort.

TODAY'S POLICE ORGANIZATION IN THE FEDERAL REPUBLIC OF GERMANY

The 1949 constitution, known as the Basic Law (Grundgesetz) of the Federal Republic of Germany, contains few provisions related to central government authority in police matters. In cases of emergency, the government of a state may request the aid of police forces from other states or of the Bundesgrenzschutz (the border police). If the state government does not request aid and the federal government finds that a state of emergency exists, it may federalize police from that state and other states to deal with the emergency. Likewise, the federal government may use the armed forces to supplement police where they are not able to handle emergencies themselves. All such actions must cease upon the request of either house of the legislature (*Grundgesetz*, Articles 35, 91). The federal government is given the authority to set up a border protection police, central police data and communication agencies, and a federal criminal investigations agency (Article 87). The federal government may make cooperative arrangements with respect to criminal investigation, protection against internal subversion, and international law enforcement (Article 73.10).

These constitutional provisions allowed the establishment of the Federal Border Police (Bundesgrenzschutz, or BGS) in 1950. The federal criminal detection effort has been institutionalized in the Bundeskriminalamt (BKA), with headquarters in Wiesbaden. The BKA, which is similar to the American FBI, acts as a communications center for information on crime rates, fingerprints, criminal histories, and other criminal information. In addition it is responsible for research on forensic subjects, and it acts as the German center for Interpol, the international police agency. BKA agents may be called on by the local police for help in criminal investigations (Kosyra, 1980).

Administratively, such federal police efforts emanate from the offices of the Ministry of the Interior. A medium for cooperation among the states and between the states and the federal government in police matters is the Standing Conference of Interior Ministers that meets several times each year and includes the ministers from all the states.

Federal government support is crucial for the Bereitschaftspolizei. By agreement with the federal government, the states provide for personal services costs, room, and board for the recruits of these forces. The federal government provides for vehicles, communications facilities, sanitary arrangements, and arms. The effect of this involvement is that the federal government is a major force in the planning of police strength in the states, since the Bepo has not only an order-maintenance function but also a recruit-training function, and since almost all regular police personnel start their careers in that subdivision of police. The federal government also supports state police organizations by exempting police recruits from the compulsory one and one-half years of military service required of young German men. Furthermore, the peculiar nature of

German criminal law, that, in the case of major crimes, comes from the federal parliament, to be administered at the state level, also creates a large measure of federal influence over state criminal processes. Finally, the German Constitutional Court, through decisions about criminal law, and especially criminal procedure, exerts a national influence on local police departments.

In essence, however, the police of the Federal Republic are organized, recruited, and controlled at the state level. This means that there are some organizational differences among the states. Differences in organization, in fact, are more pronounced than differences in function and training. Berlin, which is still nominally under foreign control, also presents a special case, although in general the rules that apply to the states of the Federal Republic are also in effect for Berlin. Figures 1-3 show varied police organizational arrangements for two states, Lower Saxony and Rhineland-Palatinate, and for one city-state, Bremen. These charts show the differences in organization among the three states, but they also show the five basic organizational divisions of the police of the various states: (1) Schutzpolizei, or uniformed street police, (2) Kriminalpolizei, or criminal investigations force, (3) Wasserschutzpolizei, or navigational police, (4) Landespolizeischule, or police schools, that handle training for the middle ranks of the police (mittlerer Dienst and gehobener Dienst), and Bereitschaftspolizei, the units that combine social order control work with training of recruits.

A major variant of this organization occurs in Bavaria, which has its own border police (Bayerische Grenzpolizei) and does not contribute recruits to the national-level BGS. Bavaria also is not pledged to take 20 percent of its street police from among the ranks of the federal BGS, as are the other states. Recruitment from the ranks of the BGS is, for other states, the major exception to the normal path of police service through the Bepo. In recent years, however, Bavaria has agreed to take a certain number of BGS personnel into its police.

The BGS itself has been a controversial agency because of its military character. Despite objections from some quarters (Werkentin, 1984: Ch. 4) the BGS has remained within the police sphere. In 1972 and 1976, federal legislation created closer ties to state police. BGS training, salary, and service rights were put on a par with those of state police forces. These changes made possible the easy integration of BGS personnel into state forces and the easy use of BGS troops in civil order control emergencies.

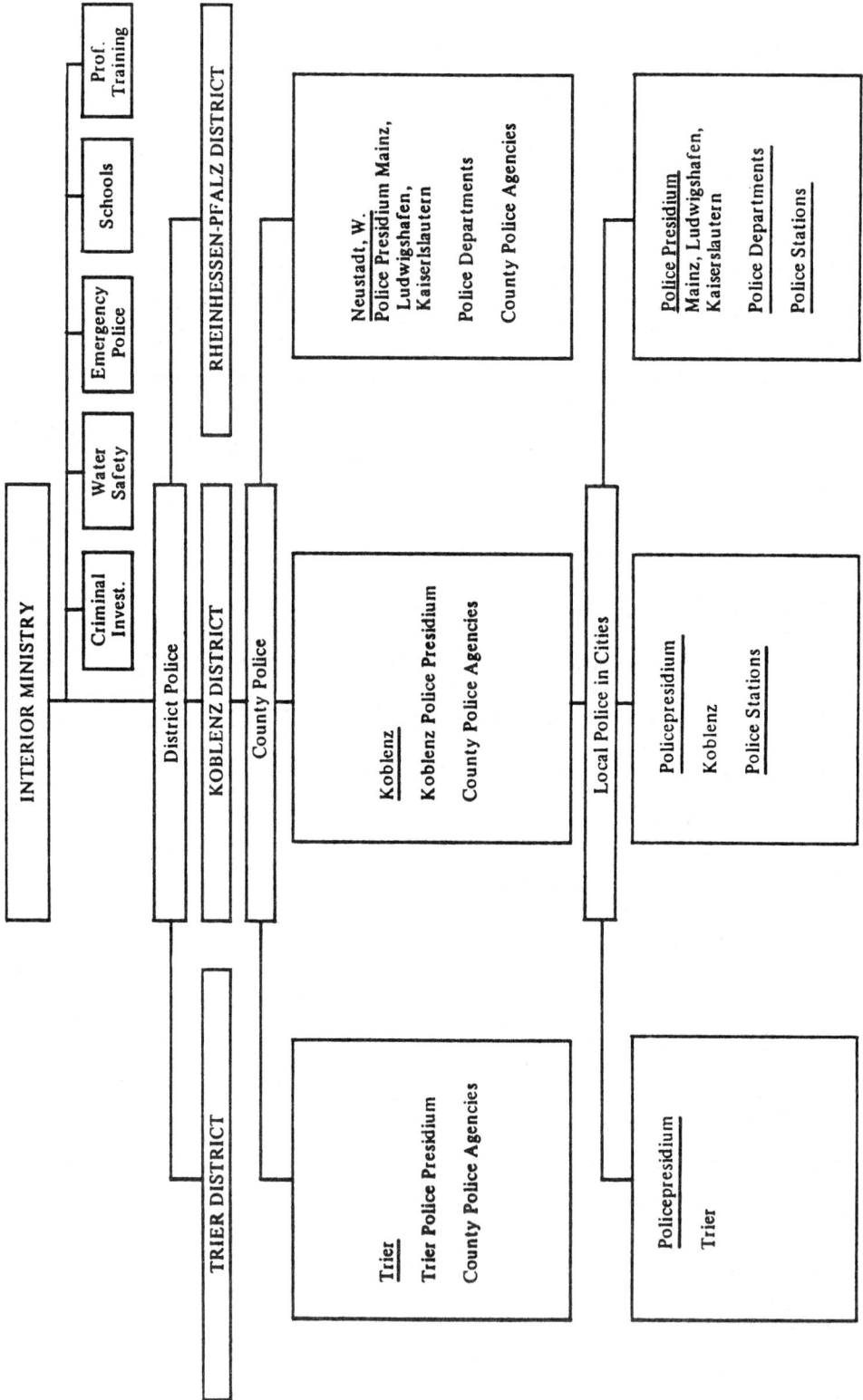

Figure 1. Organization of the Police in Rhineland–Palatinate

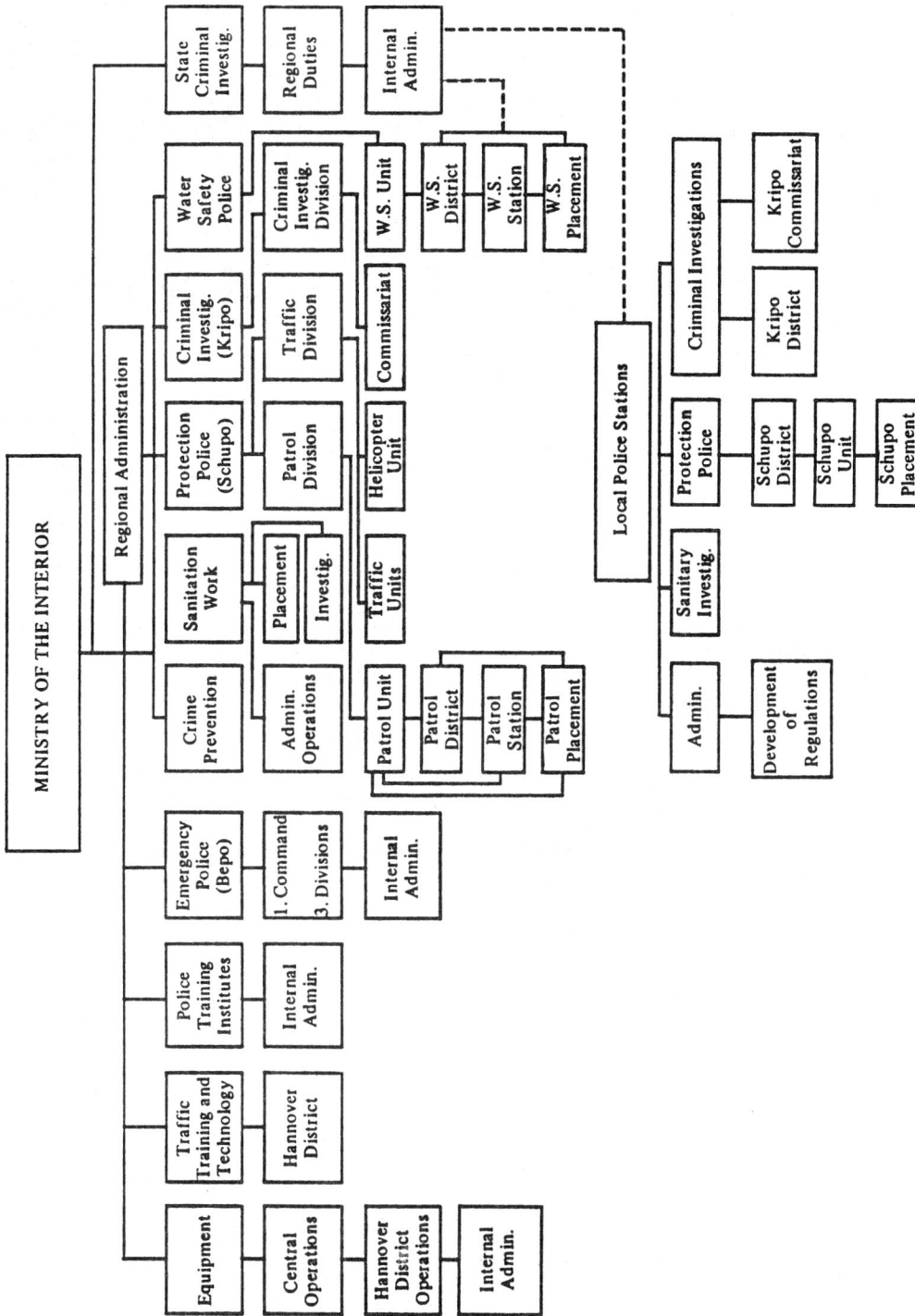

Figure 2. Organization of the Police in Lower Saxony

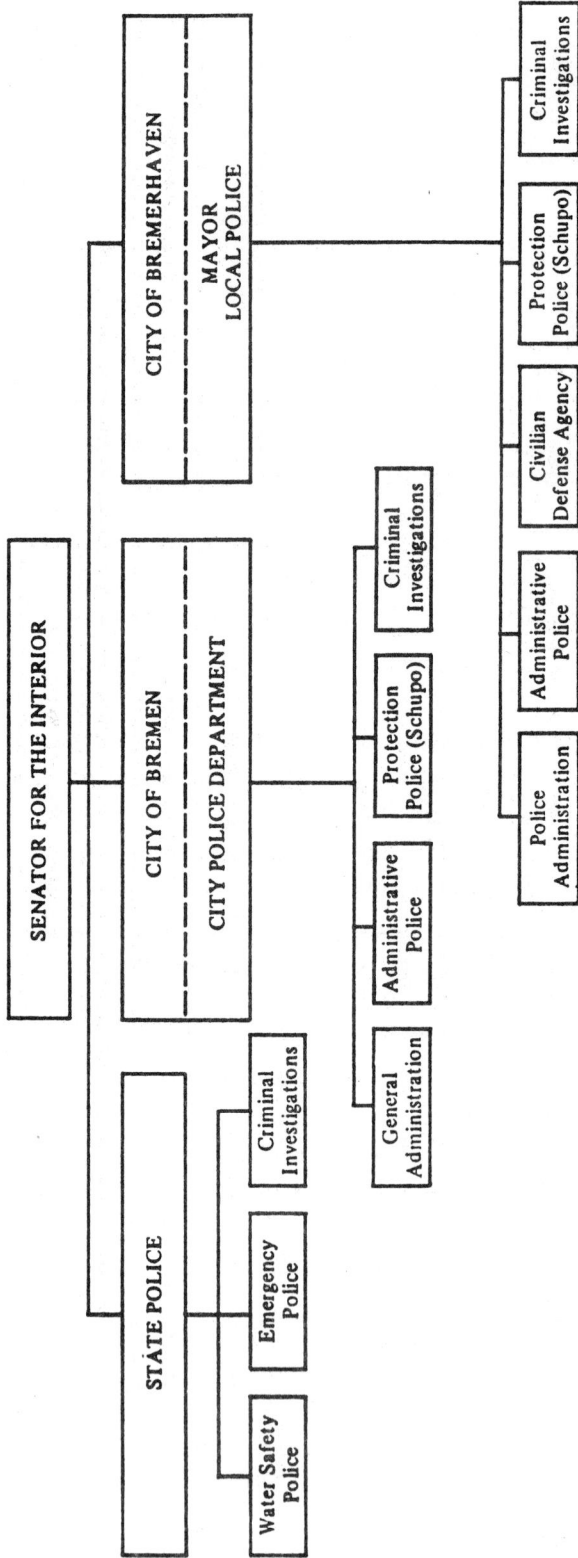

Figure 3.   Organization of the Police in Bremen

Civilian leadership is an important facet of police administration in Germany. In addition to the interior ministers of each state, many police presidents, or police chiefs, of local subdivisions are civilian political appointees. Most of these civilian individuals have a legal education and have held other positions in the interior ministries or in the justice system.

Detective work is a coveted goal for many of the police recruits, and there is great competition for entrance into the ranks of the detective forces when basic training in the Bepo and basic street work are completed. For this reason the detective forces are able to be very selective and it seems inevitable that many of the most capable individuals will serve their police time as detectives. Since there is no attempt to rotate officers between detective and patrol work, as there is in some agencies in the United States, the division between these two remains great despite the efforts to have them work closely together.

German police training has often been praised for its thoroughness and professionalism. In a country in which the larger civil service has generally been divided between an elite leadership and a common rank and file, the police service offers an opportunity for officers to advance from the lowest to the highest ranks entirely on the basis of examinations and of the personal ability that is shown at each stage of the process. Although there are some variants to the pattern, the general track that officers follow from the lowest to the highest rank takes them through three major periods of training in the course of their career. After the first two to three years in the Bepo, of which the first is devoted to basic training, while the second and third combine training with peace-keeping functions, recruits go to the police school that exists in each state for another six months of training preparatory to assuming individual street-level assignments. Much of the training in this final six months is in law, legal procedures, and general demeanor of police in relation to citizens.

The officer who completes this training enters into the middle ranks of the German civil service (mittlerer Dienst). After six years those who did well on the examinations for the middle service, who are outstanding in street work, and who do well on a further examination then go on to another two or three years of schooling at higher police schools or at colleges for public administration in each state. Graduates of these schools enter into the higher civil service (gehobener Dienst). Depending on the state, 15 to 20 percent of the police of the Federal Republic are in the higher civil service.

The final step into the highest police leadership (höherer Dienst) entails another two years of schooling of which the first takes place in the officer's home state. Candidates for this highest rank then spend one year at the Police Leadership Academy in Münster-Hiltrup in the state of North Rhine-Westphalia. For the last year of training, then, the police officer lives and studies with the best elements of the police of all the states. Between 1 and 3 percent of the police make it into this highest service.

Counting back, one can see that in order to achieve the highest rank, the police leader must have gone through at least seven years of training. This formal training is in addition to the numerous continuing education courses in various aspects of police work that all German police take part in. Some officers also take further outside courses in specialized topics such as accounting and computer science. To an outside observer the old saying that "half the Germans are in school and the other half are teaching them" seems to apply particularly aptly to the police with their strong emphasis on training and education.

As of July 1, 1986, the number of police personnel in the Federal Republic is close to 200,000 in a population of about 62,000,000. In 1978, total police strength was 179,121. Thus, there has been an increase of 11 percent in the past decade. In 1950, shortly after the adoption of the Constitution, police strength stood at 88,000, with a population of 45,000,000 (Dierski, undated). Thus the proportion of police to citizens has risen from 1/500 to about 1/300 in the past 35 years. Table 1 shows the distribution of police by federal government and individual states. Table 2 shows the ratio of police to citizens in the various German states. Of the total federal police there are about 22,000 in the Bundesgrenzschutz and about 5000 in the other federal forces, Bundesverfassungsschutz and Bundeskriminalamt (Constitution protection force and federal criminal investigations agency). The Federal Republic, then, with its heavily urbanized and industrialized population, has a ratio of police to population that is comparable to that of more rural France (1/276), but higher than that of Great Britain (1/408) (Stead, 1983: 4). In rural Denmark, with only one large city, the ratio is 1/500. In the United States, the general averages for small cities are from 1/576 to 1/776; for large cities, 1/502, for state forces 1/149 to 1/2248 (*Schriftenreihe,* 1980). In addition, authorities in the United States are able to call on National Guard and military troops in case of major demonstrations and catastrophes. Although the Constitution of the Federal Republic allows for the use of military troops in extreme emergencies, the actual use of such troops internally would be unthinkable because of Germany's history of militarism, according to the Director of the Police Leadership Academy. At most, according to this official, it would be possible to use the army in natural catastrophes.

Table 1

POLICE STRENGTH IN THE FEDERAL REPUBLIC OF GERMANY

STATE[1]	SCHUPO[2]	KRIPO	IN TRAINING SCHOOLS	TOTAL
Baden-Württenberg	18,784	3,367	1,086	23,507
Bavaria	(breakdown not available)			31,357
Berlin	11,394	1,772	—	13,166
Bremen	2,709	478	169	3,356
Hamburg	6,311	1,308	430	8,049
Hesse	10,588	2,247	1,338	14,173
Lower Saxony	14,373	3,296	972	18,641
North Rhine-Westphalia	34,132	6,166	(not available)	40,298[3]
Rhineland-Palatinate	7,205	1,480	115	8,800
Saar	2,647	441	257	3,345
Schleswig-Holstein	5,416	951	320	6,687

TOTAL STATE POLICE	171,379
Federal Police, including Bundesgrenzschutz	27,000[4]
TOTAL	198,379

1. State figures are as of July 1, 1986
2. Presumably including Bepo
3. Not including training positions
4. Approximate

(Source: Unpublished Interior Ministry Figures for state figures; estimates gathered from journal articles and official reports for federal figures)

Table 2

RATIO OF POLICE PERSONNEL TO POPULATION
IN THE GERMAN STATES
(as of January 1, 1986)

1. Berlin	1 : 135	
2. Hamburg	1 : 197	
3. Bremen	1 : 197	
4. Saarland	1 : 314	
5. Bavaria	1 : 360	
6. Schleswig-Holstein	1 : 389	
7. Lower Saxony	1 : 387	
8. Hesse	1 : 391 (30.9.1985)	
9. Baden-Württenberg	1 : 394	
10. North Rhine-Westphalia	1 : 411	

(Source: Unpublished Interior Ministry Figures)

Compared to the Federal Republic, police strength in the German Democratic Republic, which is naturally of great concern to those in the West, is relatively high. In 1977, that country had about 96,000 regular officers, (Ruhmland, 1977). It also has 50,000 border troops that are included in its military forces (Lapp, 1986). With a population of 17,000,000, the police-citizen ratio in that eastern country is about 1/176 and would be even higher if we counted the border police, as is done in the Federal Republic. Crime incidence in the Federal Republic, as reported by police to the *Bundeskriminalamt* (Bundesrepublik Deutschland, 1985), shows an increase of 135 percent between 1965 and 1985. The crime rate (crimes per 100,000 population) during the same period rose from 303 to 690, an increase of 128 percent. By contrast, the crime rate in the United States rose from 2449 to 5031 between 1965 and 1984, an increase of 105 percent from a base that was about eight times that of comparable crimes in the Federal Republic (Bureau of Justice Statistics, 1986: 365).

Criminality started to level off about 1983, probably for reasons of crime-prone age structure, as in the United States. The 7.2 percent of the population who are not citizens committed 18 percent of the crime in 1985. This population group is younger and on the average poorer than the German citizen population and is the object of a good deal of social and economic discrimination. The increases in crime rate seem inordinately high to most Germans and police have been under continuous pressure to deal more effectively with crime in general and particularly with crime by foreigners, including a large proportion of Turkish guest workers.

CONCLUSION

What can we conclude from this short history of police in Germany? In many ways the history of the German police reflects the history of Germany since 1918. During the ruthless Nazi dictatorship, a ruthless and brutal police force was developed to support the leadership. During times of prosperity and good feelings, police operations emphasized friendliness, helpfulness, and community education. In times of social stress and disorder, the police response has been one of increasing alienation from the public and a siege mentality. In Germany stressful times have also reopened the old wounds brought about by the failures of the police in the two previous governmental eras.

A short history, however, cannot explain the details of organizational response to particular situations, nor can it show the impact of historical changes on organizational ethos, structure, and leadership. We need to look at these facets of German police in the light of the ideal of democratic policing for a democratic society that was proclaimed for the postwar German police. This ideal was to be realized through some very specific changes: demilitarization, decentralization, and internal organizational reform. Each proposed change, which seemed so simple at first, became gradually metamorphosed to a form that was congenial to the traditional German public service culture. The efforts to bring about change were also deeply affected by two major developments in post-war German history, the cold war of the 1950's and the movements of social protest of more recent years.

CHAPTER THREE

DEMILITARIZATION: THE GRAND IDEAL

I know that some parties wish to impute to me the desire to make a new Wehrmacht out of the police . . . . However, those who have some true knowledge of the situation know that it is not at all possible to create an army out of a police force.

Former Wehrmacht General Kurt Grassner, shortly after being named as head of the new Bereitschaftspolizei.

STRATEGIC AND ORGANIZATIONAL DEMILITARIZATION

THIS CHAPTER ends with the suggestion that a paradox exists in today's German police: by creating a more highly militarized police force than was envisioned in the Yalta program, a less highly militarized state presence becomes possible in the Federal Republic of Germany. Understanding this paradox requires critical analysis of the concept of militarism in police forces. It also requires some description of the German situation with respect to the organizational and situational components of demilitarization as they have developed over the past forty years. These matters, in turn, are closely connected to a major concern of this book: the role of police in modern social order crises.

Since the middle of the nineteenth century, demilitarization of police in Germany is an ideal that appears to founder constantly on the rock of historical circumstance. Demilitarization was one of the highest priorities for the new police in 1945, as it was after the disorders of 1848 and 1918. In post-World War I days the Prussian police under Interior Minister Carl Severing took the lead in developing a police that, according to police writer Eugen Raible, were "not engaged in militarism and military adventures" (Raible, 1963: 11).

Even in the conservative state of Württemberg, the issue of demilitarization was of concern in the early post-World War I era. For example, in 1919 the newsletter of the union representing the rural police in Württemberg, known as *Landjäger,* demanded of the Interior Minister that the military-like organization of the Landjäger be disbanded and that all Landjäger personnel come under the 1876 civil service law. Another demand was that uniforms be simple and that military-like insignia be abandoned (*Der Württembergischer Landjäger,* July, 1919: 7).

In today's Germany, as in those previous eras, the existence of external threat, internal unrest, and terrorism, however, have created counterforces that have led inevitably to increasing concern with security and combatreadiness in police forces. They have led also, on the part of the police, to increasing defensiveness and even anger about criticisms of the use of police power. Countering these forces, however, have been changes in the general outlook of the younger generation of police officers, those who have grown up in a viable democracy. These officers do not respond well to the kind of military discipline, leadership, and tradition that was typical of German police and that continued, despite massive structural demilitarization, during the earlier post-war years.

The issue is clouded by the fact that demilitarization has both *strategic* and *organizational* implications. By "strategic demilitarization" I mean rendering the police incapable of acting as an adjunct military force in times of armed conflict. Organizational demilitarization, on the other hand, refers to the effort to deemphasize military-like rank, discipline, and decision-making in police organizations, the so-called "military model" of police organization.

In Germany the debate over demilitarization has always been dominated by strategic considerations. The recurring question that followed the major upheavals of 1848, 1918, and 1945 concerned the degree to which the police was actually an adjunct military force that could be used against foreign enemies. Efforts to civilianize police were tied to efforts to decrease the general military potential of the Germans.

These supranational considerations have given the militarism/demilitarism debate a peculiar intensity. They have led to imposition of outside solutions and also to charges and counter-charges at high levels about the potential military strength of the police. In 1932, for example, at an international disarmament conference, French representatives accused the Germans of having a police that had military capability and that should be counted as part of German military strength. The

German outrage was strong. "Only people of bad faith would believe the French claim," said one author (Elster, 1933). "There is no German police, only Länder (state) police. The great difference between the forces of the Länder can be seen by their variety of uniforms. These police have absolutely no common leadership and no bonds to each other. The strength of the German police is also not a serious question — in any case it was ordained by the victor powers. This strength has not been exceeded by one head." The author, Botho Elster, contrasted the civilian status of all high German police officials with France "where the police are under the Ministry of War and in battalions that correspond to army corps." Furthermore, he said, police armament was not excessive in Germany: three men shared each rifle and 500 men shared one machine gun. With increasing indignation he continued, "Isn't it enough that they took away our means of protecting ourselves against foreigners? Should protection against internal crime also be taken away?" (Ibid.: 79). Ironically, within a few short years of the time that this controversy was aired the German police had become a ruthless adjunct military force — an indication that talk about police accountability becomes superfluous in a dictatorship.

Fears about the military potential of the police are exacerbated in Germany by the fact that the police are so much more highly centralized than are the police of the United States, with their large number of independent jurisdictions and variety of organizations. Furthermore, despite the recurring efforts to civilianize police operations, the actual heritage of the German police, as was true of other continental European nations, was one of militarism and emulation of military forces (Riege, 1959; Liang, 1970: 28). Prior to the creation of the Empire in 1871, the state police of each German state was a contingent of the military. In France and Italy today, this tradition lingers with the Gendarmerie and the Carabinieri, who continue to be part of the defense establishment despite strong rival forces under the Interior Ministries.

Germany effectively abandoned such a pure military connection in the latter 19th Century. Nevertheless, the typical "Schutzman" of the Empire was a former noncommissioned military officer with twelve years of military experience (Raible, 1963: 11). Police of the Empire were imitative of the military, asserting their comparability in bravery, discipline, and effectiveness. They were also jealous of the greater prestige of the military forces (Liang, 1970: Ch. 1). Thus, moves toward civilianization were made in the context of strong traditional ties to the military.

From an organizational as opposed to a strategic standpoint, demilitarization involves a change of values and the abatement of the paramilitaristic structure that is generally characteristic of police organization. The question is: "Is it effective and wise to invest police personnel with the appearance of being an army?"

The advantages that are generally cited for a paramilitary structure are important ones. [In large-scale emergencies involving disasters, riots, or terriorism, police leaders are able to be more effective if they have highly-disciplined, well-trained "troops" who will respond quickly and efficiently to orders and strategies devised by the leadership. Military demeanor and appearance are also presumed to increase the authority of police in dealing with the general population, thus decreasing the dangers to the individual officer that are inherent in police work. A military *esprit de corps* and emphasis on professionalism, according to advocates of paramilitarism, cut down on general laxity of behavior, poor working habits, and amenability to corruption that can bring the police into poor repute.

On the other hand, one can argue that a paramilitary police is alienating and dysfunctional (Guyot, 1977; Goldstein 1977: 260). Police are not at war with citizens, nor do they perform extranational functions. They are part of the justice system and therefore should be concerned with the rights of those suspected and accused of crimes. They are dependent upon cooperation from the public in performing their tasks of crime prevention and control. The police officer on the street practices a great deal of discretion in dealing with citizens, and should be well trained in the use of persuasion, nonlethal force, and legal principles rather than in blind obedience and military maneuvers.

Seen simply, these organizational dilemmas are related to the differing functions of police. In executing highly-charged civil order control tasks police are expected to act with military-like discipline, exercising restraint, obeying orders, and moving in rehearsed formations. Often, this kind of police work begins to resemble a war, with tensions and hostilities escalating on both sides. Deviance control and deterrence of crime, on the other hand, require the more casual, discretionary approach that emphasizes service to the public and cooperation between citizens and police. Looked at from this perspective, the French and Italians, with their separate police for riot control and for crime control functions, would seem to have solved the organizational problem of militarism in policing.

The reality is more complex, however. Organizational structures can have important effects on attitudes. In a democracy that strives for an accountable and responsive police, an order-control army is immediately suspected of being the tool of a ruling class that is losing legitimacy. Furthermore, the distinction between a public order situation that demands calling in a specialized riot police and one that can be handled more naturally by calling in a few street police officers is sometimes vague. Overreaction by police can precipitate much higher levels of tension than necessary in many such situations.

The optimal organizational configuration for a deviance-control force is itself a controversial topic. During the 1920's, at the same time that German police were promoting demilitarization, American police reformers like August Vollmer and Orlando Wilson promoted a "military analogy" in police organization in order to counteract the politicized, corrupt, inefficient, and generally lax organizations that typified large city police forces in the United States (Fogelson, 1977; Walker, 1979). These Progressive Era reformers hoped to make police more disciplined, prouder, less discretionary in their operations, and more professional in their outlook. This was to be done by promoting paramilitarism with its connotations of discipline, order, and hierarchy. Despite the fact that a new wave of reformers is now calling for a deemphasis on the military analogy, it has become thoroughly incorporated into the organizational style of most modern police departments.

In Germany, demilitarization of police has had both strategic and organizational dimensions. The two have tended to become confused in the post-war era, with both the Germans and their erstwhile conquerors playing roles in bringing about change. The basic reality, however, is that of an ideal, a grand ideal in many ways, that has become the victim of both historical circumstance and organizational culture.

THE PLAN FOR DEMILITARIZATION

Paul Riege, a police leader in Weimar and author of a leading history of police, wrote an article in 1958 in *Der Polizeibeamte (The Police Civil Servant)* that helps us to understand the position of some of the older police who continued to serve after the war, usually after years of hiatus during the Nazi period (Riege, 1958:113). "Uniforms," he said, "and rank insignia follow fashion and change with its changes. Uniforms are sometimes green, sometimes blue, sometimes gray; rank insignia are sometimes on the shoulder, sometimes on the arm. It would be wrong to try to set one-self up against this kind of fashion. But what always remains, what is immutable, is the professional ethic of the police officer, the internaliza-tion of his professional trust and task, of his special and wonderful duty to be the 'friend and helper of the people.' A man who gives himself up to drink, who permits himself to be bribed, who shrinks from performing an unpleasant duty, has never fit well into the uniform of a police officer. At all times such an individual would quickly be identified and removed from police service."

Riege goes on to compare unfavorably the police organizations built up after the Second World War with those that existed after the First: "After the First World War a strong reaction quickly took place against the early signs of public unrest. The State created a new police that was tightly organized, well-armed, and had tactically-experienced leader-ship. This force was used in every way successfully to struggle against both large and small disturbances against public order and security" (Ibid.: 115). After the Second World War, says Riege, it was otherwise. Despite the fact that they were not all NS followers, behaved coura-geously in the war, and were in large part opposed to the Himmler take-over, the old police ended up taking a large part of the blame for the atrocities of the Nazi regime and were disbanded. The new people who were taken in were ill-trained and had no sense of professional ethics. The post-war goal was to make the police powerless, and it was only af-ter many police lost their lives in the line of duty that a partial rearma-ment was allowed and "only after years that the so-crucially-needed public order troops (Bereitschaften) were finally reconstituted" (Ibid.).

This statement tells us a good deal about the feelings of police veter-ans with respect to the demilitarization of the police. It shows nostalgia for the pre-Nazi police institutions, including heavy armaments, police living in barracks, and professionalism as symbolized by militaristic bearing, language, and rank. More importantly, it shows the strong identification of police function with social order control. Despite the statement about police as friends and helpers (which Riege puts in quotes) the selection conveys a message that strength, combat-readiness, and discipline are the hallmarks of a professional police force.

The statement expresses also the fear (perhaps reinforced by observ-ing the operations of American big-city police) that without military dis-cipline, all order and commitment break down and the organization becomes corrupt and demoralized. A British officer's letter in 1947 to Herbert Kalicinski, head of the Police Institute in Münster, also addresses this concern of the Germans (J. A. S. Selwyn, 1947, quoted in Schorn, 1955: 200):

> Since much misunderstanding exists in the German police about the concept of demilitarization, I would like to explain the British impression of this idea. The Germans tend to see demilitarization as a denigration of one's personal pride in attitude, as corrupt and worthless behavior, and careless demeanor. This is naturally a totally false impression. I know that the police officers who behave with a certain polish and who have good discipline in the ranks are tagged as militarists. The concept of capacity to work (Leistungsfähigkeit) and militarism are thrown together in the German mind because of their former connection. The result has been that professional behavior and discipline are much under a desirable standard in the German police today.
>
> *Military* discipline is the strong control of a group of men by officers without whose permission no actions may be taken. *Police* discipline, on the contrary, is the self-control of the individual officer, who through his knowledge of the laws makes his own decisions. His appearance and his behavior must be of the highest standard if he wishes to receive recognition and attention to his requests from his fellow citizens. No measures that are used to achieve this type of discipline can be characterized as "militaristic."

The prime purpose of the demilitarization effort was to render the German police powerless as an external military threat. More disinterestedly, a secondary purpose was to create a force that in tone, manner, and organization was more appropriate for policing a democracy than had been the National Socialist police. The plan for demilitarization, as conceived by the Allies, addressed four major concerns: armaments, uniforms, communications, and police troop concentrations. The prescriptions were as follows:

1. Armor and equipment were to remain simple, with no heavy arms or sophisticated communications equipment. Total disarmament of the police on the British model was a short-lived experiment that came to an end when it became clear that unarmed police could not deal with the chaotic conditions and rampant crime that followed the collapse of the regime at the end of the war. The use of occupation forces to handle crime control problems was not in the long run satisfactory and the need for rearming the German police soon became evident. Nevertheless, allowable weapons were limited to sidearms, a certain quota of rifles, and truncheons. Heavy armored equipment and sophisticated communications equipment were forbidden (Military Government Gazette, 1945).

2. Police uniforms were to be civilianized. The high collars, boots, and military insignia of the Third Reich police were to be abandoned and more casual styles of uniforms were to be developed. This change occasioned some great expectation on the part of at least one police leader, who described the change this way: "The closed uniform-collar gave way to the open jacket. The breast was exposed to the fresh winds of the newly-achieved democratic freedom. Along with the old strict style of uniform, the police officers left behind internal conformity and each one became accustomed to thinking in individualistic terms, to living according to his own principles and, above all, to developing his own political ideals" (Schutzinger, 1951: 5).

3. On a more subtle level, demilitarization meant abandonment of military terminology in training, organizational literature, and day-to-day interchanges within the organization. This internal organizational aspect of demilitarization proceeded more slowly than the others and probably was not effectively realized, if at all, until the second generation of post-war recruits was hired. As one police official explained to the author, it would be impossible today to treat the young recruits in the harsh, demeaning way that was typical of police training and socialization in the 1950's. Thus changes in organizational style were driven by outside forces as well as internal commitment.

4. For the Germans, the most radical facet of the plan for demilitarization of police was the abolition of the police recruit troops who lived in barracks and who were used as riot control and crowd control agents even before the advent of he Third Reich. These troops had been under the jurisdiction of the various state governments during the Weimar Republic and had been incorporated into the military at the time that the Nazi regime created a unitary government for all of Germany. This branch of the police in each German state was known as the Bereitschaftspolizei (literally, "readiness-police") and was distinguished both from the Schutzpolizei (literally, protection police), the regular street police, and from the Kriminalpolizei, the criminal investigations police. These three branches of the police are commonly known as Bepo, Schupo, and Kripo.

There is a rather complicated history behind the development of the Bepo during the Weimar period (a summary of this history may be found in Chapter Two). Even then, there was some ambivalence about the true nature of the Bepo. Eugen Raible, in his history of German police, tells us quite matter-of-factly that after World War One the army was limited to 100,000 men and *therefore*, it was necessary to develop a "garrison police" (Raible, 1963: 15). By the time of the Nazi takeover in 1933, the Bepo was a well-established branch of police in all the states and was the major force that was supposed to control the increasingly volatile and violent situation in the urban centers of Germany.

From its earliest days, however, the Bepo was also the entry-level organization through which police recruits passed on their way to regular street duty. Tenure in the early Bepo was long and arduous. In Baden, recruits, starting between ages 19 and 22, spent one year in basic training and then seven to twelve years in this force prior to moving into the Einzeldienst (individual duty) (Ibid.: 40). The length of duty testifies that the Bepo was in essence a civil order control police at that time. Nevertheless, it was also considered a valuable arena in which the young recruits would not only receive training, but also would develop the kind of maturity that is necessary for street work, a maturity that only additional years can bring. The garrison regimen was essentially paternalistic: room and board were provided, strict rules about hours and behavior were enforced, and recruits were not allowed to marry while in the Bepo.

The Bepo's duality of function appeared to constitute a happy mixture to the Germans. That the structure, training, and mentality of the Bepo was essentially military in nature was seen not only as a way to optimize the execution of the police mandate to deal with riot and other forms of civil unrest, but also as a way to exert discipline and control over the young recruits.

In the Allied effort to demilitarize the German police, it was natural that any organization that resembled the Bepo should be strictly forbidden. In the short run, even the new German police leaders, who objected strenuously to some of the Allied plans for the police, were not unhappy with this proscription. There were several reasons for this. First of all, the training and maturation functions of the Bepo, that previously had been so important, could not be a major factor in the development of the post-war police, since the emergency conditions that existed and the small number of police personnel did not allow for much emphasis on training. Furthermore, since most of the police officers were former military personnel (as were, to be sure, almost all young and even middle-aged German men), the kind of training that was given in the Bepo was presumably already a part of their background. When some training academies were started after the war, the training that they gave was similar in length and content to that which American police receive, and the Germans did not attempt to incorporate any of the kind of paramilitary training that had been received in the Bepo.

As for the police function of maintaining civil order, provision for which was not really included either in the post-war police organization or in any other organization, it was not of great immediate concern. In the earliest post-war period, this function was handled by the military forces of the Allied powers. As Germany gradually moved toward greater self-government, however, and as a new constitution was developed in the western sector, there was another reason why the lack of a special police force to handle social unrest was not a major problem to most Germans. This reason was that Germany during the late 1940's and the early 1950's was going through a period of great national re-building, economic development, and increasing prosperity. Despite the aftermath of recriminations, investigations, and hardship that followed the Third Reich, or perhaps because of them, the often volatile and fractious German public practiced a kind of subdued and conservative consensus politics that seemed to preclude the need for police forces to be engaged to any large degree in the control of social unrest.

As was explained in Chapter II, the 1950's witnessed an increasing preoccupation with traffic control. Other problems faced by the police leadership were the development of cooperative ties with other European police, rehabilitating the image of the police in the eyes of the German public, and in general trying to live down the reputation that the police had earned during the Nazi period.

The period of Adenauer's leadership following the war was an era of good feeling in German internal affairs. It was a period in which the police mission was primarily one of deviance control and, as such, cooperation and empathy with the public were the means of choice to insure effectiveness. Paramilitary training, separation of police and public, and sophisticated weaponry would have been counterproductive in carrying out this mission.

RE-CREATION OF THE BEREITSCHAFTSPOLIZEI

Ironically, it was not the Germans, but rather the Allied High Commission, meeting in New York in 1950, that reintroduced the Bepo in Germany (Blum, 1976). And it was not the need for better training or for some form of riot police, but the need for German military capability, that inspired this change. Although Chancellor Konrad Adenauer strongly supported a build-up of German military forces, the Allies were not yet ready for such a potentially threatening development. Nevertheless, the realities of the cold war and the desire to have the Germans themselves assume some of the burden of defense were the prime determinants of the redevelopment of the Bepo. The somber fact was that in East Germany, the Russians had encouraged the development of a *Volkspolizei,* or People's Police, whose strength was estimated at 100,000 personnel, much of it massed near the borders of the Federal Republic (Dierski, undated). Estimates of the strength of the East German People's Police varied tremendously. One account in 1950 had this strength at 240,000 (van den Bergh, 1950).

From the standpoint of military strength, the Allied plan was quite modest. Each German state was to be allowed to set up Bepo units; the combined strength for the states was to be no more than 20,000 individuals. In addition, a 10,000-man federal Border Protection Police (Bundesgrenzschutz, or BGS) was to be formed to patrol and protect the border with East Germany. The BGS was a compromise: there had been some discussion about setting up a 10,000-man federal Bepo. Today the BGS is in effect a federal police force, used not only at the borders, but throughout the country as needed for order maintenance. Arms and equipment for the state Bepo forces were to be supplied by the federal government in Bonn which in turn would be allowed to ask for their help in emergencies. When these plans were further developed, the states wanted only 10,000 individuals in the Bepo and the rest of the quota of 20,000 militarized police was given to the BGS, giving it a total of 20,000 (Raible, 1963).

The Allies saw this arrangement as the best that could be hoped for under the circumstances. The feared German army was not to be reconstituted. John McCloy, Allied High Commissioner, declared (somewhat cynically, given the circumstances): "We will not allow the development of an army or of military—like troops under the pretext of building a police force (*Die Welt,* September 22, 1950).*

The federal nature of German government, with most police powers concentrated at the state level, and with a major portion of the new police forces under state control, ensured that the Germans would not be able to pose a threat to western Europe. That they also would not be able to pose a major threat to the Eastern forces was passed over or rationalized in terms of the greater German need for protection against

---

*This article and the following cited newspaper accounts may be found assembled in *Bereitschaftspolizei-Zeitungsausschnitte,* a folder of clippings in the Historical Collection of the Police Leadership Academy in Münster-Hiltrup.

the east, which would presumably result in greater willingness of the
states to commit their police troops to defense of threatened areas.

From the point of view of police organization and police objectives, the
purpose of establishing these new forces had nothing to do either with conventional police operations or with control of internal social unrest. As such,
this redevelopment of the Bepo met with virulent criticism on the part of the
press and also within some political circles. The leader of the opposition Social Democratic Party accused the government of trying to slip in a remilitarization of Germany and to make of the Bepo a force that would become a
kind of Bonn palace army ("einer Art 'Bonner Hausmacht' "). The Bonn Interior Minister countered with the assurance that the police and military
would be kept strictly separate (*Die Welt*, September 17, 1950; *Die Neue
Zeitung*, November 8, 1950). Earlier the Mannheim local paper had also reported that a large majority of Baden-Württemberg's Parliamentary Committee on Internal Affairs had declared itself opposed to an barracked police
(*Mannheimer Morgen*, April 4, 1949). The states of Hamburg, Bremen, and
Lower Saxony were reported to have serious reservations about setting up a
barracked police, with its large measure of central control (*Hamburger
Abendblatt*, November 17, 1950).

There was also some public outrage. The letter of a high school principal, returning the Bepo recruitment posters, that showed a young man
in uniform, is typical: "We teachers were asked to warn youth against
becoming impressed with uniforms (literally: uniform-happy) and con-
formism, and we have taken this advice to heart" (HS, EA 2/11 202, Bd.
1, #79).

Whether the new forces were in conformity with the constitution was
another question that was argued at length in the Parliament and in the
press (Werkentin, 1984: Ch. 2). The original plan called for a 10,000-
man federal Bepo and it was argued that a constitutional amendment
would be required for such a force since the Basic Law of the German
state made policing a responsibility of the individual states. "The national government has police problems. The Constitution is an impedi-
ment," proclaimed a headline on September 26 (*Hamburger Abendblatt*).
Under the final plan, the federal Bepo was abandoned and the states
agreed to set up Bepo units that would be recruited and whose salaries
would be paid at the state level, while the federal government would
supply them with arms and equipment (*Die Neue Zeitung, Frankfurt*, November 23, 1950; *Westfalische Rundschau*, November 24, 1950; Dierski,
undated). The federal government, however, would set up a border police, which was clearly permissible under the Constitution.

The controversy was exacerbated when Kurt Grassner, a former Wehrmacht general, was asked to take a leave from his business in order to lead the new Bepo. According to the *Westfalische Rundschau* of November 22, "the suitcase of General Grassner will contain books on infantry staff training and training for the use of Stiel Hand Grenade 24." Grassner himself protested against some of the criticism, insisting that it was not as a general but as a police officer that he made his way to Bonn. "I know," he said, "that some parties wish to impute to me the desire to make a new Wehrmacht out of the police . . . . However, those who have some knowledge of the true situation know that it is not at all possible to create an army out of a police force" (*Die Neue Zeitung, Frankfurt,* Nov. 23, 1950).

General Grassner was not the only controversial leader, however. In October *Die Neue Zeitung* reported that Bonn was disturbed because previous Wehrmacht officers were secretly encouraging other officers to offer themselves for Bepo service. According to this account, Chancellor Adenauer gave former Weimar Interior official Walter Abegg the responsibility of overseeing the development of the force because it was believed that someone like him would insure that the democratic spirit of the new government would not be violated in the Bepo (Ibid.: October 1, 1950). Nevertheless, the SDP continued to make accusations about the former Nazi and even SS connections of the new Bepo leadership (*Die Neue Zeitung,* January 24, 1951).

In October a major police union protested against the use of previous Wehrmacht officers in the Bepo, especially singling out the appointment of former General Kreuzer to handle training of the new Bepo leadership recruits. In addition, the union objected to calling the new force "police" since it did not have a true police mission (*Hamburger Abendblatt,* October 4, 1950; *Die Welt,* October 4, 1950).

Details of the new organization were provided by the newspapers. Indeed, according to the *Göttinger Tageblatt* (November 27, 1950), "The setting up of the new Bereitschaftspolizei has filled the columns of newspapers and journals in the past few weeks as no other internal political matter has. Even in America many accounts with large pictures have appeared that, however, are less designed to report the facts than to feed the fantasies of the readers."

Light machine armaments and "full motorization" were anticipated for the Bepo (*Die Neue Zeitung, Frankfurt,* November 23, 1950). Compared to the regular police which at that time had approximately one pistol for every three officers, this was a major increase in armaments.

Details of financial obligations and leadership continued to be discussed, and it was declared that one-third of the Bepo personnel should be ready for action at any time.

The actual organization that was established, however, was a familiar one, and one that the Germans could accept as a police organization performing traditional police functions. And it is as a police organization concerned with the dual function of training and control of social unrest, rather than as a military organization designed to protect West Germans from their eastern former countrymen, that the Bepo has developed since 1950.

Nevertheless, the Bepo has been military in organization and operation. Recruits live in barracks. Their first year is devoted to classes and other kinds of training (such as driver education, drills, and weapons training). During their second year, while undergoing further training, they are available for crowd control assignments. After two and one-half years (or more in some states), they go through another six months of training at one of the training academies located in each state, and then finally they are assigned to regular street duty. The civil service ranking of police officers follows from these stages. Successful passage through the Bepo training and the preparation for street work puts police officers in the lower middle rank of civil service (Mittlerer Dienst).

In 1950 Bepo recruits started at age 18 or older. In the 1960's the entrance age was lowered to 16. This lowering of the starting age results from the peculiarities of the German education system coupled with the many employment opportunities available to German youth during the years of high prosperity and economic expansion. Students who are not in an academic high school (Gymnasium) normally finish their general education at age 16 and then go into specialized trade schools or apprenticeships. The police was finding it increasingly difficult to attract young people, many of whom already had spent two years preparing for another vocation. For a 16-year-old, however, police service is an extremely attractive opportunity since he or she is paid the normal entry-level civil service salary during the years spent in the Bepo. In addition, the Bepo provides room and board. Furthermore, service in the police excuses one from the one and one-half years of compulsory military service that is required of German youth. In fact, the comparatively large amounts of money available to the officer during the first few years of police service are in serious contrast to the comparatively smaller amounts of available money that are available for luxuries when he or she must begin to pay for housing, food, transportation, and the like upon moving into the Einzeldienst (individual service), or patrol officer position.

The youth of the recruits makes the maturation function of the Bepo much more important than it had originally been, since the adolescent recruits need further schooling in basic subjects, such as German and driving, and in addition must be encouraged to keep their ties to home, family, and community while living in barracks. Police journals speak of Erziehung ("bringing up") as one of the most important aspects of Bepo training (e.g., Mikutet, 1970; Hohn,1952). The first year of training is seen as one of "Schuler" and "Lehrer" (pupil and teacher) rather than one of would-be professional and instructor (*PFA Schriftenreihe,* 1970, p. 223; 1980, p. 226). A 1980 article in a police yearbook provides us with an example of this paternalism. The author says that, with a larger proportion of 16-year-old recruits, upbringing becomes an important aspect of police training. Further, he says, young men, especially in these complex times come into the police without a clear sense of values. "Sixteen-year-olds in particular have a moral sensibility that must be nurtured by all means" (Ibid.: 227). Certain kinds of character traits, however, including "lack of enthusiasm for the job, lack of punctuality, and lack of self-discipline" cannot be helped by police training. The length of the training program helps to weed out black sheep, while living together in the police establishment promotes consideration, tolerance, and "the feeling of belonging together . . . . Many outsiders are trying to make us abolish this kind of training, but it would be very unwise to give in to these demands, especially since the training as it is set up in no way leads to social isolation of the trainee" (Ibid.: 229).

Police training for young recruits also contains formal course work in ethics, usually presented by clerics. For example, a speech by Bishop Gerhard Pieschi (Pieschi, 1980) to the heads of the police academies of the various states was entitled "The Unity of Upbringing and Education." "It is the responsibility of the government," he said, "to insure the ethical upbringing of the police officer" (Ibid.: 285). "The basic ethical principle that the state supports is the worth of the individual . . . . Therefore, there should not be a 'special ethic' for police, but rather they should adhere to this basic principle" (Ibid.: 286).

Although few people think that age 16 is an ideal starting age for police officers, there seems to be little effort to raise this entry age. This is so despite the fact that the police are frequently criticized for this use of youngsters, and despite the fact that there are now a large number of applicants for each vacant police position.

The reestablishment of the Bepo and the establishment of the Bundesgrenzschutz would seem to have constituted a major force for remilitarization of the police of the Federal Republic. As such, they have been bitterly criticized (see, e.g., Werkentin, 1984). The German police, however, saw the Bepo as a way to reintroduce the amount of training that they felt was necessary for a police officer. At the same time they assumed that the recruits were engaging in military-like maneuvers at an age when they are impulsive and in need of stronger discipline than regular police work would provide. By the time they were engaged in street patrol work they would take on the service mission that was so strongly stressed during the 1950's. And indeed, the German police at that time developed a reputation for professionalism, service to the public, and democratic operations, including civilian leadership, employee participation in decision-making relating to personnel matters, and citizen advisory groups to help make police policy (Berkley, 1969; Panaat, 1960).

THE INCREASE IN PUBLIC ORDER PROBLEMS

The Federal Republic has had serious problems of social unrest during the past twenty years. Student demonstrations and riots in the 1960's have given way to environmental protection disturbances, occupation of vacant houses by the homeless and their supporters, and protests against American missile deployment on German soil. From a relatively peaceful and prosperous society concerned with growth and expansion in the 1950's, the social and economic picture has changed, with unemployment, inflation, and anxiety about the future as major problems. In such an atmosphere, the containment of manifestations of social discontent becomes a preoccupation not only of those in power but also of the police leadership.

The change did not come about suddenly. Perhaps the earliest case of serious disturbance was the 1962 "schwabinger Kravalle," which started when a group of celebrating students blocked a street in the university district of Munich. The police tried to break up this incident and demonstrations and rioting quickly ensued and continued for several days (Schreiber, 1965). Student demonstrations became particularly severe in the latter 1960's, paralleling the movements in France and the United States.

Police problems have been exacerbated by terrorist activities throughout the 1970's and 1980's. The environmental defense movement and the anti-nuclear movement also have triggered major riots and demonstrations in the Federal Republic. Two of the most devastating of these were the 1981 demonstration at the Brockdorf nuclear power plant in the state of Schleswig-Holstein and the 1982 protest against building a new runway at the Frankfurt International Airport. In both of these cases, police resources were strained to the limit. The situation in Brockdorf was made worse by the fact that the demonstration was scheduled to take place on the same day as the pre-Lent Carnival celebrations, which normally require the deployment of large numbers of police in most German states. Police leaders not only had to provide for policing their local parades, but each state had to send some of its Bepo forces to Schleswig-Holstein to deal with the disturbances there. In this situation, all Bepo troops, even those in the first year of training, when they are not supposed to be used in action, were utilized and many were injured in the ensuing riots. A similar situation existed in Frankfurt, where the police were not successful in preventing violence and injury.

The Brockdorf demonstration was particularly traumatic, but it was also instructive for police in that it was the first in which major strategic planning involving police, including BGS troops, from all over Germany was involved. After this event *Bereitschaftspolizei Heute,* the Bepo journal, featured news about the demonstration in a major cover story that gives some measure of the excitement that surrounded the engagement (Brockdorf, 1981). All Bundesländer (states), as well as the BGS, had promised to help Schleswig-Holstein, says this story. "By train (from Bavaria), by highway, even by helicopter the forces moved north, ready for action" (Ibid.: 4). A real problem of coordination was involved since most of the police personnel had to go through the tunnel under the Elbe River to get to their destination. The police were quartered in schools as well as in the atomic plant itself. Each state was responsible for its own care, and the logistics of cooking, sanitary accommodations, etc. were formidable.

On February 28, more than 10,000 police "with countless motorized vehicles including air and water conveyances, and with the most modern leadership and action supplies assembled in the Wilster Marsh in Itzehoe as well as in Brockdorf" (Ibid.). Positions were taken at the early hour of 4:00 A.M., "for the German police does not allow itself to be taken by surprise" (Ibid.).

Although police searched all potential demonstrators for weapons at road blocks leading to the site of the nuclear plant, the marshes, frozen at that time of the year, at first made it possible to bypass the barricades and bring weapons to the site. The police, according to this account, using water cannons and tear gas, and bringing in helicopters and reserves, were able to stop this advance.

Police estimated the crowd at 50,000 demonstrators, while the demonstrators estimated it at 80,000-100,000. In the end 127 police were wounded, 7 seriously, and 40 demonstrators were wounded. "Amazingly," according to this police account (Ibid.: 6), the press acknowledged that the police had done a good job, especially since the demonstration, which had been refused a permit by the local authorities, was illegal. Police leaders, however, were worried about the fact that some of the young recruits, pushed beyond their limits by overwork and crowd hostility, were being reduced to fits of crying.

The number of incidents in which police have been required to quell unruly crowds has grown steadily. In the state of Baden-Württemberg, police statistics show that the number of mobilizations has increased dramatically in recent years. In 1981 police handled 557 demonstrations, of which 75 were described as "not peaceful." This compares to a total of 283 demonstrations in 1980. SEK teams (Special Action Commando teams, roughly equivalent to Special Weapons and Tactics Forces) were called on 179 times in 1981, as compared to 106 times in 1980. (*Die Polizei Zeitung Baden-Württemberg,* November 11, 1982). In the Federal Republic as a whole, demonstrations increased from 1300 in 1970 to 7453 in 1984 (Ruckriegel, 1986). In 1986, of those demonstrations that involved more than 400 participants, 109 were classified as "nonpeaceful" (*Süddeutsche Zeitung,* January 26, 1987: 6).

Inevitably, the increased police activities to control demonstrations, riots, and terrorism led to charges of police brutality and overreaction. In the course of the 1970's a series of books and case studies appeared attacking police methods, organization, and leadership. Shades of the National Socialist era were evoked and the Bepo and BGS, in particular, became the targets of virulent attack. "Is the Federal Republic a Police State?" is the title on one prominent publication of the times (Roth, 1972; see also, e.g., Humanistische Union Berlin (ed.), 1975; Bolle et al, 1977).

Even in the academy, the police apparatus was suddenly the subject of studies which exposed police organization and methods to open scrutiny. Some of these studies were informed by a Marxist ideology and came to the conclusion that the police were tools of the capitalist order (see, e.g., Goeschel et al., 1971). Some sociological studies of the time resembled the American studies of police that had been done a few years previously (see, e.g., Feest and Blankenburg, 1972; Murck, 1976). The police, who had cooperated with sociologists in these studies, felt betrayed by the results, which they interpreted as being unfair and anti-police. Attacks by academics were particularly resented because the police establishment itself had started on a period of major organizational reform in the early 1970's. These reforms included greater openness to reseachers, organizational democratization, reform of the BGS, and banning the use of weapons such as hand grenades and machine guns.

Police reaction in general has been pedictable. The strain on resources occasioned by the public unrest brought about demands for increases in police strength, especially within the Bepo. According to one commentator, "The terrorism of the past few years led to greater arming of the police than all the other problems of the past twenty years . . . . The need to establish police as a symbol of order also leads to a more militaristic stance" (Blankenburg, 1976: 529).

Within police organizations, control of civil unrest has become an increasingly high priority. Research on improved nonlethal weaponry such as water cannons and tear gas projectiles has become a major activity. Better ways to deploy police forces in demonstrations are constantly being developed. In the federal Interior Ministry, a special department was set up in 1978 to handle "major situations and serious disturbances against internal peace" (Gebauer, 1982: 13). Seven staff units were set up: deployment, leadership, development, ordinance, public relations, civil defense and catastrophes, and environmental protection. The need for an effective communications network among states was stressed. Specifics of training for leadership in handling police troops has become an important topic of conversation and of comment in police journals.

Even the *Gewerkschaft der Polizei,* the major police union, which normally calls for moderation and restrictions on arming the police, became concerned about police safety and reputation in the face of increasing public order problems. At its 1982 convention the warmest topic of discussion was a resolution demanding legislation to prohibit demonstrators from wearing masks that hid their faces (a somewhat ironic demand in view of the union's adament opposition to all efforts to have German uniformed police wear name tags). A further demand of the union was that all "political, scholarly, and technical means should be furthered to develop better public order control techniques that will meet police needs and at the same time will take account of the principle of restraint (Verhältnismässigkeitsprinzip)" (*Deutsche Polizei,* 1982: 8).

Ronald Reagan's visit to Berlin in 1982 occasioned a large demonstration in which some people were hurt. This, according to Günter

Schroeder (1982: 10), the head of Gewerkschaft der Polizei, was due to the fact that it was not possible to move reinforcements freely from other states to Berlin without permission of the Allied powers, who still control military and police maneuvers in that city. Furthermore, Schroeder claimed that Bepo units as now constituted are not efficient for large demonstrations. Despite these problems Schroder rejected as undemocratic the alternative of developing a specialized police (Sonderpolizei) to handle disturbances.

Concern for legality and formal rationality in dealing with citizens are also part of the preparation for crowd control. Bepo troops are cautioned about violating constitutional rights of demonstrators. After a particularly serious encounter with the public in Kreuzberg, the state police director in Berlin promulgated a series of rules for behavior in such engagements. These rules were adopted shortly afterward also by the state of Hesse. Included were:

1. Be calm
2. Don't allow yourself to become provoked
3. Always remember the prohibition against excessive force
4. Practice cooperation but not friendliness ("Üben Sie Kameradschaft aber keine Kamaraderie")
5. In cases where it is not clear what the preferred action should be, trust your leader
6. Watch what you say and secure witnesses.
   (*Der Tagesspiegel*, Berlin, January 11, 1981, reprinted in Borner, 1982).

The police have established Identification and Documentation troops (Beweissicherung und Dokumentation, or Bedo). Their purpose is to photograph violent incidents during demonstrations, and identify the law-breakers in court (Otto, 1984). According to the Interior Minister of Hesse, the general task of the "Bedo" troops is "the filmed, photographed, and acoustic determination of criminal acts. As much as possible, incidents should be able to be proved and reconstructed" (Ibid.: 7). Such materials are especially useful in presenting evidence in court, says this official, but are also useful as a means of instructing police in problems encountered while dealing with demonstrations.

Excessive photographing and documentation on peaceful demonstrators, however, is the real danger that accompanies the development of structures such as the Bedo forces, and reinforces the apprehensions of those who fear that the police is gradually becoming an internal spying agency. Despite restrictions imposed by the German Constitutional Court on police photographing during demonstrations, this problem continues to exist in the minds of many Germans.

Among police personnel, the sense of outrage at attacks on police, and frustration about the misunderstanding of police problems has multiplied in recent years. In a 1981 story entitled "Die Polizei Hat die Schnauze Voll" ("The Police Are Fed Up"), *Der Spiegel* (#48, 1981), the major weekly newsmagazine, described some of the problems and also the police reactions to these problems. This article was written after 109 police officers and many demonstrators were wounded in a battle with 100,000 demonstrators who were protesting the new runway at the Frankfurt airport. The article quotes a high commissioner of the Bepo: "After 200 hours of overtime, my colleagues have an intense anger even against peaceful demonstrators, and cannot stand any runway opposers" (Ibid.: 28). Other leaders lamented the fate of the police effort to develop close ties with the public: "An optimistic development toward a citizen-friendly police has been interrupted and turned back." "Arming the police as if one is fighting the Russians" is not a salutary development. "The more police react with new technological capacity, the more the people will find the line between police and public to be a war front" (Ibid.: 31).

The upshot of all this is gradual hardening of attitude toward the public by the police, a sense of frustration at being the targets of the public unrest although they are only fulfilling their duty to provide order, and a developing organizational defensiveness. "We must place our heads on the block for the sake of political decisions made by others," in the words of one leader of the Bepo (Ibid.: 28). Ralf Dahrendorf's comments to the *Gerwerkschaft der Polizei,* quoted at the beginning of this volume, echo these sentiments.

THE FATE OF DEMILITARIZATION

As we have seen, organizational and strategic militarization or demilitarization has conjoined throughout modern German history, with the need for combat-ready police forces a priority of both police and national leadership. To speak of militarism as a problem of German police provokes strong negative reaction among police leaders of the Federal Republic, however. This no doubt is because the issue of strategic militarism among police has played such a prominent role in police history, even in the immediate post-war period, with the re-creation of the Bepo in 1950. In addition, contemporary pressures on the police because of the large numbers of peace-keeping actions that must be undertaken make it difficult to contemplate the peculiarities of the organizational aspects of the military model in a dispassionate way. Nevertheless, an analysis of the situation in the Federal Republic leads to certain insights into militarism in policing and especially organizational as opposed to strategic militarism. These insights can be categorized in terms of the organizational elements of structure, ethos, and leadership that were described in Chapter One.

With respect to militarism, major changes in structure, ethos, and leadership definitely were planned for the German police. Police troops were to be abolished, uniforms were to be changed and aramaments were to be modified. With respect to ethos, military demeanor, military language, and military discipline were to be relaxed. The discredited leadership of the Nazi past was to be purged and a new leadership, dedicated to a responsive, nonmilitary police was to be developed.

Structural Change

Apparently, the most dramatic failure has been that of the redevelopment of a barracked police. The Bepo, with a strength of 26,000 (Domnik, 1981: 3) constitutes a large portion of the total police strength of about 200,000. Today's Bepo is in conception a throwback to the Weimar Republic. Although this force was re-created for strategic reasons, it has become integral organizationally to the police of each German state since it serves the upbringing and maturation function that the Germans find so necessary for their young police. The actual training for street work that is comparable to American police training is generally done in a six-months period at the end of the recruit's years in the Bepo.

The present arrangement for the Bepo, however, has both advantages and disadvantages for structural demilitarization. By separating the peace-keeping forces from the conventional police forces within the total police organization, the Federal Republic ostensibly has developed an organization that can deal with both needs without causing the kind of organizational dilemma that is created in the American police apparatus when faced with major peace-keeping tasks. Also, by having the peace-keeping force double as a recruit-training and education device, the impact of the military influence would tend to be mitigated. Under this arrangement, the conventional (i.e., non-Bepo) police forces in the various states of the Federal Republic, ostensibly freed from the need to be a primary force in time of emergency, are able to concentrate on developing a citizen-friendly police with large amounts of civilian input and civilian control.

There is a certain advantage to this organizational arrangement also from the standpoint of a strategic as opposed to an organizational perspective on demilitarization of police forces. Without the separate Bepo, living in barracks and, in normal times, essentially invisible, the Federal Republic would probably find it necessary to increase considerably the strength of the other police forces in order to deal with the numerous crises that occur. Such a large police presence would tend to raise once again the specter of German militarism as an endemic cultural reality, and would diminish some of the efforts to create an open and democratic society.

There are at least two problems with this organization, however. In times of stress, it lends itself to increasingly single-minded concern with control of an unruly population by providing a command structure, weapons, and tactics that are specialized toward that end. In an occupation that is in any case geared toward action and the possiblity of the use of force, such a development has an important effect on the conventional police forces. In effect, the "military" arm of the police becomes the more important agency and gets more resources and attention than do the "civilian" units. In the United States, where a crisis often results in the mobilization of the National Guard or the military, it is easier to maintain the distinction between conventional police work and suppression of disorder. The fate of the Bereitschaftspolizei of the Weimar Republic, which was incorporated wholesale into the military after the advent of the Third Reich, serves as a reminder that police organized into paramilitary troops can be manipulated and used for military purposes more easily than conventional police.

The second problem is the effect on the young recruit of being initiated into police work through involvement in the most highly militarized arm of the police. The hallmark of police professionalism in an organization that is moving away from paramilitarism as a form of control is the wise use of discretion by the individual at the service, or street level. After several years of living in barracks, training in military-like maneuvers and discipline, and learning to respond unquestioningly to commands of superior officers, it becomes more difficult for the police officer to move easily into a situation where independence of thought and concern for citizen problems become higher priorities than proper dress and demeanor.

In terms of organization, conventional police forces in the Federal Republic are not less governed by the military analogy than are most of those of the United States. The Bepo experience, however, tends to reinforce this organizational militarism rather than to mitigate it. German police and jurists contend that discretion is not practiced in the German criminal justice system to the extent that it is in the United States and that police, like judges and prosecutors, are pledged not only to carry out the law, but also to adhere more faithfully to it when they are actually on duty. Police, however, much more than prosecutors and judges, have no choice but to make important discretionary decisons frequently in their work, and the only real question is whether or not their decisions are directed at constantly improving service to the public.

These problems regarding the Bereitschaftspolizei have received some attention from the German police leadership. In 1977 a group of sociologists at the University of Saarbrucken was commissioned to do a major study of the vocation of police officer. One of the recommendations of that study was that consideration be given to separating the training function of the police organization from the order-maintenance function (Helfer and Siebel, 1978: 1137). This recommendation has not found favor with police leaders, however, because of the radical restructuring of the organization that would be involved, and because of the many disadvantages that would accrue to the organization from such a change. Not the least of these would be the need to establish a more completely specialized crowd-control unit within each state police, with all the implications of creating true paramilitary organizations within the regular police apparatus. Such organizations exist in both France and Italy, but they are not regarded as salutary by the Germans.

The Bepo itself, however, is undergoing some changes that may change its character (Domnik, 1981; Busch et al, 1985). Although civil order crises have increased, the need for new street police officers has actually decreased because of a stable population and a generally young police force. Therefore, most states of Germany now have action-ready units of the Bepo that are actually finished with their police training but are not yet involved in street work. They are expected to spend at least one year in these units. Because of their greater experience and maturity, these troops are the ones that are most likely to be used first in cases of civil order disturbances, with the younger and less seasoned officers brought in only if the occasion demands more personnel. Thus a larger distinction between training and civil order control is developing at the same time that a larger civil order control police is being established. Nevertheless, all of these police continue to be in a status that is preliminary to work in the Schupo.

More problematic and less ambiguous than the Bepo with respect to structural militarism is the Bundesgrenzschutz (BGS), the border patrol police that was also established in 1950, with the clear mission to protect against external enemies, especially those on the eastern borders, rather than to police internally. This federal agency, along with its Bavarian counterpart the Bayerische Grenzschutz, is difficult to justify as part of the conventional police forces. Nevertheless, BGS troops may be used to supplement state police in cases of need. They are, in fact, used in most major demonstrations.

The stark contrast between military operations and police operations is exemplified in the law regarding the Bundesgrenzschutz. In times of peace, the BGS is part of the police, and is bound by all the strictures of domestic law. Since it is a federal agency, however, BGS personnel are not controlled by the state police laws. Their general training is in the Model Police Law recommended by the Conference of Interior Ministers. In time of armed combat, however, the BGS assumes combat status and is bound only by the international law of war (Walter, 1983: 48-50; Rasch, 1980: 42). This schizophrenic arrangement, which actually represents a compromise with those interests who, in the decade of the 1950's, hoped that the entire police would be able to take on combat status in emergencies, has never been put to the test, since the BGS has never been used in armed combat. The situation is hardly a comfortable one, however, and provides fuel for accusations about militarism and repressive potential in the German police. One textbook also describes this status as potentially detrimental to the social benefits accruing to BGS pesonnel: "The critics of [the BGS' two-sided obligations] have good cause to remind us of the tragic fate of the German police divisions in the Second World War, that were put into unsalutary action situations by an irresponsible leadership, so that the participants in these divisions could not lay claim to their civil service rights after the war" (Walter, 1983: 48).

During the 1970's efforts were made to integrate the BGS more closely with the state police forces. Service, salary, and career rights were put on a par with state police. BGS training was made to be more closely equivalent to police training. The police of each state except Bavaria are committed to accept 20 percent of those who enter their Schutzpolizei from the BGS, usually after eight to ten years of service.

The federal government is in a position to exact such a commitment since it gives crucial support to state Bepo units.

These BGS personnel, frankly military in spirit and trying to build an image as an elite force, represent a throwback to the days when most German police personnel were people who had served for years in the military forces. For the federal government, promising an eventual police career enhances the effort to recruit young people into the BGS. The possibility of incorporating the BGS into the military, where it would seem to belong more naturally, was discussed at length during the 1950's and, in 1956, BGS personnel were given the opportunity to choose between remaining in the BGS as part of the police apparatus and entering into a military career. Forty-two percent chose to remain in the BGS, and it has been developed and strengthened as a police force ever since (Ibid.: 17).

Maintaining the Bundesgrenzchutz as a police organization, however, represents a peculiar compromise with both the constitutional strictures against a national police force and the ideal of a nonmilitary police organization. The BGS remains the most controversial structure within the German police and is regularly denounced by critics of the police (see, e.g., *Bürgerrechte und Polizei*; Werkentin, 1984). It is evident that by now the BGS is no longer just a border and customs police but is used rather freely throughout the Republic in civil order crises. Through this development the BGS ostensibly has become somewhat softened because of the police-like training it now receives and because of certain restrictions on weapons that have been imposed. In fact, however, the BGS suffers from severe problems of morale and conflict within its leadership and between the leadership and the Interior Minister. These conflicts are occasioned by its militaristic atmosphere and its efforts to become an elite tactical force within the police (see, e.g., *Der Spiegel*, 1987, #24: 112-113).

The other facets of structural demilitarization, uniforms and armaments, have also undergone some evolution since the original plan was promulgated. The states gradually moved toward the use of a common color and style of police uniform. The Schupo officer today presents a rather casual appearance to an American observer. Often bearded, or with hair that is longer than is conventional for military personnel, he or she wears a forest green jacket, brown pants, yellow shirt, and white hat with visor.

Greater homogeneity of dress is the most obvious change in uniform that has occurred since the police arm-bands of the early post-war days were replaced by uniforms. A common uniform does not necessarily connote militarism in clothing; nevertheless, it does have some effect on police operations. When the federal government mobilizes police from all the states for the purpose of dealing wih major incidents of civil disorder or large assemblies of protesters the effect of a single uniform is one of greater solidarity and strength than if the personnel from the states were clothed in varying styles and colors. The similarity in clothing also enhances the sense of solidarity that the individual police officer has with police from other states. It becomes easier to consolidate forces from various states, use portions of particular state forces with portions of other state forces, and employ other such effectiveness-enhancing strategies. On a more speculative level is the argument that the entire police apparatus becomes easier to take over as the result of this rather simple symbolic change in uniform.

Name tags for police officers have been fiercely resisted both by the police hierarchy and by the police unions on the grounds that individual officers would become the target of frivolous or malicious accusations (Sommer, 1952; Haber, 1965). The lack of name tags, however, is one of the major discontents with police that are voiced by radical groups, student groups, and others who are unhappy about police actions (*Bürgerrechte und Polizei,* CILIP 26, 1987, Nr. 1).

The degree to which police are armed and the amount of heavy armor that police agencies have at their disposal is a subject of controversy in Germany. Even excepting the frankly military nature of the police during the Nazi period, the traditional German police of both the Empire and the Weimar Republic were heavily armed (Jacob, 1963: 88; Liang, 1970: 56). Nevertheless, a clear goal of the post-war reform was to cut down on police armaments.

After a period of unarmed policing for the first months after the war, the Germans rearmed their police, but with strict limitations on the kinds of weapons that could be employed. Side arms for street police and a quota of rifles and submachine guns for particular emergencies were allowed. With the advent of serious terrorism and with increasing social order problems in general, however, armaments were again a matter of concern. The Gewerkschaft der Polizei continued to oppose heavier arms for police, with the exception of special anti-terrorist commando forces. Werner Kuhlmann, former head of the GdP, fought long and hard for legislative control of police weaponry. "All weapons that police may use should be enumerated in law," he said (Kuhlmann, 1969: 218). "Explosive materials like hand grenades and grenade launchers are not police weapons since their only purpose, contrary to that of the police, is to destroy life. The police function is not combat and victory, but rather protection and service."

Some commentators disagree with these sentiments, maintaining that heavy armaments are necessary to carry out the tasks of the organization. As one author puts it: "There are always people who find that the organization and weaponry of the Bereitschaftspolizei is too 'military.' The question keeps coming up whether machine guns, grenade launchers, hand grenades, and armored vehicles should be allowed. The answer is simple. We can never know with certainty about the degree of threat there may be to public security and order. The functions of the police, however, vary from warning of citizens to capturing of armed robbers, from dispersing a curious crowd to stopping a violent and serious 'Putsch.' For this it is necessary to be prepared and armed. The better the public knows how well armed the police is, the greater the deterrent effect of this arming, and the easier it is for police to carry out its critical work" (Raible, 1963: 186).

Armamants used in military engagements are problematic in all cases when used against the citizens of one's own country. Kinds of weapons and the nature of their use are subjects of debate in police departments in all western nations. Even Britain, with its unarmed Bobbies, is moving ever more toward an armed police, although it is not doing so without controversy. Likewise, the use of deadly force by police officers is much researched and discussed in the United States (Fyfe, 1978).

What is particuarly interesting in Germany, however, is the degree of research, development, and training that goes into nonlethal crowd control weaponry such as water cannons, tear-gas pistols, and special shields. There is a kind of arms race here: as demonstrators and other protestors use new tactics and weapons against the police, police are developing new counter-strategies and antiprotest weapons. This is, of course, more salutary than firing into crowds, as is done by less-scrupled forces such as those in South Africa. Nevertheless, the amount of energy and resources that are devoted to such development of arms suggest an increasing tension between police and public that leads to greater paranoia on both sides. Further, the use of CS gas and rubber bullets is often denounced by critics of the police because these weapons can injure seriously and in any case cause a great deal of distress (Busch et al., 1985).

A further controversy, this one about the status of police in major national defense emergencies, broke out in the 1960's, with the Interior

Ministers first suggesting that all police should have combat status in case of war, and then retreating from this position in the face of strenuous objections, especially from the GdP and its leader Werner Kuhlmann (Paschner, 1970: 124-127). The compromise, that the BGS should be able to be used as combat troops if hostilities occurred, created a situation at that time in which BGS personnel were not welcome in the GdP. Despite the program in the 1970's to make the BGS more police-like, former BGS employees, upon entering conventional police work, tend to go into the more conservative Deutscher Beamtenbund (German Civil Servant's Association) rather than the GdP, where they do not feel particularly comfortable (Bramshill, 1981).

In general, the conflicts regarding armaments and use of police in potential combat situations show how close to the surface the conception of strategic miltary use of police forces remains in the minds of German leaders. These controversies, coupled with the obviously strategic considerations that occasioned the creation of the Bepo and the BGS in 1950, are indicators of the sense of strategic vulnerability that pervades German politics and indeed German life. Despite the strongest efforts of police unions or other concerned individuals to separate policing from territorial defense, the dynamics of German geography and political reality seem always to provide a counterforce that pushes for strategic strength and reserve capacity for police forces.

On balance, one cannot say that the Germans have followed closely the plan for a structurally demilitarized police force. When compared to the police of comparable European nations such as France and Italy, however, the Germans do not have a particularly martial organization. The most controversial aspect of German police structure — the induction of 16-year-old adolescents and their several years of socialization into barracks life and paramilitary modes of action — is tempered by the fact that numbers in this corps are restricted by future manpower needs for conventional street work. Furthermore, the fact that these relatively inexperienced troops move on to other responsibilities as they move into adulthood means that the Bepo cannot be a force of trained veterans who become better and better at their work. The emphasis within the Bepo itself on general education and on the importance of the police work that the recruits will be doing in the future also gives it a milder aspect than might seem if one regarded only the barracks, uniforms, and drills. The use of the Bepo is indeed a far cry from the years of military duty that were a prelude to police service in the times of the Empire or even the more numerous years of Bepo work in the Weimar Republic.

Ethos

Organizational ethos, or spirit, is a more elusive reality than is structure. Nevertheless, it penetrates more deeply into the consciousness of the members of the group and has greater effect on their modes of interaction among themselves and with others outside the group. For the Germans, demilitarization of police meant that the soldierly discipline, ideals, and bearing that had been so much a part of the organization would be deemphasized and replaced with a more relaxed, participative, service-oriented force.

An American finds it difficult to understand the degree to which military modes of speech and discipline were part of the ideals of the German police. Furthermore, the language of struggle, combat, and victory became so much a part of the German environment during the Nazi years (Craig, 1982) that the police were caught up in a general hardening of speech that it would take years to change.

Nevertheless, a major change has taken place. As one respondent explained, the atmosphere within the Bepo has changed radically since he first joined in the mid-1950's. At that time, and with a former Wehrmacht general in charge of training the new officer corps, the old style of training and discipline were reinstituted. Today, recruits are treated with greater respect. They are reasoned with, are encouraged to go home on weekends and in the evenings, and the attempt to "toughen" them through harsh discipline, deprivation, and degradation rites has been modified. The retreat from a military ethos has also taken place in the Schutzpolizei where employee participation, wise use of discretion, and restraint in relations between superior officers and subordinates have become the ideal, if not the norm. The nonuniformed Kriminalpolizei has never used a militaristic style in its post-war operations.

Whether these changes are due to conscious efforts by the police to become less military in ethos, or whether they represent a response to changes in general German culture is an important question. The fact is that in today's Germany, a country that has a large measure of prosperity and democracy, the old police ethos probably would not work. Recruits would not be inclined to respond favorably to an atmosphere of repression or unduly harsh discipline. There are too many alternatives for German youth today and too many years of education behind them to make it possible to revert to the old organizational atmosphere. Some recruits are involved in the very movements, such as the Green Party, whose adherents often confront the police in situations involving civil order control. The police, in its efforts to attract and retain personnel, and in order to keep from alienating a public that has largely grown up in the post-war years, has had to become more congruent with majority German thought.

Countering the changes in organizational ethos that would suggest that demilitarization has been successful in that arena is a growing sense of paranoia and frustration that one detects in the police literature. This literature suggests that the police are moving more and more to the belief that they must do their duty in spite of public hostility. If insititutional paranoia, always a threatening force in police operations, becomes severe, organizational ethos may indeed begin to swing back to a martial mode more in keeping with an organization under siege.

Leadership

A military style of leadership contributes to a military atmosphere in an organization. Such a style emphasizes command, respect for rank, insistence upon strong hierarchical consciousness, and unquestioning obedience by lower ranks. In return for obedience, it also implies a certain paternalism and loyalty to those under one's command and a sincere concern for their welfare.

Military leadership style is endemic in most police organizations throughout the world. The real issue seems to be one of degree rather than kind. In the German situation the notion of a changed leadership style was important to those who envisioned a new character for the German police. Such a change, however, was antithetical to the tradition of the police and did not take hold easily.

Demilitarization of German police leadership should not be confused with denazification. There were some claims, in Germany and elsewhere, that the new police had taken in former Nazi personnel and that they were little different in composition from the pre-war days. In Bavaria, for example, the head of the Bavarian Landespolizei was accused of developing a militaristic police and of hiring previous National Socialist police. While insisting on his own opposition to a militaristic police and especially to a Nazi-like police, he replied to his critics by pointing out that, although his organization took in former police who had been forced into military service, these rehired police had all been cleared acording to the denazification process (*Süddeutsche Zeitung,* October 31, 1947). At about the same time the legislature of the then-state of Württemberg-Baden discussed a Swiss charge that many of its police were former military men. The answer to this charge was that it was only natural that many previous soldiers were in the police. "Who was not a previous soldier?" the legislators asked (HS, EA 2/11, 173: #214-223).

A further issue was the leadership of the Bereitschaftspolizei when it was reconstituted in 1950. Amid the claims that many of the new Bepo leaders were tainted by former Nazi ties, a special program of psychological testing was set up in North Rhine-Westphalia to insure that only people with a desirable psychological profile would be chosen as Bepo leaders. For eight weeks psychologists from Bonn shared living quarters with the leadership candidates, attempting to assess their frame of mind for the task before them. Although the candidates were somewhat hostile to this scrutiny, and the psychologists had to break through their "iron curtain," according to one account "it was worth it, for they (the psychologists) experienced an insight into the internal spiritual composition of a portion of the population (whether guilty or not we do not try to determine) that has a lot of baggage to carry in relation to the lost war, and out of whose ranks . . . the skeleton of any new German rearmament effort must come" (*Süddeutsche Zeitung,* December 3, 1950).

This latter remark suggests once again the close identification between strategic military function and police function held by many Germans. The leadership training, however, was designed to insure ideological acceptability in terms of the new regime. "The general course of instruction," according to one paper, "that mainly takes the form of discussion, should assure that each candidate has a positive attitude toward the democratic state" (*Westfalische Nachrichten,* October 18, 1950) (HS, EA 211, 173: #212-214).

Despite the undercurrent of anxiety that one detects in these newspaper accounts, the evidence is strong, as was explained in Chapter Two, that under the scrutiny of the Allied High Command the general police leadership was purged of Nazi elements, and even that most rank and file police personnel had not been actively involved in Party activities. The result, however, was that there was a leadership vacuum, and that inexperienced and untrained personnel were elevated to positions of leadership. Some few prewar police leaders who had lost their positions or resigned during the Nazi era, such as Herbert Kalicinski, were rehabilitated to police work and soon assumed important positions. Nevertheless, the large number of military veterans who were in the police assured that the style of leadership was still very much in the military mode.

As a new generation of leaders made their way to the top, however, the military style became softened. This generation was brought up on the new principles of a friendly and accountable police. Training at the central police executive training school in Münster-Hiltrup has emphasized participative management. The major textbook on organization behavior that is used emphasizes organizational experiments that have demonstrated the efficacy of techniques geared toward maximum utilization of individual human potential within organizations. In 1973, for the first time, a civilian director was put in command of this executive training school, known as the "Polizei-Führungsakademie," or PFA.

In this regard, a 1970 article in *Die Polizei* (Mikutet, 1970) gives us some insight into the new leadership ideals. The article, written by a police commissioner in the state of Baden-Württemberg, was entitled "What Reforms are Needed in the Bereitschaftspolizei Training?" This article had one section on "style of training" in which the author addressed the matter of leadership style. "We must start with the premise," he said, "that no trainer in our day can develop the personality of a young and still immature youth in a way that will allow him to carry on his police duties in a friendly, humane, clear, and yet decisive manner, under circumstances of strong hierarchical dependency. Modern social psychology has discovered the interesting and useful fact that the demeanor of the individual police officer will reflect the example of his superiors" (Ibid.: 222). He went on to urge less distance between officers and men in the Bepo, and told his readers that even in the military, with its ever-greater technical and specialist demands, team-building has become an important organizational innovation. In the army "the task of the leadership is no longer to enforce discipline, but rather the encouragement of greater initiative and better morale that come especially from strength of conviction and group spirit. How much more must this attitude hold for the civilian arena of the police, that controls a higher sophisticated technical apparatus and uses a large number of specialists" (Ibid.).

Nor should these changes await the retirement of the older generation of Bepo leaders, said the author. This older generation can learn to be more "up-to-date" (sic) in its approach and has, in addition, the advantage of years of experience.

Finally, the author explained that the most useful way to change is in one's style of speaking and in the use of words. If a leader is insulting, overly critical, distant, unconcerned for the feelings of his subordinates, he cannot achieve a positive result with them (Ibid.).

Is the more accommodating style of leadership doomed by the pressures on police caused by the threats of terrorism and public discontent? Inevitably, the leadership of the Bepo, with its troops and barracks, is more military in character than that of other police agencies, which are more closely in touch with the civilian population. This question is tied to the larger question, however, of whether the Bepo will continue to increase in importance within the police or whether new, more professional police troop arrangements will rise to replace the basically amateur Bepo. Already elite squads known as Speziale Einsatz Kommando, (Special Action Commandos), or SEK, and Mobile Einsatz Kommando (Mobile Action Commandos), or MEK, are used in emergencies, such as terrorist operations and large demonstrations, that require special skills and training. The BGS also has an elite antiterrorist unit known as GSG-9.

It should be remembered that the highest leadership in German police organizations is civilian. Traditionally, police are under the Interior Ministry in each state. In the post-war years, however, there is also civilian leadership at the local level. The local police chiefs, known as *Polizeipräsidenten*, are political appointees. Usually they are trained jurists who have served in other high civil service positions such as prosecutor or judge. Occasionally a career police officer is appointed to the position of police chief, but as a political appointee. More unusually a civil servant from a nonlegal background, including a business background, is appointed as police chief.

The relations between the civilian chiefs and their career police subordinates vary from excellent to poor. In talking to career police, one gets the impression that the political leadership does not know the ins and outs of policing and should concern itself only with public relations, high policy, and securing of resources. The more a civilian police chief gets involved in the day-to-day operations of a police agency, the more he is likely to incur the resentment of the career officers. This is so despite claims that a police officer "should not feel he is a member of a military troop, but attached to a civilian department" (Knocke, 1954). It is a classic situation that can be compared to the efforts to maintain civilian control over the military in the United States.

This is not to suggest that civilian leaders of police in Germany are figureheads. They are actively involved in the policy-making process as well as in the various boundary-spanning activities that are important for the development of an organization. When it comes to day-to-day decision-making about street work, detective operations, crisis control, and other conventional police activities, however, close control by the civilian leadership would be seriously resented.

CONCLUSION

At the beginning of this chapter a paradox was posed: by creating a more highly militarized police force than had been envisioned by the Allies, the Germans have made possible a less highly militarized state presence. The realities that constitute the elements of this paradox have been described piecemeal in the course of the chapter. It remains to explain how they come together.

As is the case with so many nations, geography has had an important role to play in German history. Situated in the center of Europe, unprotected by natural boundaries, Germany has often been the locus of armed conflict in Europe, and German governments have traditionally played on the fear of the people that they would be conquered, especially by Slavic peoples from the East. A visitor cannot help but notice that in some parts of Germany the devastation of the Thirty Years War, fought three hundred years ago, is still a lively topic of conversation.

In such an atmosphere, exacerbated in modern times by Germany's vulnerability to the colossal Russian nuclear and conventional warmaking machine, a large and visible military presence is more likely to occur than in a country that feels more secure in its location or its strength. In post-war Germany, however, such a military presence has not developed for various reasons, not the least of which is protection afforded by the American, French, and British military presence. Another important reason is that the German leadership, sensitive to Germany's unfortunate reputation as a militaristic nation, and eager to bring about a change in national image, has made efforts to keep Germany free from the appearance of strong military influence.

Along with the fear of foreign penetration, however, one senses a certain uneasiness among Germans about the capacity of their fellow citizens to practice the pragmatism that is involved in democratic decision-making. Nor is this uneasiness totally without foundation. Despite its reputation for being obedient and marching in step with its leaders, the German public is actually quick to respond to frustration, whether economic, social, or political, by resorting to direct confrontational tactics. This was notoriously so during the Weimar Republic, with its extremists of left and right battling each other regularly in the streets. As was explained earlier, however, social unrest manifested by demonstrations and riots has become increasingly a problem also of the Federal Republic.

The natural response to increasing public order disturbances would seem to be to increase the forces that can be used to quell such disturbances. There is little agreement on whether or not this has actually happened in the past. Gurr (1976), in his study of historical trends in the administration of justice in four major world cities, shows that increases in police forces tend to follow increases in public order crises rather than increases in crime. Bayley, (1985: Ch. 4), using other evidence, does not support this claim. Nevertheless, in the short run, increasing public disorder does suggest some decrease in legitimacy of the elite in a nation and will lead to escalation of force in order to prevent major upheavals. Public order disturbances, however, may also be the favored tactic of an extreme minority that has little support from the public at large. In any case, the logical result of such disturbances is an increase in police presence.

In the Federal Republic, the peculiar nature of the Bepo, antithetical as it may be to the hopes and designs of the post-war architects of a new German police, deters the development of such a greater general police presence. The fact is that by keeping a large percentage of the German police resident in school for several years makes them a good deal less visible to the public than if they were on the streets.

Another way of looking at this is to say that the Bepo makes it possible to have a larger number of police available than might otherwise be tolerated. Despite claims of the police hierarchy that only two-fifths of the 26,000-person Bepo is "combat-ready" ("einsatz-fähig") at any one time, the entire force represents a back-up in times of emergency. Since there is no equivalent to the National Guard or any other militia in Germany, and there is genuine horror at the thought of using military troops in internal disturbances, the Bepo presents a rather innocent face to the majority of Germans. In times of stress it is available for action; in more peaceful times it is just a training program. Indeed, for the majority of Germans the lengthy training in law, citizenship, and history that Bepo recruits undergo is very much in the German tradition of having highly trained workers and civil servants. The long apprenticeship thus makes the police appear more trustworthy and increases the respect they are accorded by the public.

One could also argue that the amateur nature of the Bepo, with all troops rotating out regularly, and with training as the major objective, actually has a mitigating effect on the militaristic aspects of this force. The size of the force is constrained by the needs for street police three years later. Recent drives to increase Bepo numbers therefore tend to aim for rather modest increases despite what is seen by many Germans as major public order problems. This reality tends to decrease even further the police presence in the Federal Republic.

The recent policy of keeping personnel in the Bepo for an extra year of civil order work that does not double as training may change this situation somewhat, and may result in having more seasoned individuals handling many of the crowd control assignments. Nevertheless, the Bepo remains essentially an amateur agency when it comes to crowd control, i.e., this activity is not its major occupation.

In the eyes of those Germans who are critical of police, however, the Bepo continues to contain the seeds of a strategic military force, just as it did in Weimar. The obviously strategic motivation that resulted in the re-creation of the Bepo in 1950 reinforces such claims. This historically-determined suspicion remains part of the modern legacy of the German police. In times of crisis, this suspicion becomes particularly acute, with recriminations and dark reminders of police history becoming increasingly frequent.

A further problem is that an essentially amateur Bepo is not usually useful in delicate operations involving terrorists and hostage-takers, and a whole new apparatus of special tactics forces has been developed for these purposes. The increasing integration of the BGS with the regular police forces and the ability to use the BGS internally, in contrast to its original pure border functions, combined with the existence of these tactical forces may well lead toward making the Bepo increasingly irrelevant as a social order control force. If this happens, the dubious aspects of recruiting veritable youngsters and developing them as police during their late adolescence may become all the more evident.

In sum, the German police apparatus, despite sincere efforts to become more civilianized, continues to excite controversy with respect especially to the strategic aspects of militarism. Probably the greatest hope for a major change in direction would be an extended period of social tranquillity in which decision-makers, relieved of the atmosphere of crisis and tension, would have an opportunity to reassess organizational structure, function and basic objectives.

CHAPTER FOUR

DECENTRALIZATION AND
RECENTRALIZATION

.... that the British and American occupation authorities took the police function away from the states resulted from a clear misunderstanding of the German tradition of public administration. What legal tangles and how much confusion resulted from this can hardly be calculated.

Former Interior Military official L. Egidi, in a 1956 statement

COMMUNALIZATION AND ITS DECLINE

IT IS perfectly natural that conquerors try to export the institutions of their homelands to the conquered territories. These institutions are familiar and are cherished by those in power in the homeland and by their representatives in the occupying forces. In addition, the creation of new institutions serves to break up entrenched power structures and to atomize potential opposition. In this way the Roman and the British civil services became the model for administration in their respective empires. Likewise, the Normans imposed not only their customs and government, but also their language, on the conquered Anglo-Saxons.

Where a conquest results in a permanent takeover, or where the new institutions are particularly suited for a new regime in the conquered territory, these new institutions may become entrenched, taking on, however, an indigenous flavor suited to local conditions. The common law is a good example here. Originally the law of the king's courts as opposed to local courts, and designed to consolidate national power above local law, this kind of law gradually became an accepted vehicle for dealing with disputes. The common law courts lost their ties to the monarchy and became strongly independent, building their strength on the regularities of procedure that soon came to typify the common law, and that persists in the elaborate procedural concerns of English and American courts today.

Where the conquerors do not annex the conquered territories, however, those imposed institutions that are most antithetical to local sensibilities gradually revert to structures that are more familiar and more legitimate in the local context. This was the fate of the Allied plan to decentralize the German police. Compared to the demilitarization efforts, that struck most closely at the appalling past and were generally accepted by the new German police leadership, decentralization was met with dismay, vocal opposition, and tactics of delay and resistance.

This issue has a peculiar intensity. Decentralization and empowerment of local authorities in police matters are, in fact, structural indicators of what are deeply-rooted conceptions of the proper relations between police and public. Indeed, even the issue of minor consolidation of small police agencies is an emotional one that arouses strong conflict within the International Association of Chiefs of Police and other police organizations. Justification of smallness in police agencies also has its academic supporters, with a whole school of public choice advocates claiming as a result of their research that small police agencies are more effective than large ones (see, e.g., Ostrom, Parks, and Whitaker, 1978).

The arguments are familiar ones. On the one hand, small police agencies are said to be closer to the public that they serve because they are subject to municipal authorities who must be elected at frequent intervals. On the other hand, a larger department can be more professional, i.e., it can afford better equipment, communications technology, training, and specialization of personnel. Furthermore, it can strive to avoid the very problems of politicization that too great an accountability to elected officials may create.

In the United States these issues of accountability, professionalism, and politics are vastly more important than is the issue of a possible misuse of police by a state or national power elite trying to consolidate its power at the expense of a democratic order. Such use of local police is so foreign to the American experience that it hardly ever surfaces as a basis of argument against consolidation.

According to Bayley (1985), the fact of decentralization must be considered in the context of other realities, such as size of the decentralized jurisdictions and the existence of multiple and overlapping jurisdictions. He gives the example of France, a centralized system that is, however, smaller than the state of Texas. In France also, there are two police systems, the *Police Nationale,* that polices cities of over 10,000 inhabitants, and is under the Interior Ministry, and the *Gendarmerie Nationale,* that polices rural areas and small towns, and is under the military. In his way, centralization is mitigated by the division of powers between the two forces.

The situation in Germany is very different. Those who work in the German justice system, and especially the police, generally insist that they have a decentralized police and have always had one except during the period of the Nazi regime. When one compares the German situation to that in France and Italy, whose police forces are thoroughly nationalized, there is some justification to this claim. Before 1921 German police forces consisted of municipal police responsible to municipal authorities and a state militia that handled small towns, the countryside, and civil order disturbances. The municipal police, however, handled only minor law-breaking and order problems. With the Police Law of 1921 all police forces came under the state Interior Ministries (HS, EA 2/11, 173: #267). Common recruitment, training, and operations became the norm and, again with the exception of the nationalization under Hitler, have remained the norm ever since. The German claim is that such decentralization to the state level is about as much as would be compatible with German traditions and ideals of public service.

One American writer, George Berkley (1969), agrees with this German view. In fact, Berkley's contention is that nations with police forces centralized at the state or national level, have a more "democratic" police that do the Americans. He claims that a central government has the power to hold police more accountable, has greater capacity to deal with crises that threaten the fabric of the state, is more able to promote professional standards, and has the means to provide police with better training and equipment than could a local government.

Whatever one's position on centralization or decentralization of police forces, the issues at stake are accountability, professionalism, and political power. Are police responsive to local needs for safety and security? Are they well-equipped and trained to do the tasks that are required of them? In the final analysis, who makes decisions about deployment, strength, and general use of police forces?

The Plan for Germany

The Allied powers, meeting in Yalta and later in Potsdam, agreed in 1945 that German police administration would have to be decentralized.

There was to be neither national oversight of policing, nor national attempts to influence police organization or deployment. Police were to be concerned with purely "police" tasks: defense of life and property, upholding of law and order, crime prevention and control (Dierski, undated). However, no specific plans concerning the structure or nature of this police were developed during the early discussions about the administration of post-war Gemany (Werkentin, 1984: Ch. 1).

Despite the agreement, a strong centralized police was set up in the Russian zone. In the West, however, decentralization meant different things to each of the three victorious powers, and therefore each imposed, in its respective zone, a different police organization. To the French, decentralization meant that police forces would be organized at the level of the Länder, or states, essentially the same arrangement as the Germans had had previous to the Nazi era. To the British, decentralization meant a regionally-organized police, with civilian Police Authorities such as exist in Great Britain. To the Americans, it meant police that were organized and controlled at the community level (Bottscher and Schafer, 1949).

The Germans also had to give up the Administrative Police (Polizei Behörde) that had made the police appear to be such an ubiquitous presence in pre-1945 Germany (Ibid.). This change was very unpopular with the Germans, who tried to explain to the military government that the functions of the administrative police had always been performed in separate divisions, and not by the regular, or executive, police (Vollzugspolizei). Administrative police functions included interior administration (passports, registration of citizens, street cleaning and upkeep, traffic engineering, control of fireams, public health regulations, building codes, etc.), business regulation (advertising control, price control, production control), agricultural regulation (fish and game, public waterways), traffic regulation (bus lines, shipping rules), and culture regulation (truant laws, municipal concerts). In August, 1947, several German police leaders in the American zone protested once again this peculiar requirement of the authorities. According to the Germans, persistence in this order made control of the extensive prevalent black market activities extremely difficult (HS, EA 2/11 173: #154, #157).

Particularly distressing was the separation of registration of population (Meldewesen) from the close ties it formerly had with executive police authorities. The states continued to require that all people be registered and that they report to the authorities when they changed residence. The ties of the registration authorities to the regular police were no longer strong, however, and this development was seen as especially detrimental to the investigation of crimes. According to one author (Booz, 1953), this separation resulted in a certain lack of energy on the part of registering authorities, who previously had kept up their interest in their work because of their frequent interchanges with police. Furthermore, said this commentator, ". . . today there are women who are carrying out the registration function. With all due good feeling toward women employees, what do they understand about the police? . . . . What do they know about human nature, a knowledge that veteran police officers only achieve after many years in service? For a woman, Herr X may seem to be a decent fellow, that could not act illegally, only because he represents himself that way to her . . . . " (Ibid.: 25).

Nevertheless, the separation was insisted upon. An arrangement was worked out that provided for cooperation between former administrative police and the conventional police, where administrative police would enforce regulations up to the point where an arrest or search would be necessary, at which point they would call in the executive police (Gerecke, 1963).

The Development of Local Police Forces

Of the three Western plans, the American plan, with its communal police agencies, represented the most radical departure from the German organizational norms. It was also the most optimistic plan with respect to the hopes for creating a democratically-controlled police force. At the same time, it was the plan that would have the effect of crushing most completely the potential for utilizing the police as an adjunct to the military.

In the American zone, which consisted of the states of Hesse, Bavaria, Bremen, and the then-existing Württemberg-Baden, orders were issued that, among other things, forbade police to: (1) deprive citizens of "life, liberty,or property without due concern for procedure, (2) issue ordinances, (3) adjudicate offenses, or (4) "exercise any kind of restrictive control over the political activities of the German population" (HS, EA 2/11, 173: #280). Mayors were given the responsibility of setting up local police forces and providing for arms, clothes, and supervision. Criminal investigation units were to have parallel organization in regular local police departments (Ibid.: # 283).

In North Württemberg four cities (Stuttgart, Esslingen, Heilbronn, and Ulm) and thirty-seven smaller localities set up local police forces.

Towns with less than 5000 population and the countryside were to be policed by a state police, or Landespolizei (Aufbau, 1970). The Director of the Landespolizei was to be loosely tied to the state Interior Ministries, but was to have operational control of his agency. The new arrangements, in effect, were carefully designed not to reallocate the same police powers to the various Interior Ministries that they had had prior to 1933. These ministries, however, were inevitably brought in to handle coordination, record-keeping, and other integrative tasks. According to the American plan, the jurisdiction of the Interior Minister was to be "in part informational, in part controlling in nature" (HS, EA 2/11, 173: #2). He was to represent police interests to the Finance Ministry, coordinate administrative police functions through ordinances, and deal with substantive legal matters through blanket laws ("Mantelgesetzen"). The Director of the Landespolizei, on the other hand, was to do the household plan, social order control action plan, training, discipline, organization, and operation of the state police.

Working out the details of the reorganization was not a simple task. Working through the state-level authorities, U. S. military headquarters required each mayor to submit a copy of the operating rules developed by police agencies in his municipality, making certain that these rules conformed to the general guidelines regarding weapons, due process of law, abolition of military ranks and insignias, and purging of Nazi elements (Ibid.: # 26).

There was a host of immediate problems. What would happen to those who were in police schools and thus not active in particular cities? Who would take on former police officers who were returning from prisoner of war camps? What help could the cities get from the states in starting up municipal police forces? Other problems involved coordination between mayors, Landespolizei officials, and Interior Ministry officials. Borrowing of police forces in cases of emergency, like the 1947 demonstrations related to higher prices, needed clarification (Ibid.: #1-12).

Since the Reich had nationalized the police in 1933, there was the problem of pensions for disabled war veterans and widows of deceased veterans (Ibid.: #5-7). Needless to say, the cities did not want to take on this financial burden. The case of E. B.* of Mannheim was typical. After serving with the police from 1913 to 1945, E. B. was let go in

---

*At the request of Hauptstaatsarchiv Stuttgart, the names of individuals mentioned in agency correspondence and personnel records are not revealed.

Mannheim because of his Nazi Party membership. He subsequently found work in Germersheim. When he retired the question was: Who would pay his pension? No one seemed to be able to answer this (Ibid.: #77). Another case was that of K. S. who, under the nationalized police, had become a permanent civil servant in 1945. Upon his request that he be taken into the municipal police in Karlsruhe because of this status, the city claimed that it had no responsibility for him. When the central government took over the police by the law of 1937, said the Karlsruhe authorities, it took over all these responsibilities. Now that the cities unwillingly have been forced to take over the police because of a rule of the military government, there is no reason why they should have to honor these old commitments. If anything, it should be a responsibility of the states (Ibid.: #74-76).

In January, 1948, the Interior Ministry in Württemberg finally said that it could not be responsible for regular aid for former police officers, but could help with one time subsidies. A law was proposed to deal with the problem (HS, EA 2/11, 137: #41). For regular police operations, there was also the question about possible subsidies from the state for the new local police. In Hesse the Landtag decided upon a state subsidy of between 2500 and 3000 marks for each police officer (Ibid.: #31-33; #42-44).

Because there had been no census since 1939, many towns did not know if they came under the prescription to set up a local police. Furthermore, the large numbers of homeless refugees, estimated by one author at 19,000,000 individuals (Kosyra, 1980), artifically inflated the populations and the police problems of the towns and cities. In any case, 5000 seemed like a excessively small threshold limit for the creation of local forces. The military authorities were petitioned unsuccessfully from numerous sides to raise the figure to 10,000 (HS, EA 2/11, 173: #73-83, #143-147). Additional difficulties stemmed from confusion about local and state police jurisdiction in the use of officials who formerly would have been under the Administrative Police and were now in separate agencies (Ibid.: # 174-176). Police corruption, the much-anticipated consequences of local police, became an issue and, in 1947, several proposals for combatting corruption were put forth (Ibid.: 182-186).

Coordination of local police was done through the Interior Ministry and reports went through the Interior minister to the military authorities. These reports included information on organization and personnel of the new communal forces. From the small town of Wasserfingen the mayor forwarded this report in April of 1946: "In this town there is at this time a Landespolizei unit with a strength of 17 men. This strength must be seen in light of the fact that we have right now 1800 Poles quartered in private residences and that furthermore we also have a refugee shelter in this area. We cannot afford to carry all this through a municipal police force and would like to request that the Landespolizei be permitted to stay at least until the Poles leave" (Ibid.: #18-19). The mayor's statement represents a particular fear of, but also a certain attitude toward the Polish refugees, most of whom had been imported as slave labor during the war.

Gradually the delineation of responsibilities was clarified. Central criminal files were to be kept at the state level in order to facilitate communication. Local police forces would be able to call on the state police for help if the highest civil authority in the town requested this help and if the Interior Minister found that the local police were unable or unwilling to deal with a particular situation (Ibid.: #7). Despite the gradual normalization of the situation, one continues to find in the German correspondence at this time a real unhappiness with the local police forces. The Bürgermeister of Wendlingen complained that, in his town of 6340 residents, he did not want a town police (Ibid.: #82). A letter from the head of the Württemberg State Police to the Interior Minister in Stuttgart also typifies this feeling of discontent (Ibid.: #9). The author tells us that two major considerations should inform the development of new police forces. The first is the practical problem of building the police to the place where security and order can be upheld in all of Württemberg-Baden. The second is the political problem of assuring that the police forces as a group and as individual officers stand firmly grounded in the belief in democracy and that they cannot again become a gathering-place for reactionary elements.

"The easiest solution to these problems would be to have a well-organized state-level police with outstanding leadership. The development of such a police, however, is not possible because of the existing American guidelines." Under these guidelines the state police loses power and prestige. Some of the disadvantages of the communal police forces, however, could be overcome with the development of an oversight office in the Interior Ministry. "In other words, an office should be created in the Interior Ministry that will carry out (1) the duties of former staff officers of the Schutzpolizei, (2) part of the duties of the former Ministerial Directors of Police, and (3) part of the duties of the former Federal Police Directors." This office, according to the author, would develop overall plans for police work in the state, would determine standards for police strength in the various cities (this is important because "countless" local governments, in order to save money do not employ enough police), would regulate salaries in order to make them coincide with those of the state police, would regulate kinds of ranks in each department, and would approve of all promotions and dismissals from service.

Exactly one month after this letter was written, the Interior Minister wrote to the U. S. Military Government about the possibility of setting up a special section in the Interior Ministry to handle police matters. The problem, according to this letter, is that the state police is independent, the local police forces are independent, and the Interior Ministry, which has the responsibility for bringing all this together, should also have the power to do so. In fact, says the letter, "there is a great need for a new police law" (Ibid.: #11). This request for new power at the state level was disapproved by the Public Safety Branch of the Military Government on March 3, 1946 (Ibid.: #12).

At the same time that the Interior Ministry and the state police authorities were bemoaning their lack of power, there is mixed evidence about the response of the municipalities to their greater powers. Police chiefs were to be chosen by city councils and the fear of political influence was heightened. The new letterhead of the mayor of Heilbronn proclaimed this individual to be "Der Oberbürgermeister der Stadt Heilbronn, zugleich oberste Polizeidienststelle" ("Mayor of the City of Heilbronn, as well as Head Police Station") (Ibid.: #9a).

Other mayors were trying to ascertain how much power they had over the police (Ibid.: #5). The Landrat (county executive) of Schwäbisch Gmund, on the other hand, complained that it was not possible to give control of the police to mayors and county executives, since they were not trained to do this kind of work. The state police, he says, should have all the police duties. "At least there should be the possibility for contracting with the state police to do the policing for local governments" (Ibid.: #4).

Return of Partial Control to the Germans

In 1949, the same year that the German Constitution was approved and the occupation was winding down, the Allied High Command issued further directives for the "organization, control, and administration of the police of the states" (HS EA 2/11, 173: #289). Each state was to set up police forces with due concern for the restrictions included in the Basic Law. There was to be no consolidation of police over two or more states. Police were forbidden to strike, to engage in political activities, or to join "nonpolice" organizations. Strength and weaponry of the police had to be decided by elected representatives of the people, subject to the veto of the Allied High Commission. Any attempts to consolidate police forces would have to have the approval of the Allied High Command and in no case should a German police force have more than 2000 personnel. Police chiefs could only be dismissed if their technical or organizational talent was not great enough to fulfill their duties.

Return of responsibility to the German authorities did not mean that there would be no further monitoring of police by the military. In a letter from the Office of Military Government to Dr. Reinhold Maier, Minister-President of Württemberg, the new guidelines for supervision were made explicit (Ibid.: #187). There would be no effort to supervise the day-to-day operations of the police. The general policies of decentralization, freedom from militarization, and denazification, however, must be adhered to. Certain reports, communications channels, and rules for working relationships were also established.

Difficulties with the new organization did not evaporate after the partial return of responsibility to the Germans. Some localities continued to resist the whole idea of communal police forces. Likewise the 1949 yearly report of the Landespolizei Württemberg contains this statement: "Our experiences the past few years show that the development of communal police forces in small towns is totally impractical and has not proven to be worthwhile." The example is given that prosecutors take cases that should have been handled by local police to state police forces instead, since they trust the state police but not the local police (Ibid.: #260). Prosecutors, it should be mentioned, continued to be state officials, a further complicating factor in the situation.

Other police chiefs pointed out contradictions within the orders themselves — did they really mean that there would be local autonomy or would the state authorities have some jurisdiction? In Heidelberg, the newspaper reported confusion among the people because police were wearing two different kinds of uniforms. The paper explained that people didn't realize that there were two different police forces at work, rural state police and communal police. In Heilbronn, the mayor complained that it was not clear to what extent police officers could engage in politics (Ibid.: 286-288).

In a lengthy letter to the Interior Minister of Württemberg, the mayor of Stuttgart tried to get some clarification of the 1949 orders. Did they mean that earlier orders were no longer in force? Did the ban on political activities mean than police could not vote? If it did, it would be a violation of the new Constitution. Did the ban on joining nonpolice organizations mean that police unions could not affiliate with the national labor organizations? To what extent does the Bundeskriminalamt (the national criminal investigations agency) have power over the state criminal investigations officers? To what extent do the state-level officers control the communal ones? It is important, he said, to avoid having all criminal investigations activities centralized at the state level because this would cause a rupture between detectives and patrol officers, since the latter are communalized. Another problem is that of mobilizing police for action in case of civil unrest. It is not clear what the relation of the Interior Ministry and the local police will be in these matters. Furthermore, the Landtag (state legislaure) should give out guidelines for the optimum strength of police forces, since the guidelines of the military authorities may no longer be binding.

The communication from Stuttgart goes on with a general discussion of communalization. This is a reality by now, says the mayor, but it would be much better if the smaller cities would be allowed to join with the state police. In that way the great fragmentation of effort in combatting crime throughout the state would be mitigated. The experience with these little town police forces has not warranted continuing them. What is really needed, according to this official, is a rethinking of the whole matter of police organization, and a commission should be appointed to accomplish this task (Ibid.: #307).

In October, 1949, the Interior Ministers of the various states held a conference in Bonn during which their power over local police was a prominent topic of discussion. They decided to petition the Allied High Commission to allow greater Ministry control over deployment of police in emergencies. Decisions about the degree to which police are armed, furthermore, should also be made by the Interior Ministries. A major need for a codification of police law was asserted (Ibid.: #298, 300).

Police Vice President Ludwig Weitmann, in a speech at a "Police Day" in Ludwigsburg on March 18, 1950, summed up the difficulties as perceived by police executives. The cities, he said, were not overjoyed to have to take on the support of police forces, which entailed huge new costs, especially for larger cities. As the police became subordinate to the local powers, some friction developed. Since police chiefs are chosen by city councils, politics becomes involved in police operations. Furthermore, the leadership of the police chief is undermined in those cities where the mayor is trying to become involved in running the police department. Training is not emphasized because of lack of funds, especially in the smaller localities.

At the same meeting, however, Oberburgermeister Rolf Engelbrecht of Ludwigsburg, who was the ultimate authority over the town's police, declared that there were no major problems in the 30-man Schupo force and the 5-man Kripo force in his jurisdiction. Nor was there any major difficulty in separating the executive police from the administrative police.

The American authorities tried to help with technical assistance from American police. In August, 1949, a training official from the Oregon state police toured Baden, Württemberg, Hesse, Bavaria, and Berlin, meeting with state police officials to help them with their new duties (HS EA 2/11, 173: #285).

Decline of the Communal Police

In November, 1950, the Allied High Commission decided that state governments should be allowed to centralize their police forces at the state level. Those cities that had communal forces and wished to keep them, however, should be allowed to do so (*Westfalische Nachrichten*, November 15, 1950).

This new opportunity was followed by renewed calls for reorganization of police forces under state rather than local control. Within a few months a request was made from the Baden-Württemberg police union to the Interior Ministry in Stuttgart that the communal police be integrated into the state police. The present system, according to this request, did not give equal benefits to all police officers.

In 1950 *Deutsche Polizei,* the leading union journal, also voiced criticisms of the communal forces in several articles. In one article, entitled "Quo Vadis Polizei" (Muller, 1951), police leader Wolfgang Muller complained that the small communal police in the three zones could not of themselves deal with police problems in the "crowded, narrowly defined borders of the Federal Republic of West Germany" (Ibid.: 29). At the least, he said, there is need for clear laws in each state in accordance with one model law given out from the central government.

In the same year another article in this journal, entitled "Communal or State Development of Police in North Rhine-Westphalia" (Sperrer, 1951), makes the point that "The danger of political influence is immeasurably greater in local police forces than in state forces where the Interior Minister is responsible to parliamentary control" (Ibid.: 76).

Furthermore, the local police, according to this article, is not efficient from a financial standpoint and should be abolished.

In the first of a series of articles on police reorganization, the problems faced by lawmakers in reforming police organizations were analyzed (Hohn, 1951). Disadvantages of the present organization were detailed: the civilian character of the police has not worked out well, the Interior Minister needs to have more control, there is no clear understanding about the nature of police work, the communal police do not have clear civil service standing as either local or state employees, and elected police chiefs are not responsive to the Interior Minister. The article concludes with a call for centralizing all police leadership at the state level. Other arguments presented in favor of a centralized police emphasized the fact that new technology and complicated intercity traffic make localized policing impractical (Gerecke, 1963).

Some opinion was more mixed. Württembeg-Baden's Interior Minister, for example, in a speech at a police function (Ulrich, 1951), praised the police forces set up in 1945 for dealing effectively with a chaotic and dangerous breakdown of security and order following the war. "We suffer still in the federal territory from an all-too-strong decentralization of the police, and we suffer under an all-too-strong fragmentation." If security is to be provided, he goes on, it will be necessary to work for a new organization that coordinates the various police entities. However, it would not be good to disturb the development of local self-government too much. The solution to the problem would be to accord greater power to the Interior Ministers to use the communal police and to coordinate the work of the communal forces in case of need. "Democracy is threatened," he concludes. "We can only protect ourselves through harmonious and meaningful common endeavor of individual police organizations."

Gradually, the smaller cities gave up their local police forces. In Baden-Württemberg a new law allowed cities with a population of over 75,000 to continue with local police. The state, however, retained the right to determine the size, armaments, and training program of city police. Under those rules, Pforzheim, Stuttgart, Mannheim, and Karlsruhe continued their city police under the direction of their mayors (Gerecke, 1963).

In due order, each state passed police laws that regulated the activities and organization of its newly centralized police. The nature of these laws shows the persistence of the Weimar institutions despite the trauma of the intervening years. Riege (1959: 59-77) tells us that:

— In Schleswig-Holstein the 1931 Prussian Police Administration Law was used as the model for the delineation of police duties,
— In Bremen, "the police law was crafted from the principles of the Prussian Police Administration Law of 1931,"
— In Hamburg various laws about organization and operations were passed. "These laws are equivalent to Paragraph 14 of the Prussian Police Administration Law of 1.6.31."
— In Lower Saxony, the 1951 police law "is equivalent to Paragraph 14 of the Prussian Police Administration Law of 1931."
— In North Rhine-Westphalia, the 1953 police law established "entirely new basic principles." Tasks of the police, however, were taken from the Prussian Police Administration Law of 1.6.31.
— Hesse and Rhineland-Palatinate passed police laws in 1954, again with the Prussian law as model,
— In the Saarland, the 1950 police law provided that the Prussian Police Administration Law of 1931 should be in effect, "to the extent that it does not conflict with the state constitution."

Only in Baden-Württemberg and in Bavaria, neither of which had been part of Prussia or sympathetic to the liberal Prussian government of the 1920's, were there police laws that did not consciously go back to the Prussian law. Nevertheless, says Riege, in the Bavarian law "the tasks and obligations of the police are essentially the same as those in other German states" (Ibid.: 88).

Baden-Württemberg, indeed, had particular problems in that this state was created out of the three southwestern states (Baden, Württemberg-Baden, and Württemberg-Hohenzollern) that had been occupied by both the French and Americans. Thus, there were varied police organizations that had to be consolidated, as well as the independent communal police in the American zones that had to be integrated into the state forces. According to a documentary of this period (Gerecke, 1951), this reorganization was not without pain occasioned not only by giving up separate organizations but also by giving up the historically-grounded places associated with police leadership and training in the earlier states. "But finally," says the author, "the understanding prevailed that in a federal country a unitary state police must be brought together and built up" (Ibid.: 51).

By 1955, all of the northern German states had completed the reconstruction of their police in a way that, with few exceptions, mirrored the philosophy of policing that was enshrined in the police law promulgated in the latter days of the Weimar Republic. By the end of the 1950's the few remaining communal police agencies in Baden-Württemberg had become part of the state organizations. In Bavaria, where greater diversity was constitutionally allowed, the city of Munich continued with a communal police until 1975 (Werkentin, 1984: Ch. 3).

The following passage illustrates the intense relief felt by German police at being able to return to their pre-1933 system of state control (Raible, 1963: 189-190):

> The development of the German police after 1945 in the various zones was handled by the occupying powers in accordance with the philosophy and reality in their own countries. No consideration was given to the historically-determined outlook of the German people. From this some measures were taken that Germans could not understand. They would not have taken place if the occupying powers had been more knowledgeable about German circumstances.
>
> About 1950, the occupying powers gave the states more freedom . . . and therewith the possibility of creating a police that would be appropriate for German needs and today's circumstances. The leadership of the German police once again could cultivate close cooperation with the public. Police training once again could stress development of each one's personality, correct behavior, good decision-making, and humane behavior whenever police strength must be employed. This development soon showed that the German police once again could earn the good reputation of being a democratic police, and that it was better to unify police authority once again in the hands of the states.

The author of this passage, Eugen Raible, goes on to explain why people are wrong who think that the state-based police should share the blame for the Nazi takeover. In fact, he says, it is only a state-based police that can guarantee "domestic security, peace, and order." The danger is that a centralized police will become high-handed, or will not be used sufficiently or usefully, rather than that the organization will be dangerous. Only the constitution and laws can guarantee against the dangers that people fear from the police. In fact, he concludes, it is precisely radical decentralization that brings about a situation in which the police is not useful or trustworthy. It depends on the local authorities for salaries, benefits, and work conditions and thus becomes dependent on the authorities. This creates extreme difficulty in trying to use police from various communities in a cooperative way.

A further difficulty, according to Raible, is that the military is not useful in dealing with domestic crises, since it has preemptive NATO obligations and cannot easily be used for domestic purposes. Thus a communal police would leave the state helpless in case of disorder (Ibid.).

The fear of uncontrollable disorder that Raible mentions is one of the themes that seems to predominate as one goes through the histories and documents. Other themes are the desire to restore exactly those police institutions that existed prior to National Socialist times, fear of political influence over police, and need for certainty about lines of command, responsibility, and accountability. Each of these themes assumed the status of accepted wisdom within a short time after the decentralized police was established.

Fear of uncontrollable disorder touches upon the civil order control function of police forces. The ad hoc approach to this function that is practiced in the United States and in Great Britain seems strange to the Germans. Indeed, the ease with which American leaders make use of militia troops such as the National Guard and even regular army troops in case of serious disorder (Higham, 1969) is totally antithetical to the German experience of the 20th Century. Furthermore, the fact that a regular standing army had not yet been developed in 1950 increased the insecurity of the Germans with respect to serious order control problems.

The need for coordinated order-control capacities goes deeper than the inability or disinclination to employ army troops, however. It goes back to the conception of German society itself as unstable, volatile, and likely to erupt in disorder at the slightest provocation. In such a situation the police become the force that provides protection against encroaching chaos. The experiences of the Weimar Republic strengthened this fear of disorder. As will be explained later in this chapter, however, there is at root also a deeper conception of the relation between state and citizen with the state as protector/enforcer and the police as supporters of the power of the state. Why, however, were the Germans so content to reestablish the police law of 1931, the same one that had lasted only a few years? One critical commentator says: "It is noteworthy how the fascist police, and also the police established by the Allied occupation forces were contrasted with the 'healthy world' of the police organization of the Weimar Republic. One seemed to forget the easy transition of Severing's Prussian police into fascism — only 5000 out of 85,000 police were let go — and the build-up of the Wehrmacht with the help of the police troops of the Weimar Republic" (Werkentin, 1984: 68).

As explained in Chapter Two, however, this law of 1931 was the culmination of an effort of at least fifty years to arrive at a new concept of police, a concept that stressed restriction on police power, as opposed to the rather broad conception of those powers that existed before (Raible, 1963). Whatever the organizational and ideological failures that followed the development of this law, the law itself remained a monument to a "new police" in the eyes of those who were searching for a way to anchor the post-war police in some kind of stable ground. Nostalgia for some aspects of the Weimar police may have been misplaced, but the fact is that the Prussian law represented a conceptual democratic alternative to the aborted efforts at structural democracy imposed by the Allied powers.

The German fear of political influence over the police was related to local control by mayors and other elected officials. American cities in which political machines controlled recruitment and used police to do political favors, poll-watching, and other chores provided the bad example that was to be avoided. Community police, that come out of a community and that are more responsive to community needs than state or national police seemed to be beyond reckoning in this distaste for a politicized force. In the German bureaucratic tradition the state represents the law and is thus the more benign entity than the more obviously political locality. Indeed, as will be explained more thoroughly later in this chapter, there was little interest in the spirit of communal policing, or the philosophy under which it developed in the 19th Century in Great Britain and the United States. This Anglo-Saxon philosophy was one of citizen responsibility and citizen control: the fear at that time was of excessive state power.

Finally, the need for certainty about lines of command, responsibility, and accountability contrasts again the German bureaucratic tradition in which the police took part, with the seemingly chaotic mix of jurisdictions, powers, and organizations that make up the sum of American police forces. Although concerns about efficiency and responsibility are often strong in the United States, the general ability to interact, to "make do," to use what is available, to live with inefficiences, and to cooperate, is the product of years of evolution. Small wonder, then, that the Germans were not able to take on this complex and subtle mode of interaction in the few short years that they had communal police forces.

In the final analysis, communal police forces were imposed upon the Germans in the name of democracy, but were seen by them as efforts to destroy the effectiveness and power of the police. One sees little effort being made to let the idea take hold, to allow it to develop, and to see it as a strong step toward a democratic social order. With the Western powers increasingly concerned about the Soviet threat, there was in any case by 1949 a certain willingness to let the Germans strengthen their police with the understanding that its function would be strategic in case of armed conflict.

NATIONALIZING INFLUENCES SINCE 1950

Since 1950, not only has communal policing died, but the trend in Germany, as in fact in other countries, has been toward greater national government influence and control, as opposed to the state government control sought by the Germans in the early post-war years, over police operations. There are at least ten indicators of this increasing nationalization of police power:

1. With the exception of the top civilian leadership, the highest leadership—i.e., the top 1 percent—of German police officials receive one year of intensive training at the Police Leadership Academy in Münster-Hiltrup. In addition, the leadership frequently attends short-course training sessions at the Academy. Although the Academy is technically under the state government of North Rhine-Westphalia, it is largely supported by the federal government.

This training assures that every two years a cohort of police who have studied together, lived together, eaten together, and been in constant communication with each other and with their instructors, is sent out to all parts of Germany to take over leadership positions in police departments and divisions. It is to be expected that, in addition to the training received, they have also developed mutual solidarity and a nationwide network of contacts. Many of these graduates train other police in the state police schools and Bepo installations throughout the country. Furthermore, the curriculum used in the state police schools is developed at the Police Leadership Academy.

2. A Standing Conference of Interior Ministers brings together the highest police representatives of each state several times each year to make plans and to exchange ideas about the police and crime problems. Most major planning for police training, equipment, and operations comes out of this Conference. The Conference has also developed a Master Plan for Internal Security (Bundesministerium des Innern, 1977) and has proposed model police laws.

3. The Bundeskriminalamt (BKA) in Wiesbaden acts as a major clearing-house for crime statistics, criminal histories, communications with states, and assistance with respect to forensic matters and criminal investigations. It also conducts and commissions research on crime control. The Kriminalpolizei of the various states, in conjunction with the BKA, is developing constantly stronger inter-state and state-national ties (Stumper, 1976). In fact, the ever-increasing technological capabilities for oversight and covert observation that the BKA possesses are the target of a good deal of concern, with the fear that a "Big Brother" type of citizen observation may soon develop (Sternsdorff, 1983; Busch et al, 1985).

4. The Bereitschaftspolizei receives (as it has since its inception) major support from the federal government. In turn, the federal government employs a national director for the Bepo, standardized weapons are used, and the national government has the right to oversee the deployment of Bepo troops on an inter-state basis.

5. Each state, with the exception of Bavaria, is required to take 20 percent of its Schupo recruits from the Bundesgrenzschutz, or Border Control Police. These BGS troops do not go through the Bepo training in state schools; rather they have their own training schools for both rank and file and for officers. Thus a federally trained and federally financed organization provides a substantial input into street-level local police.

6. For years there was a movement to pass a national police operations law (Einheitliches Polizeigesetz) that could be adopted by all the states and the federal government. This law was proposed by the Standing Conference of Interior Ministers in 1976. The law included sections related to police procedure in encounters with citizens, cooperation with other authorities, and use of weapons. It was met by a storm of protest by certain groups, who claimed that it infringed on human rights, especially in the matter of weapons use. Thus, to take an extreme example, Rote Hilfe (Red Help), a Berlin group, mounted a campaign against the law, claiming it would further militarize the police, allow shooting to kill, even of children under fourteen, allow for forty-eight hours of police detention prior to the appointment of an attorney, allow for searches and seizures without warrants, and similar depredations. Well-organized resistance to the law was also undertaken by groups in Dortmund, Frankfurt, Hamburg, Mainz, and Munich (Bibliothek für Zeitgeschichte, 1976).

Although the proposed law was amended to deal with some of the criticisms, it was defeated in the federal parliament in 1979 (Jesse,

1980). Nevertheless, in its general provisions it became a model for new police laws and regulations in several of the states including Baden-Württemberg, Bavaria, North Rhine-Westphalia, Rhineland-Palatinate, and Lower Saxony (Ule and Rasch, 192). In 1986 the Interior Ministers Conference proposed a new but still controversial version of this law in hopes that it would be adopted by all the states as well as the federal government. If this or a similiar law is adopted by all the parties, police operations will become highly uniform throughout Germany, although police organizational arrangements will continue to differ from state to state.

7. Since 1979 police from all over Germany wear the same uniform. Where formerly there was a variety of colors and styles in the various states, the standard police uniform throughout Germany now consists of yellow shirt, forest-green jacket, brown pants, and white cap. Green, silver, and yellow stars on the shoulder signify different rank levels.

8. In Germany a national criminal law with regard to felonies is administered by state police forces. This is in no way a new development. In fact, national laws administered locally are a legacy of the system built by Bismarck in the late 19th Century, according to which the local aristocracy assumed the positions of high public administrators within the states, but the newly-centralized Empire strengthened its power through policy-making in important substantive matters (Jacob, 1963). This arrangement, however, serves to strengthen the federal government in relation to the states.

9. Through interpretation of the laws and Constitution, the courts, and especially the Federal Constitutional Court (Bundesverfassungsgericht, or BVG) help to strengthen a national standard of police procedure and action. There are some similarities to the situation in the United States, although criminal procedure in general, as well as substantive criminal law, is regulated by federal law in Germany. A recent example was the BVG determination that it is a violation of the constitutional right to peaceful demonstration if police gather excessive nonarrest-related information about individual demonstrators (i.e., lists of demonstrators) (BVG 69.315, 349). Recently also the Court asserted the right to demonstrate peacefully even if police determined that some violence is likely to occur at a demonstration. This decision was related to the (unsuccessful) effort to forbid the 1981 demonstration at the Brockdorf nuclear power plant in Schleswig-Holstein. With respect to the census law passed in the early 1980's the BVG held that cross-checking of census records and police records was unconstitutional.

In addition to the BVG, the Federal Supreme Court (Bundesgericht-shof, or BGH) helps to regulate police conduct from the national level. For example, this court decided in 1985 that indiscriminate arrests at demonstrations were illegal (Dietel, 1985).

10. The increasing unrest in Germany itself has increased the degree of centralized police operation. As one police official explained, the security emergencies of the 1970's led to a rethinking of many aspects of police work. The unthinkable—that police of North Rhine-Westphalia would be used in Bavaria, or that police of Bavaria would be used in Schleswig-Holstein—has become a normal, if not frequent occurrence. According to some critics, in fact, the police apparatus has used the threat of terrorism as an excuse to increase police strength and technical capacity, tighten national control over police, and justify dubious police encroachments on privacy (Busch et al., 1985).

In sum, there has been a tendency towards increasing nationalization of police power in Germany. With problems of terrorism, unrest, and instability, the German people themselves appear to be ambivalent about the locus of police power. In a public opinion poll run by the EMNID Institute in Bielefeld, when respondents were asked whether police tasks of fighting violent crime or terrorism should be handled by the states or by the federal government, 50 percent opted for federal government control and 49 percent for state control (Tacke, 1982).

With impressive new technology, communications possibilities, and easy traffic of criminals from state to state, the drive toward nationalization in modern police departments seems almost inevitable. In Great Britain similar, in fact more, nationalization has taken place in the past fifteen years (Brogden, 1982). In the United States, however, much of the nationalization that has taken place has followed time-honored American lines of development: grants-in-aid for equipment, training, education, and experimentation, as well as widespread exchange of knowledge and ideas. The FBI, as a center for information and technical advice, has developed along much the same lines as the BKA in Germany.

CENTRALIZATION AND CIVIL ORDER CONTROL

What does the increasingly centralized German police organization connote for civil order control? In a country that only uses police, as opposed to military forces, to quell disturbances against public order, would a communalized police be able to deal with these disorders? Does the present organization facilitate, as some claim (Werkentin, 1984), the ruthless suppression of peaceful dissent by a threatened governmental system?

These are difficult questions to deal with, largely because there is little in German experience to provide points of comparison. By the time major post-war civil order problems had developed—i.e., the decade of the 1960's—the state police reorganization had been thoroughly developed.

Obviously the German leadership, both in and outside of the police, saw localized police as a major obstacle to civil order control. In the police journals and the media, this matter was brought up during the discussions about reorganization of police in the early 1950's (Müller, 1951: 29; Hohn, 1952; *Die Neue Zeitung,* München, October 29, 1949). In correspondence among police leaders concerns about the problems of civil order control are also evident (see e.g., HS, EA 2/11, 173: #307). The political leadership also found decentralized police to be a hindrance for public security and order (Werkentin, 1984: Ch. 4).

The larger question of whether or not a localized police actually can deal effectively with public order problems can best be examined in light of the British and American experience, since both of these countries rely extensively on local street police to handle civil unrest. In the United States, small-scale demonstrations and even some large but peaceable ones, are handled by local police and, in some cases, state police. These forces generally receive minimal training for such kinds of work.

When there are critical social order problems, however, there is easy recourse to the National Guard or to military troops. Since the state Guard can easily be nationalized by order of the President, the Guard itself is essentially a national militia that is, if not a first line of defense in crowd control (the police assume that role), at least an easily available one. Thus, for example, President Eisenhower in 1957 nationalized the Arkansas Guard, which was being used by Governor Faubus to hinder desegregation of Little Rock High School. Eisenhower used this same Guard, with help from regular military forces, to enforce desegregation. Likewise, in 1962 President Kennedy used the Mississippi National Guard to enforce the enrollment of James Meredith at the University of Mississippi. In Watts, Detroit, the other cases of major disorder in the late 1960's the Guard and the military were freely used.

According to some experts, the use of the regular military is in fact preferable to using the Guard because of the better training and discipline of the standing army. The military itself, however, does not have specially-trained riot control forces and is not schooled in dealing with confrontations in which the use of force needs to be minimized. Furthermore, for the military itself there is little prestige and much uneasiness involved in engaging in conflicts with other Americans (Williams, 1957).

Thus the picture is a mixed one in the United States. On the one hand, Americans seem to accept the use of military troops for social order control with some equanimity, a situation that does not exist in Germany. On the other hand, most demonstrations, whether peaceful or not, are handled by local police forces with little training.

The situation in the United States, however, is not as acute as it is in the Federal Republic of Germany, which in 1983 had a total of 9,237 demonstrations, of which 274 were "nonpeaceful" (Busch et al., 1985: 322). In the United States, even large demonstrations are generally peaceful and do not call for a massive police presence. In Germany, with the fear of violence and the confrontational attitude that clouds these manifestations, it is not unusual to have far larger numbers of police than of demonstrators, as in Nurnberg in early 1987, where 4000 police stood guard over a rally consisting of 1500 anti nuclear power plant demonstrators (*Die Welt,* Jan. 18, 1987: 1).

In Great Britain local police forces have generally handled crowd control in this century, although there is an earlier tradition of military or militia involvement. According to F. C. Mather's (1967) description of British government action during the Chartist uprisings of the 1840's, the usual British practice of having a magistrate read the Riot Act to crowds before engaging magistrates or militia troops was not found to be effective in the massive unrest of the time, nor was the militia itself a very useful force. Mather claimed that only the London Metropolitan Police had the training, discipline, and morale to deal effectively and nonviolently with the Chartist demonstrators. In the end, however, it was the military that contained the disorders.

The military was last used to maintain public order in Britain during the labor unrest in the 1920's; all more recent disturbances have been handled by local police. The urban riots of the 1980's, however, in which hostility toward the police played an important part, have led to serious reappraisals not only of police role and behavior, but also of their capacity to contain unruly or violent crowds (Scarman, 1985; Brogden, 1982).

How the Germans would have dealt with social order control if localized police forces had become institutionalized, and whether they would have developed a pattern of inter-agency cooperation or of military intervention, remains an open question. Whether such local forces would have maintained friendlier relations with dissident groups than is now the case is another open question. One thing should be remembered, however. Public order problems in Germany are not manifestations of anger or despair by an economically deprived underclass, as were the urban riots in Manchester and London, or the riots in many American cities in the 1960's. Most social order control problems in Germany, in fact, are occasioned by environmental concerns of various kinds and by the NATO deployment of atomic weapons on German soil. Many of the demonstrators are thus young, intellectual, idealistic, and of upper middle-class background. The police, with a more conventional and conservative working-class background, are in a similar position with respect to these demonstrators as were American police with respect to Vietnam War opponents. On the one hand, there is police resentment against the often privileged status of demonstrators. On the other hand, there appears to be some ground for cooperation and some mutual interest in peaceful protest. Locally-controlled police forces, in cooperation with local political authorities, would not necessarily be less effective in these circumstances than state-level ones.

ORGANIZATIONAL ELEMENTS IN DECENTRALIZATION: STRUCTURE, ETHOS, LEADERSHIP

Structure

In all the talk about centralization and decentralization, it is often forgotten that German police organizations until 1921 included communal police forces that performed a watchman function in most municipalities. Although these police forces were tied in various ways to the Interior Ministries, they operated basically as local entities. State police (Gendarmerie or Landjäger) handled rural areas, emergencies, and other general police duties. Thus it can hardly be said that communal forces were so foreign to the German tradition of police that the impossibility of digesting them should have been a foregone conclusion. Why had the state police forces as developed in the Weimar Republic become such an entrenched institution?

The answer to this question probably lies in the efforts to professionalize and modernize police that were undertaken after the First World War. For the first time police were given the treasured and respected status of "Beamte," or civil servant. They were carefully selected, and were given extensive training and modern armaments. Unions of police officers became important bargaining agents for the rank and file. Compared to the often feared but also often ridiculed communal Schutzmann of the Empire, who was usually a former military employee, the status of police in their own eyes and in those of the public were much enhanced. In effect, police took on a new tradition, that of the German bureaucrat, with all its significance in terms of organization and outlook. The police hierarchy was paralleled by other state bureaucratic hierarchies, including those of the various Ministries of Justice, with which the police interacted frequently.

At the same time, in the Weimar Republic, the concept of democracy itself was meaningful to the Germans chiefly in terms of a Rechtsstaat, or law-based state, as will be explained more fully in the next section of this chapter. The more nebulous, but also more fundamental democratic concept of community power was foreign to German thought, and indeed has never become integral to German ideas of democracy. Thus the legacy from Weimar, comfortable as it was to the Germans, deviated fundamentally from the American concept of politics and democracy.

Two further structural aspects of decentralization also need to be considered. The first is the strategic significance of a centralized police. The second is the reality of a large degree of pluralism that exists in the German police structure, giving it a kind of *de facto* decentralization different from that envisioned in 1945.

By the late 1940's both the German leadership in Bonn and the Allied leadership were increasingly concerned with Germany's weakness in the face of the Russian and East European powers. With little else to go on, they looked to the police as a force that would help the Allies protect Germany against possible Eastern incursions. As explained in Chapter Three, these strategic concerns were paramount in the decision to recreate the Bereitschaftspolizei. At the same time, any other measures that would make for a strengthened German police were looked on with favor by the Bonn govenment. Thus there were actually three forces in the drive to centralize the police at the state level. First the Allied powers, never too clear in any case what decentralization of police was to mean except in the crudest structural sense, lost their interest in this particular reform and made little effort to institutionalize it. Second, the

German federal government, for strategic reasons, was eager to strengthen the police in any way possible. Third, the actual police authorities and most of the communities involved, for reasons of tradition and operational ease, were not comfortable with decentralized structures in either the American or the British zones and thus made no effort to support them. The grand hope for democratizing the German police through community control became a victim of strategic and bureaucratic priorities.

This rather bleak assessment of the fate of localization of responsibility for police must be tempered by consideration of the structural reality of police operations in Germany today. The German police apparatus is not a monolithic structure that can be easily manipulated from the center. In fact there is a large measure of pluralism built into this apparatus as it exists today. This pluralism in police operations constitutes a *de facto* decentralization that is not inconsiderable.

At the most basic level, the fact remains that in day-to-day operations the German police is decentralized to the state level. In a country that is no larger than some American states, (albeit with a population of 60,000,000) this fact in itself represents a good deal of decentralization. As in the United States, there is often rivalry rather than cooperation between various police organizations. As one respondent explained it, absurd situations can develop, with agents of the various federal agencies (i.e., BGS, BKA, BND, and BVS) all spying on each other. Further, although there is much uniformity in police operations, the actual organization structures vary considerably from state to state. This variance in organization makes communication between state police organs somewhat more difficult than it would be otherwise (Stumper, 1976).

Within each state, there are also strong forces for a pluralist operation. Once the initial period of near-universal street-level police work is over, the career paths of Kripo officers and Schupo officers are quite separate. There is pressure within Kripo ranks to increase this separation and to elevate the status of the Kripo relative to the Schupo. This is so despite stringent efforts by the general police leadership to insist on the concept of the "single career path" (einheitliches Laufbahn) within German police, and to counter the centrifugal tendencies of the Kripo with insistence on integrated training at the Police Leadership Academy, similar pay scales, and other integrative efforts. There has indeed been some bitterness on the part of the Kripo about what is seen as repression of their branch, and a separate Kripo union broke off from the major police union, the Gewerkschaft der Polizei, in 1969 (Lehr, 1975).

Unions themselves are a force for pluralism. Almost all German police officers belong to one or another union. The most important of these is the Gewerkschaft der Polizei (GdP), which counts 90 percent of sworn police among its members, and which is one of the seventeen major union groups that constitute the national Deutscher Gewerkschaft Bund (equivalent to the AFL-CIO). An older and more conservative union to which police belong is the Öffentliches Transport und Verkehr (ÖTV). The previously-mentioned union of Kripo officers is a small but militant group that is considered by the GdP to be a major threat and force for fragmentation (Bramshill, 1981; Kuhlmann, 1969).

The mix of civilian chiefs and career police in the leadership cadres must also count as a force for pluralism in German police. As explained in Chapter Two, the civilian leaders in the Interior Ministries and at the local level do not have a career police background, but are most likely to be career civil servants in other parts of the justice system. Although they are not likely to get involved in the technical aspects of policing, they do provide a bridge between the career police leadership, most of whom have been in a rather inbred track of police training and service for many years, and the nonpolice world.

Some of the internal structural forces for pluralism will be discussed in greater detail in Chapter Five. Taking the forces just mentioned into consideration, however — varied organizations, unions, civilian leadership, internal factions — it seems reasonable to conclude that the structures of the German police today are of a variety that would tend to belie some of the more radical criticisms by those Germans who see only a monolithic, highly militarized and centralized force, the chief function of which is to conduct a civil war, or "Bürgerkrieg" against the citizens (Werkentin, 1984).

Ethos

Section One of the Prussian Police Administration Law of 1931 says "Die Polizei ist Angelegenheit des Staates" ("the police is an institution of the State"). While few people would dispute this fact, its significance is really in the meaning that such phrases have meant in the context of police history in Germany. In effect, the police emanate from the *state,* not from the people, in philosophy as well as in practice.

Once again we need to return to the term Rechtsstaat or "law-state," a term that one encounters constantly in reading about German law and justice institutions. Since the late 18th Century, this concept has been a guiding principle in German legal and governmental philosophy. The word itself has assumed enormous symbolic proportions and means different things to different people. Indeed, one sees the word so often in books, speeches, newspapers, and other offerings that it begins to sound like a slogan to a foreign observer. At the risk of oversimplifying, it can be said that, under the Prussian monarchy and then under the Empire, Rechtsstaat was meant to indicate that the rule, even of autocratic monarchs, was bound to a regimen of duly-promulgated laws. The contrast was with the earlier philosophy of a Polizeistaat, or police state (not to be confused with the modern totalitarian police state), a paternalistic but intrusive public order in which the state was supposed to rule for the good of the people (see Chapman, 1970; Michaelis, 1980 for further discussion of these concepts). In many ways the Rechtsstaat of the monarchy was a German response to the Enlightenment theories of contract government that were so influential in the establishment of the American system of government, although the German form of contract tended more to the ideas of Hobbes than of Locke or Rousseau. The monarch had the obligation to rule through law, but not through democratic procedure or participation by the people. In both the Weimar Republic and the Federal Republic, the term Rechtsstaat is generally coupled with the terms "freie" and "demokratische" ("free" and "democratic"), in other words, a *democratic* law-state in which there is public participation through the selection of representatives to make rules for the governance of the people. In the Federal Republic it has also become common to speak of a "soziales Rechtsstaat" or "socially-conscious law state" to suggest the ideal that the state has some responsibility for an active role in assuring the social welfare of its citizens.

Rule of law (and especially democratic rule of law) rather than arbitrary and lawless rule is certainly not to be underrated, and it plays a large part in the philosophy of democratic government everywhere. The difference between the ideal of democratic rule of law and that of community power is a subtle one. Understanding this difference, however, is crucial to understanding the situation in Germany with respect to decentralization of police forces. The fact is that the Germans failed to see the significance of community power as long as they had democratic rule of law. This may have been natural considering the history of German governmental institutions. What was less natural is that the philosophy of community power seemed also either not to have been understood by the Allies, or not considered important enough to warrant an effort at education. To them, decentralization was a structural reality that had to be carried out, not a philosophy of organizational or political power. Even more, the disorganized and uncoordinated way in which different types of police organization were built up in the different zones of occupation suggests that little forethought or planning had gone into most crucial aspects of changing the German police organization (Müller and Kroger, 1960).

Both sides, then, saw the decentralization effort as one that was directed chiefly at fragmenting German police power rather than at creating a new form of empowerment. For the German people themselves, perceiving the police as an organ of the state seemed like a more logical and natural state of affairs than the more complex and even disturbing ideal of community power.

Leadership

It has been stressed in this chapter that the police leadership had little interest in perpetuating the structure of decentralization imposed by the British and American forces. What of the political leadership? The dedication of many of these leaders to a democratic social order had been sharpened by years of exile or oppression during the Nazi era. Were they unable to see the advantages of police power that would be an adjunct of community power?

In a manifestly hostile critique that nevertheless contains important details about the historical development relative to recentralization of police, Falco Werkentin (1984) blames Social Democratic Party elements for leading the effort to "anchor the authority of the new republic in a highly-armed, militaristic police" responsive to central control (Ibid.:58). Carl Severing himself, the Social Democratic Prussian Interior Minister and police leader in the Weimar Republic, was a leading voice in the push to recentralize the police. According to Werkentin, only the Social Democrats, with their clear anti-fascist backgrounds, could have brought about the abrupt and massive recentralization, especially in North Germany (Ibid.: 61).

Within the police apparatus itself an important point to remember is that, with the decimation of the police leadership in 1945, many of the new leaders were Weimar police officials who had been trained, and whose careers had gotten under way, at the crucial point in German police history where professionalization and centralization were developed as hallmarks of a democratic police force. As such, they were also carriers of the bureaucratic traditions of the German Rechtsstaat. Such

individuals were not likely to be imbued with a passion for the complex-
ities of community power as opposed to state power. Herbert Kalicinski,
head of the Police Institut in Hiltrup and former police leader in Weimar
explained this perception in a speech in 1950: "We have the task to develop the profession of police in the good old tradition of the Weimar Republic under the leadership of our honored Minister Severing, and we
thereby put ourselves in sharp contrast to the concept of police as it was
developed in the Third Reich . . . . " (Kalicinski, 1950).

This is not to say that the police leadership was lacking in dedication to a democratic social order, but rather that their conception of how
to police such an order was based on an earlier experiment, one that was
rather short-lived. Indeed, and despite the redevelopment of strategic
forces through the Bereitschaftspolizei at that time, reading the police
journals shows that, in terms of training, publicity, and philosophical reflection, there was much concern for the development of a police that
would be appropriate for a democracy. Furthermore, the strong emphasis on a citizen-friendly police in the 1950's was part of this effort to be
accepted by, and to build cooperative ties with, the citizenry.

Finally, the working relationships that developed among the varied elements of the police organization and described earlier as a form of
pluralism, suggest that the ideal of decentralization was not totally dis-
carded. Rather it had assumed a comfortable form that was in conformity with the German bureaucratic tradition.

CHAPTER FIVE

DEMOCRATIZATION

Without exaggeration I can say that the German police has reached a point where it has no equal among police forces throughout the world. This is attested to by the many foreign police officers who attend your seminars and schools, as well as by the world-wide reputation that your police has earned among police leaders in other countries.

American Brigadier-General E. F. Panaat, at the opening of the German-American Police Conference, Heidelberg, June 22, 1960.

FOUR D's—Demilitarization, Denazification, Decentralization, and Democratization—were the occupation goals for the German police (Kemperer, 1953: 407). In addition, the police were to engage no longer in judicial, legislative, and inappropriate administrative functions. Inappropriate administrative functions were those general governmental functions, such as public health, fire fighting, and registration of citizens that were performed by administrative police (polizei Behörde) as opposed to executive police (Vollzugspolizei). Judicial and legislative functions were those far-reaching powers assumed by the Nazi police as it became the major governmental agency that ran the death camps and otherwise spread terror throughout Germany and the occupied countries of Europe.

As we have seen, demilitarization and decentralization were not carried out as planned, although peculiarly German versions of both have survived in the present-day police organization. The denazification effort, although a serious one, also had mixed results in the early post-war years, before a whole new generation of police took over in the 1960's and early 1970's. Separation of administrative and executive functions, that the Germans claimed was based in any case on a misunderstanding of the word "police" in German governmental history, has survived in some states. However, the states of Baden-Württemberg, Bremen, Hesse, Saarland, and Rhineland-Palatinate have returned to the original terminology and organization of administrative police (Rasch, 1980:48).

DEMOCRACY IN POLICE ORGANIZATIONS

When it comes to democratization, however, there is a problem of definition. What exactly does "democratization" mean for organizations in general and for police organizations in particular? What did the Allies mean by "democratization" as distinct from the other three "D's?"

To take the second, and easier, question first, there is little evidence that the occupying powers had a clear conception of what democratization was to consist of. In fact the general lack of coordination among even the three Western allies with regard to police administration in their various zones of control suggests little planning or little agreement on internal organizational constructs. The Allied powers were in agreement on several points: the general need for decentralization, disarmament, getting rid of fascist elements, outlawing of the SS, SD, Gestapo, and police troops such as the Bereitschaftspolizei. As the plans for police reform developed in each zone, and despite exhortations about the importance of a democratic police, it became evident that the Allied plans went no further than external structural change and leadership change. It seems clear that the highest priority in all this was to render the police relatively harmless and insignificant as a fighting force or a governmental power.

Democratization, however, demands changes in operations that go beyond basic structures. The thornier question of what a democratic police organization actually would consist of involves analysis of three somewhat different constructs: democracy in general, democracy in organizations and especially police organizations, and policing a democratic society. An extended discussion of these three matters, that occupy a major place in the modern literature on police organizations (see, e.g., Goldstein, 1977; Reiss, 1972; Wilson, 1969) is not possible here, but a few points can be made about each of them.

The Concept of Democracy

The core principle of democracy is meaningful participation in decision-making by those who are part of the society. In large groups, including nations, some form of majority rule is incorporated in this principle. All other precepts follow from this one. Degree of democracy can be measured largely by the degree of such participation, and by the degree to which diversity and conflict can be accepted and contained within the structures of participation.

Modern Western societies also measure democracy in terms of two further principles: enumerated individual rights apart from the sphere of collective decision-making, and relative equality, both with respect to law and with respect to social and economic relations. Equality presumes also that governing functions, whether executive, legislative, or judicial, will not be exclusively the task of one class, gender, or ethnic group, but rather shared by different groups in the population.

Democracy in Organizations

In general, democracy in organizations, whether private or public, also can be evaluated in terms of adherence to the above three principles. The nature of participation by organization members — e.g., whether or not they participate in those policy decisions that actually lead to change — is important in making this assessment. There needs to be opportunity for free exchange of opinions and airing of controversy. Conflict must be open and not destructive of the organization as a whole. Furthermore, the makeup of organizational personnel, whether they represent a diversity of classes, sex, and ethnic background, is a clue to the openness and concern for equality that exists within the organization. Respect for the individual rights and dignity of organization members is also part of the complex of democratic indicators.

The literature on democracy in organizations, however, is concerned with a further variable, that of effectiveness with respect to productivity. Thus the "human relations" approach to organization, that basically involves applying democratic principles to organizational operations, is legitimized in terms of costs and benefits. The human relations school, however, also recognizes the fact of hierarchical structure and relationships and their usefulness in certain situations. Therefore, this school of thought is concerned with reconciling democratic ideals with traditional organization structure. Democracy is to be achieved through a relaxed and open leadership style, decision-making by committees and small groups, concern for the welfare of organization members, and easy communications among members (Kassem, 1976). In a society where technological expertise is of extreme importance, such an *ad hoc* approach to decision-making is particularly useful, since it provides opportunities for participation by the newer organization members, who are often those with the most up-to-date training (Bennis and Slater, 1968).

Police organizations traditionally have been hierarchically structured and para-military in style, with little concern for participation by the rank and file. This structural reality has masked the fact that many actual decisions about day-to-day actions are made at the lowest level of the organization, i.e., by the patrol officer. Such low-level discretion is not organizational democracy, however, except to the extent that it is structured and concerned with changing the atmosphere in the organization as a whole.

In the United States, with few exceptions, internal democracy has not played a large role in police department operations, although programs to increase the ethnic, racial, and sex diversity have promoted the equality norm. The question in relation to Germany is to what extent the German police, under the reform impetus of the 1940's, and laboring under a greater tradition of status inequality and command-centered operations than would ever have been tolerated in the United States, was able to achieve a degree of adherence to democratic principles of organization.

Policing a Democratic Social Order

As important as the matter of internal organizational democracy in police departments, however, is that of an appropriate way to police a democratic social order. Using the same criteria as explained above the questions are: To what extent is the public involved in decision-making operations about police operations? To what extent are public liberties and rights respected and enforced by police agencies? To what extent is equal treatment accorded to individuals regardless of status or minority characteristics?

Such considerations might well constitute the measure of any public bureaucracy in a democracy. They are particularly important when it comes to policing, however, because the most basic duty of the police is counter-democratic in nature. Police are to be enforcers, and thus to engage in conflictual relationships with the public. In these relationships the citizen has little recourse but to obey. In a democracy, however, the power and dignity of the citizen must be a consideration even in police encounters. Procedural controls on police behavior are useful in protecting citizens, but they are negative in approach and spirit. As Reiss

(1972) describes it, civility is the hallmark of a police that is appropriate to a democracy.

It seems likely that the two aspects of democratic police operations — internal organizational operations and external relationships — would work to reinforce each other. In practice, however, most concern has been with external relationships. With varying success, community control, individual rights, and equal treatment have been furthered as ways to improve policing. To the extent that internal operations are considered, the effort is to make police more representative of the people they police, i.e., to improve the racial, ethnic, and sex balance in police departments, but the actual strides towards internal democracy have been token in effect (Goldstein, 1977). In sum, then, what we are talking about when we refer to democratization in police organizations is democratization of internal processes as well as external ones. Internal processes will be considered in this chapter, external processes in the next. In each case the measure of accomplishment is the degree to which the organization adheres to the principles of democracy as they have been described.

STARTING ANEW: DEMOCRATIZATION OF POLICE IN EARLY POST-WAR GERMANY

Police Institute Chief Herbert Kalicinski, in a 1950 speech to police leaders, said "We know how little confidence the public has in the police today, as we make an entirely new start . . . . Our goal is the creation of a democratic police in the true sense of the word . . . and to make of the police leadership carriers of a new democratic ideal for the nation. Therefore we reject the use of any bureaucratic arrogance . . . No democracy can afford a police who think the people are there for the police rather than the police for the people" (Kalicinski, 1950).

Kalicinski goes on to quote from Ernst van den Berghe, former director of the police academy in Berlin-Charlottenburg, that was the Weimar equivalent of the present Police Leadership Academy in Hiltrup: "a police, whose pride it is, not to be a symbol of high-level power, but rather a friend and advisor to the people; to help them wherever possible. A police, furthermore, that feels itself in everything to be a part of the people, with whose security it is entrusted . . . a police that is not foreign to its own people or unknowing about the reality of life, but rather one that works with deep understanding and superior knowledge, with love and understanding for all things and with true heartfelt courtesy for all without discrimination as to whom is being addressed . . . " (Ibid.).

Another police leader (*Schriftenreihe,* 1957), considering the "social-psychological" and "social-pedagogical" problems after 1945, explained that the greatest need in the beginning was to deal with the fact that the authority of the police as an institution ("amtsautorität") had been destroyed, and so it was necessary to build up from the concept of individual authority: to have leaders who would inspire others by their "decent character, principled furthering of basic concepts, and ability to establish contact with the citizenry."

These eloquent pronouncements contributed to the general atmosphere of discussion, writing, and speeches about building a democratic police force. The ideal for such a force continued to be that of the Weimar Republic. This is not surprising. As mentioned, much of the leadership came from the liberal elements of the Weimar police. Furthermore, there were no clear guidelines about the meaning of a democratic police force. Perhaps most important, the total discrediting of the monstrous organization that the German police had become meant that institutional traditions and history, to say nothing of pride, had to be re-created. Reading the police journals of the time is in some ways a painful experience, as one sees the efforts to hastily denounce or pass over the period from 1933 to 1945, but not to analyze its significance. As one high police official told me, the history of that period has been suppressed, and little effort has been made to go through what documents may remain, to interview participants, and to do the painstaking historical research that would build up an archive.

The re-creation of the Weimar police, while it provided some kind of stability and model for the new police, was not an ideal solution to the matter of police organization. As explained in the last chapter, using this ideal made it impossible for the German leadership to develop real insights into the significance of communalized police. Furthermore, the Bereitschaftspolizei, that was the cornerstone of the Weimar police organization, and was reconstituted rapidly in the Federal Republic, remains in many ways the most troubling institution within the Federal Republic's police apparatus. It seems possible that, without the Weimar model, some new and perhaps less controversial organ might have been conceived and developed. An important point to remember also is that police were not able to maintain order during the incessant street-fighting and violent demonstrations of the Weimar Republic. Thus, while the present organization may be similar to that of the earlier times, the experience of Weimar and its failures as a democracy haunt the German police, as in fact they do the German republic in general.

Whatever the past, however, the question is what kind of organization the Germans have built in their desire to achieve a democratic police force. What kinds of people are found in the police? How does the organizational culture of the police—i.e., its structures, ethos, and leadership—reflect ideals of participation, equality, and individual rights? Are conflict and diversity channeled without threatening organizational viability? Answers to these questions shed light on crucial dimensions of police organization in Germany.

BACKGROUND AND PERSONALITY OF POLICE OFFICERS

Police officers are overwhelmingly men, although some of the states are now pledged to give equal consideration to women candidates, and to take women into the Bereitschaftspolizei. In the more conservative states like Baden-Württemberg, women are only found in the Kriminalpolizei, and even there as special employees not within the regular police career ladder. The pressure to hire women police, according to one police leader, will increase as the demographic reality of an ever-smaller number of working-age young men begins to affect police recruiting. By 1990, it is estimated that the number of young men eligible for compulsory military service will be about 260,000. Since Germany has a NATO commitment of 500,000, and since police service is allowed to substitute for military service, the competition for these young men will be intense.

Over the years Germany has been taking in more and more "guest workers" from countries like Greece, Yugoslavia, Italy, and now Turkey. Many of these guest workers remain in Germany and their children are born and grow up there. One of the criticisms of the police is that so few of these individuals, who form an underclass in German society, and who face serious discrimination in competition for jobs and housing, are found in police work. Statistics on minorities in police do not seem to be available. Nevertheless, their number is obviously very small. Police leaders explain that this small representation of minorities stems from the fact that all police must meet the rigorous entrance requirements regarding physical capacity and absence of criminal record, and that all police must be of German citizenship. There is no "affirmative action" such as is practiced in the United States. In fact, criminality even in one's family or among one's associates is cause for non-employment, according to one researcher (Spiegelberg, 1977).

The situation with respect to minorities does cause some uneasiness. One police leader (Schirrmacher, 1979) declared at a union rally: "Of course all Germans, no matter what their race or religion, should be allowed to function as civil servants. However, no one without citizenship should be allowed to be engaged in the field of internal security and order. German citizenship, however, should be obtainable without unusual difficulties. The real question is why foreigners are practically forced to live in ghettos. This hinders the development of citizenship."

In terms of geographical origin, the tendency in each state is to have a disproportionate number of recruits from rural areas. Since the greatest concentration of police is in urban areas, many of these young recruits are disappointed in their hopes to be stationed in or near their homes.

Information about the social class background of police officers is mixed. Brusten's (1974) analysis of the educational and previous occupational background of police recruits in North Rhine-Westphalia suggests that chiefly people with a blue collar or lower middle class background choose a police career. For them entry into the civil servant status of police officer represents an upward step on the social class ladder. This information is supported by Murck's (1976) and Feest and Blankenburg's (1972) observations of police. However, using another indicator, father's occupation, Helfer and Siebel (1975) come to the conclusion that the majority of police officers come from a middle class background.

One thing is certain: the level of previous education that police recruits bring to the profession has risen substantially since 1950, with the majority of officers now entering with a Realschul (middle-status high school) diploma, as opposed to the previously heavy preponderance of Volksschul (lower-status high school) graduates (Spiegelberg, 1977: 41).

Sociological studies of police behavior at the street level (Feest and Blankenburg, 1972; Brusten, Feest, and Lautmann, 1972; Murck, 1976) as well as the police literature, show that German Schupo offices have many of the same vocational characteristics and problems as their colleagues in the United States. Stress, in-group solidarity, discretionary behavior, stereotyping, and conservative outlook are all the norm.

In general the amount of research on police personality is not great. A study of 674 Hamburg police officers (Hornthal, 1975), that compared police to average Germans on a test of personality variables, showed police to be significantly less nervous, depressive, and excitable than the average German, and significantly more conventional and self-critical than the average. Tests of aggressiveness, sociability, self-confidence, repression, and dominance did not show significant differences.

The different interpretations of police background and personality may lead to different interpretations of possible morale problems related to upward mobility. German police literature often proclaims that the police is an open organization, where all enter at the bottom and all have equal opportunity to rise to the top. This is contrasted to the general German bureaucracy, which has historically been social class bound. One police leader also contrasted the German police organization with that of the French which, he said, is very elitist. This official said that the French police leadership academy at St. Cyr chooses from among thousands of applicants chiefly those who have legal training. These individuals look down on those who hope to work with them without having had an extensive liberal education.

The aspiration toward organizational openness is genuine. The reality, however, is not so simple. In the first place, the very fact that the highest leadership of the German police in many localities is not even police-trained, but is generally legally trained, can be considered from two perspectives. On the one hand, a "civilian" outside group holds the ultimate power over an organization, the police, that should be carefully monitored and controlled. On the other hand, as a police official explained with a certain amount of chagrin, this organizational arrangement can be seen as derivative of the German caste system, with jurists and legally-trained people in a higher class than police officers.

J. B., a former justice minister, now a professor of criminal procedure, explained it otherwise to me: "These people [the civilian chiefs] handle matters of law and administration, not matters of police technique. If the head of a police department needs to know police technique, he can pick it up." To be sure, the attitude expressed in this remark is not likely to find great favor among highly-trained professional police officers. It is, in fact, just the kind of attitude that engenders the resentment that is often felt by career police officers about being led by nonpolice personnel.

There are also other indicators of unequal access. The large majority (between 85 and 90%) of police officers in the various states are in the middle service grade (mittlerer Dienst) of the German civil service ladder. Another 10-14 percent are in the higher grade (gehobener Dienst), and only about 1 percent is in the highest grade (höherer Dienst). This is in contrast to the average levels in the civil service as a whole, with 38 percent in the middle group, 46 percent in the higher group, and 10 percent in the highest group (Murck, 1976:37). The percentage of police in the two higher levels actually increased during the reform period of the early 1970's as part of the effort to emphasize professionalism in the police (Busch et al., 1985).

For police who come from blue collar backgrounds, and for whom the middle level of service is an upward step, the limited opportunities for further advancement may not be as detrimental to morale as they are to those of middle class background. According to one police official, the German class structure is in any case more rigid than is that of the United States, and this class structure is related to educational background. Thus those who come in and remain without chances for advancement are willing to do so because they had no expectations in any case of upward mobility. Furthermore, in the German system, student grades determine, as soon as the first level of police training is finished, who will be favored to compete for advancement after a number of years of street work. Thus most officers know very soon that their police careers will be spent in street policing, and their choice to stay in the police or to move out is based on this knowledge. What this means is that the chief carriers of the police subculture in Germany, as indeed in other countries (see, e.g., Reuss-Ianni, 1983; Manning, 1977) are those who do not have a large stake in promotion to the leadership positions.

Brusten (1977), however, also shows a strong correlation between educational background and promotion without police ranks. This means that taking in larger percentages of recruits with greater preservice educational attainments may cause serious morale problems as their chances of advancement steadily decrease. For many of those who do not advance, the prospect of doing shift work until the retirement age of 60 is a grim one, leading, according to one author, to "stomach problems and sleeplessness" (Munsterman, 1980).

In a 1981 survey of 950 police in Baden-Württemberg, contentment with police work was shown to vary substantially with one's status in the organization. Among police in general, 75 percent were "generally content" with their work, while 12½ percent were "very content." Among patrol officers on shift work, however, only 50 percent were "content" and 17 percent of this group saw their relations with superiors as "poor."

Kripo officers were more content than Schupo. To the questions "Would you choose a police career again?", 67 percent of Schupo officers and 75 percent of Kripo officers answered "yes" (*Die Polizei Zeitung Baden-Württemberg,* December 31, 1981: 1). These results are similar to those obtained in a 1973 study of 461 Hamburg police officers (Stelter, 1973). This earlier study found that career satisfaction tended to increase with age, varying from 84 percent in the 51-60 age category to 63 percent in the 21-30 age category.

Interestingly, in the Weimar Republic, police officers who were not promoted to higher ranks left the service after twelve years, often setting up small businesses with the separation subsidies they received, or else going into other civil service positions. Police leaders, taking this future into consideration, tried to give enough educational opportunities to the officers to enable them to cope in the nonpolice world that most of them would be entering (Liang, 1970: Ch. 3). Thus possible morale problems among officers who did not advance were mitigated, and a young police force was guaranteed. In today's more highly professionalized police operations such an "up or out" policy probably does not seem to be cost effective.

The change in status for those who do advance is not easily digestible, either. Marital problems, stress, alcoholism, all take a toll. "There is a three-wives syndrome," said the Director of the Police Leadership Academy, as officers move from the middle to the higher and finally the highest level of police service.

In general, then, one can conclude that, despite the ideal picture of an open career track where everyone starts at the bottom and anyone can advance to the top, the system actually favors those who come from a higher status in the first place. In addition one can conclude that the German police, while not representative of the population as a whole in the sense of having a proportionate social class, ethnic, and sex makeup, is similar in composition and outlook to police forces such as are found in Britain and the United States. One important difference from the American police, however, is the degree of civilian leadership that one finds in the German system.

POLICE STRUCTURES THAT FOSTER DIVERSITY

Turning now to the effort to analyze various aspects of police work in terms of the factors of structure, ethos, and leadership, we find that the elements of structure that were described in Chapter Four as promoting pluralism within the organization are also those that, perhaps by definition, foster the kind of competition and diversity that is characteristic of a democratic organization. These structures include federalism, unionism, civilian leadership, and intraservice rivalry. Two of these structures, Schupo-Kripo relationships and union development, warrant some futher analysis.

Intraservice Rivalry

Although the rivalry between the Schutzpolizei (Schupo) and the Kriminalpolizei (Kripo) creates a further problem of status and morale, it also serves to foster competition and openness in the organization, inadvertantly (and contrary to the best-laid plans of the Interior Ministers) helping to keep it from becoming as monolithic as it otherwise would be. Police policy, as articulated in the Internal Security Plan (*Innere Sicherheit,* 1974) is that the two arms of regular police duty are equal, even though entry into the Kripo is a career move that separates the officer from patrol work for his entire working life. The fact is, however, that there is intense competition to get into Kripo work, with the result that those with higher preservice educational attainments and better records in the early years are most likely to get the Kripo positions. Kripo officers believe that their work is more specialized and requires a higher level of training, including advanced work in criminology and criminalistics, than does Schupo work. Thus they claim that they should be at a higher grade level and receive more compensation than Schupo officers with comparable time in the police.

In the 1970's, serious unrest among Kripo officers and the establishment of a separate and radical Kripo union led to a reevaluation of the police career ladder and prospects. Despite the reaffirmation of the policy of equality, the fact is that a much higher percentage of Kripo than Schupo officers are found in the higher levels of the civil service. While the average percentage of all officers in the higher grades is about 15 percent, the percentage of Kripo officers in those grades varies from 31 percent in the Saar to 70 percent in Berlin, with the median at 41 percent (Hermann, 1982).

Difficulties concerning coordination and competition between Kripo and Schupo are not new, but show up again and again in discussions about police organization in the early post-war years (Kosyra, 1980). One journal article declared that a police organization was needed in which the Kripo was not a fifth wheel of a "unified" police, but stood independently as a fully equal second pillar of the organization (Kriminalität, 1951). Indeed, the problems go back to the Weimar Republic, when the Kripo first started to develop as part of the regular police organization, rather than as an elite and highly-educated special investigations corps (Liang, 1970).

The conflict between the two branches came to a head in 1968. At that time the Gewerkschaft der Polizei, the major police union, published a tract entitled *Capitulation to Criminals? An Investigation into the Situation of the Kriminalpolizei in the Federal Republic of Germany* (Gewerkschaft, 1968). Deploring the rapid increase in crime, and basing much of their information on a survey and on discussions with Kripo officers, the union concluded, among other things, that the Kripo organization was confusing, that the training of Kripo officers was insufficient and highly dissimilar from state to state, that the Kripo did not work cooperatively with the Schupo, and that there was need to concentrate more on new crime problems such as white collar crime.

This report, which was not well received in Kripo circles, heightened the tension. That same year the Kripo started its own union. One of the goals of this union was to fight the concept of a unitary police. Membership in this union rose from 1000 in 1968 to 10,000 in 1982, about 45 percent of all Kripo officers in Germany. Between 1968 and 1978 the union organized six major demonstrations, whose purpose was to protest the lack of appreciation of the work of the Kripo (Hermann, 1982). In a bitter polemic entitled "The Destruction of the Kriminalpolizei is Threatened" (Lehr, 1975) Kripo leader Kurt Lehr denounced the Internal Security plan of 1974. This plan had reaffirmed the policy of a unitary police and had called for further integration of the two branches. He also deplored organizational changes in various states that were designed to bring Kripo and Schupo closer. "The slogan 'Unity of the Police' is an opportunistic fiction," he said (Ibid.: 2), and presented a history of separate detective work going back to 1770. A separate program of research and action was needed, he claimed.

At root are questions of pay and prestige. The Kripo union leadership believes that, by tying the two branches together, the Kripo officer is kept from attaining the status of nonpolice civil servant and remains within the sphere of the Schupo—i.e., essentially a lower class of civil servant. The problems is not new, but also echoes the situation in the Weimar Republic, where the Kripo struggled to maintain itself as a separate, highly-trained, highly-educated group with no background in

street work (Liang, 1970: Ch. 4). Much of the argument, in fact, has re-
volved around the question of whether or not the Kripo should be able to
hire well-trained agents directly into the higher grades without having
them go through the obligatory three years in the Bepo and five years in
the Schupo. Although such lateral hiring is now done in some states, the
general policy is still to promote to the Kripo from Schupo ranks.

The hurdles to becoming a full-fledged Kripo officer are actually quite
large. In the state of North Rhine-Westphalia, for example, after a police recruit has gone through his three years of Bepo training, he spends one-half
year in a regular police school. His grade on the final examination, plus his
work record during the five years of Schupo work determine whether or not
he will be allowed to compete for Kripo work. This competition consists first
of an eight-week period of application, interviews, and tests. At the end there
is an oral examination including a ten-minute speech by the candidate and a
half hour of round-table discussion. Out of every 800-900 successful candidates, 250 are generally needed for the work. The others go on a waiting list,
and rarely become Kripo officers.

The candidates who are chosen get a technical education, stressing
criminology and criminalistics, at a police college (Kriminalpolizei
Fachhochschul). After that they spend three years in a further apprenticeship before attaining the rank of Kriminalkommissar. Although,
during the years of personnel shortages, it was possible for an individual
with an academic high school diploma (Abitur) to be taken directly into
the Kripo college and thus bypass the unitary police system, this rarely
happens today since there are so many Schupo candidates for Kripo positions. Once a police officer goes through the Kripo training, he never
returns to Schupo work. If he is part of the 1 percent of the officers who
go through the training for major leadership positions, however, he will
be in the same classes with and, with some few course exceptions, receive the same training as, other police leaders.

Kripo work with its emphasis on technology, communications, and
advanced work in criminology and criminalistics, probably does require
more education than conventional Schupo work (Kripo officers tend to
be the "intellectuals" of the police service, said one Kripo officer). Thus
Kripo agents perceive themselves as "specialist" in orientation and the
Kripo officers tend to look down on the "generalist" uniformed police.
What this suggests is that the Germans, despite their emphasis on training and education, are finding that their street-level police do not have
the general liberal background that has been furthered so much in
American police departments since the late 1960's.

According to some police, and especially union leaders (Gremmler, 1986; Dietel, 1986), a major challenge is to upgrade the professional status of Schupo offices. This should be done through emphasis on professional behavior as well as through additional training in leadership, conflict-management, human relations skills, communications, and telecommunications. If these changes were effected, Schupo personnel would move more into the specialist category and their prestige would be enhanced (for a general discussion of professionalization questions, see von Harach, 1983, Hepp, 1977).

The authors of the seven-volume study of police functions and career that was commissioned by the police leadership (Helfer and Siebel, 1975) concluded that Schupo and Kripo functions overlapped at the lower levels of law enforcement but that in general the two divisions made different intellectual and personality demands on the adherents, and indeed developed different subcultures. Kripo work, according to these authors, is generally valued higher as an expert field of knowledge requiring verbal skills, memory, logical analysis, and intuitive thinking, i.e., higher "cognitive" capacity, as well as more knowledge of law, than Schupo functions. Schupo work, on the other hand, has greater danger, stress, unhealthy working hours, responsibility for public order, and need to make quick decisions, than does Kripo work. The style of operations is also different, according to this report. Kripo work is thoroughly civil in character and depends on teamwork to a much greater degree than the rather more formal, hierarchically-determined Schupo work.

Trying to integrate these two divisions further is not a simple organizational question, concludes this report. "Any unification effort that would be purely ideologically motivated and would not take into consideration the difference in tasks would therefore be extremely problematic" (Ibid., 321). At most, greater cooperation between Schupo and Kripo are possible in certain restricted matters such as searches and arrests. Further efforts to integrate the two should not be made.

This particular study does find the use of the Schupo as recruiting ground for the Kripo to be a useful device for two reasons. First, it creates opportunities for informal contacts in later years. Second, it provides an opportunity for a change of career for individuals who would not be happy with a full career in the Schupo and might otherwise leave police work.

Despite the opinions of these experts, and despite the continued problems that this policy engenders, the official stance continues to be one of a single career ladder with close integration between the two branches. Integration, according to one authority (Rupprecht, 1975) does not mean that the Kripo would be under Schupo leadership, or vice versa. The head police officer in any district can come out of either branch, and often, in fact, comes out of the Kripo. Nor should the much larger number of Schupo officers be considered a threat by the Kripo, since decisions in a government bureaucracy are not made by majority vote. Furthermore, if the two branches were separated, the Kripo would probably be swallowed or totally dominated by prosecutors' offices, a less desirable situation from the point of view of prestige or independence than exists at present. Elitist thinking by Kripo officers, according to the same official, is likely to hinder cooperative efforts, and should be discouraged. Integration means close cooperation in achieving similar goals, and the optimal degree of attainment of these goals depends on trust, understanding, and close working relationships between the two branches.

The contrast with the United States is an interesting one. In most police departments, although detective work, with its regular hours and civilian clothing, is a prized assignment, the two branches are closely allied, and leadership positions generally go to people who have had experience in various facets of police work. Research and experience in recent years, moreover, has tended to downplay the real importance of detectives in solving conventional crimes. The more complex investigative functions, however, are carried on by totally separate agencies such as the Federal Bureau of Investigation, state bureaus of investigation, or drug enforcement agencies. Entry into these agencies requires higher educational attainment than regular police work, and recruitment is not done predominantly through police departments. Thus the effective reality is that of the kind of separation that the Kripo union leadership has championed.

Employee Organizations

Employee involvement in decision-making within the German police parallels that in other German government bureaucracies. There are essentially two major organs of involvement: employee representative groups (Pesonalraten) and unions.

The history of efforts to involve employees in organizational decision-making in Gemany goes back to the 1920's, and encompasses both public and private organizations. In order to understand the functions of employee representative groups, one must be familiar with the key concept of "Mitbestimmung" (literally consultation/agreement with) that is legally mandated for German goverment bureaucracies. "Mitbestimmung" has long been a rallying-concept for union and political efforts to democratize German organizational life. The Union of German Civil Servants (Deutscher Beamtenbund), however, has some guidelines for the extent to which this concept should be operationalized among civil servants (Deutscher Beamtenbund, 1979): "We support Mitbestimmung in the civil service specifically only to the extent that it does not conflict with parliamentary powers of decision and control." In practice, Mitbestimmung has assumed a rather confined and formal place in civil service decision-making, relating chiefly to personnel actions and protection of employee rights.

Employee participation is regulated by Employee Representation Laws (Personalvertretungsgesetze) that are in effect in each state and in the federal civil service. The actual organ of employee representation in each agency is the elected Employee Committee (Personalrat). In police organizations Employee Committees exist at three levels—local, regional, and state—with the higher levels acting as appellate review levels. The Committees are elected every three years by both sworn police and civilian workers. In practice candidates are generally junior-level personnel who represent the various police unions. Thus the dominant police union, the Gewerkschaft der Polizei, has a preponderance of the members on Personnel Committees (Bramshill, 1981).

In theory, Employee Committees can have far-reaching consultative powers in relation to organization and operations of their agencies. In practice, the real power of the Employee Committees is in personnel matters, i.e., disputes about hiring, firing, promotion, training, and the like. In other words, the committee represents and protects the employee in his or her dealings with the administration. A large body of law regulating these exchanges has developed over the years. Employee Committees work closely together with unions on personnel matters. Inevitably, they are seen by many as partisan political agencies. The Social Democratic Party, to which most union members belong, is also the party of most Employee Committee members, and the politics of the Social Democratic Party tend to be supported by the Employee Committees. According to one respondent, in the states that are controlled by this party, such as Hesse, Hamburg, and Bremen, Employee Committees tend to have greater power and influence on appointments to leadership posts than in the Christian Democratic/Christian Socialist states such as Baden-Württemberg and Bavaria. This politicization of

Mitbestimmung is deplored by some police leaders as an unwarranted intrusion by outside forces in internal organizational matters. Others see it as lessening the influence and prestige of Employee Committees (Mokrusch, 1975).

The Bundesgrenzschutz, the only large federal police force, has been seriously criticized in recent years for its attitudes toward its Employee Committees. One BGS official has recommended that the Committee functions be more circumscribed by law in the BGS than in other agencies. At the same time, the BGS is also accused of designating normal shift work as action deployment (Einsatze) since Mitbestimmung is not operative in such deployment or in practice maneuvers related to deployment. Unions have threatened massive protests against BGS policies and the claim is made that recruitment for the BGS has fallen off considerably because of its poor reputation in employee rights matters (*Der Spiegel*, 1987, # 24: 112-113).

Although the influence of Employee Committees on decision making within police agencies is generally restricted to personnel matters, the involvement of unions in general police matters is quite large. In both the Weimar Republic and the Federal Republic a variety of unions developed, including, in both Republics, a separate Kripo union. Unions were outlawed in the Nazi period, but made a strong comeback after the end of the war. Civil servants are forbidden by law to strike in Germany, a point which is not conceded by some police unions. However, civil servants are strongly unionized in all the German states. At the time of the survey done by Helfer and Siebel in the middle 1970's (Helfer and Siebel, 1975: 1560), the comparative union membership was as follows: Gewerkschaft der Polizei (GdP)—60 percent; Bund Deutscher Kriminalbeamten (BDK)—6 percent; Öffentliche Transport und Verkehr (ÖTV)—11 percent; Deutscher Beamtenbund (DBB)—6 percent; no union affiliation—13 percent; unknown—3 percent.

Prior to the 1978 decision by the German Federation of Unions to take the GdP in as a seventeenth major entity, many police belonged to a separate division within the ÖTV, the union of truck drivers and other transport workers. Since 1978 the ÖTV no longer tries to recruit police. The BDK is the separate Kripo union formed in 1968. The DBB is the general union of civil servants, and is seen as more moderate and middle-class than the GdP. In terms of influence and resources, the GdP is undoubtedly the major voice for the general mass of police officers in Germany. Supervisory personnel have separate national and international organizations, although also belonging to unions in some cases.

There is another group, the Bundesgrenzverein (BGV), the union of the Bundesgrenzschutz. Because of the military character of the BGS, the GdP has not welcomed BGS employees into its ranks. Technically, the BGV, as well as the Kripo union, are allied with the civil service union (DBB) (Bramshill, 1981).

What is it that unions are trying to achieve? As a general rule, the police unions have the same goals as unions elsewhere: higher pay, better benefits, and better working conditions. Apart from the BDK, with goals of separation, higher pay, and greater understanding for Kripo workers, the general goal of the unions, according to their own literature, is greater professionalization of police in Germany. To the GdP this has meant two things: first, opposition to sophisticated weaponry and further militarization of police, and second, promotion of additional training and education for police officers (Guiesmer, 1980).

The GdP maintains an extensive public relations operation, prepares position papers, provides witnesses and speakers for legislative hearings and public occasions, publishes journals and books, and otherwise does the work of a major lobby group. As mentioned, within the police organizations its members tend to control the Employee Committees that deal with employee rights and benefits, as well as with hiring, promotion, and firing.

Although the GdP does not acknowledge the legitimacy of the legal prohibition against civil servant strikes, it generally has restricted direct action to less drastic tactics. In 1969 it organized eleven rallies in which 30,000 police participated to protest the development of a national plan for police work (Ibid.: 49). In 1970 a work slowdown of all police in Germany was organized in order to protest pay and working conditions. In 1974, however, the GdP cooperated in the first strike of public employees in the history of the Federal Republic. Higher pay and a forty-hour work week for civil servants followed this action (Ibid.: 53). The legitimacy of the GdP as the bargaining unit for police was greatly strengthened when it became the 17th major industry to be recognized as a separate entity by the German Federation of Unions (Deutscher Gewerkschaftbund).

Opposition to militarization of police has been a continual theme in the development of the GdP. "The core mission of the Gewerkschaft der Polizei was and will continue to be to define the concept of police so that it is free of military implications," said GdP leader Helmut Schirrmacher in a 1979 speech to a GdP Congress (Schirrmacher, 1979). In this concern the GdP works closely with thirteen other European countries, according to Schirrmacher. One of the major ways in which this opposition to militarism has been furthered has been through continuous efforts to demilitarize the BGS and make it similar to other police units in training and operations. These efforts met with some success during the major police reforms of the decade of the 1970's, when BGS training was made equivalent to Bepo training in all BGS installations, and when a general policy of making the BGS more like a police agency and of accepting BGS personnel into regular state police forces took effect. More recently, however, the BGS leadership has once again been criticized for its increasing paramilitarism. "Federal Interior Minister Zimmerman no longer is able to control some of the BGS commanders," complained *Der Spiegel* in a recent article (1987, #24: 112).

The GdP has also been active in furthering the prestige of police through additional education. In a 1974 attack on the prevailing system, the union called for a major change in police education. "The new citizen of the Federal Republic does not unquestioningly obey authority," said Werner Kuhlmann, former President of the GdP and a major advocate of police reform. "Therefore a new kind of police officer is needed: one who can command the respect of citizens. There is a need for an intellectualized police, one that is oriented toward learning and that is knowledgeable about social theory and psychology. In order to make the police profession more attractive to the kind of people who should be in it, this image of police must be carefully developed" (Kuhlmann, 1974).

The emphasis on learning as a way to increase the legitimacy of police in the eyes of the citizens had parallels in the American reform efforts that took place at about the same time. Despite the vaunted German system of police training, with its years of schooling, the union was calling for something different: greater knowledge of human beings and human behavior. Whether this demand stemmed from a desire for a more appropriate form of policing or from the simple desire to raise the prestige (and presumably the pay) of police officers is an interesting question. In the United States, pressure for college education for police officers became intense after the report of the President's Commission on Law Enforcement and Administration of Justice (President's Commission, 1967). This report recommended that police officers be college educated, and Congress, with the establishment of the Law Enforcement Education Program in 1968, provided federal subsidies to encourage such education. The experience of social unrest in the 1960's and the rising crime rate were triggers for this development. In Germany, a general period of self-examination and reform in policing followed the elevation of the Social Democratic Party to power and the civil unrest of the late 1960's. In any case, the unions were eager to take advantage of this reform mood to further the education of police officers.

Liberal education for all police officers is not without questionable aspects. An article in *Zeitschrift für Politik* (Hepp, 1977) explains some of the problems. Citing survey research results, the author claims that public approval of police is actually quite high. The claim of the union that police cannot be respected if they are not more highly educated really refers more to the social status of police officers than to the institution of police. If more education is required and the status of police officers is improved, however, the police will no longer be willing to do the kind of work that a state needs from its police: enforcement of laws, including the use of physical force if necesary. In other words, says the author, the monopoly of official force that defines a state would not be carried out in a desirable way. " . . . police reform shows that meeting the social status interests of civil servants can collide with the interests of the citizen. In this matter it is of secondary importance that hyper-qualified police would cost an inordinate amount of money. More important is the fact that the police institution itself may be ruined by a reform that improves the image of the individual officer. In the reform of the career image of police officers the question is really whether the government will even have an agency in the future that carries out its monopoly of legitimate force" (Ibid.: 50).

The union counterargument to this claim that police will become "soft" if they receive too much education is that resort to force, while it remains a core duty of police, is not an effective way to promote lawfulness in a modern state. Nor does the union opposition to heavy weapons mean that it is opposed to conventional arms for police or to development of sophisticated nonlethal crowd control techniques. In fact, further research on these matters is a union demand in the face of police injuries that occur at the increasing number of demonstrations and riots in the Federal Republic. The union also favors prohibiting demonstrators from using face masks and "passive weapons" such as helmets and other protective clothing (*Deutsche Polizei*, 1982: 3).

A more immediate problem related to increased liberal education for police officers, as explained previously in this chapter, is the close relation between education and promotion opportunities. As more and more officers are more highly educated, in a profession with few promotion possibilities, there probably will be increasing morale problems and instability within police forces.

Are the unions and Personnel Committees a force for democracy in the police organization? To the extent that they emphasize the dichotomy between worker and manager, they are not a force for unity. However, in an organization that continues to be hierarchically structured, with paramilitary trappings, as is the police, such devices provide legitimate and nonthreatening avenues for dissent and for participation in decision-making. In addition, they foster greater equality within the organization in that they inhibit undue discretionary wielding of power by commanding personnel. In general, they can be judged as positive factors in creating a more open environment within the organization.

Beyond these agencies and the generally pluralistic and federal structure of the police, one finds few internal structural entities that would tend to make the German police more democratic than other police organizations, or than the German police itself prior to 1933. There are some few examples of other kinds of structural democracy. For example, in the GSG-9, the elite antiterrorism squad of the BGS, problems, tactics, and decisions are considered by the entire group as a matter of course. General discussions are held each month and signs of tension between leaders and units call for immediate dialogue (Tophoven, 1984). The smooth teamwork that is absolutely critical for the delicate operations carried out by this group would seem to require such openness. The BGS itself, however, which aspires to a kind of elite status among German police forces, generally tends to be more hierarchical and military in its operations than other police agencies. Kripo operations often also work through teamwork and cooperative planning. In general, however, further indicators of organizational democracy would have to be found in nonstructural aspects of police organization.

DEVELOPING AN ETHOS OF DEMOCRACY

An outsider can easily miss the subtleties of a democratic ethos within an organization. Although it is certainly possible to probe for outward signs of such an ethos — e.g., slogans, heroes, recurring themes in organizational literature — and although it is possible to probe into these matters through interviews and surveys, the true spirit of an organization may be missed.

With the German police, moreover, there are two further hindrances to understanding organizational ethos. The first is quite simply that the history of the entire period 1933-1945 cannot be invoked and actually is suppressed in police training, socialization, and other ethos-building activities. Nevertheless, this history continues to sit like a specter at the table of post-war police development. Thus, when a police leader said with some chagrin, "We have no history . . . " he was in effect only half right. There is no history to speak of, but the history that is unspoken continues to affect the operations of the present organization. One respondent, a lower court judge with a good deal of contact with police, claimed that middle-level police officers, mindful of the consequences of cooperation during the Nazi period, have little stomach for work that involves "political" actions—i.e., policing of demonstrations and other kinds of mass protest—and even that some leaders will report sick rather than do this kind of work. According to this respondent, it is chiefly the lower level of supervisor, with no aspirations to higher office in the police organization, that exhibits this behavior. If this is indeed a common phenomenon, it suggests a certain subculture of recalcitrance that is historically determined, and that deviates from the general image of professionalism that characterizes the German police.

The glorification of the Weimar period is also a reaction to this lack of contemporary history, and may have distorted the model of a democratic police that the Germans could otherwise have developed. In any case, the historical void inhibits the development of organizational myths, stories, and long-term loyalties, as well as the stability that these characteristics enhance.

Second, each subdivision at state or local level can build up its peculiar culture that does not partake in depth of the general one. This local police culture may be affected by particular leaders, particular local conditions, or other factors that make it distinctive. Therefore in speaking of an "ethos" of German police with respect to the ideals of participation, individual dignity, and equality that we have defined as indicative of democracy, one must look for such aspects of ethos that can be attributed to the organization as a whole, and that transcend local peculiarities. Furthermore, it is only the outward signs, or "hints" of such an ethos that can be presented. Such signs may be found, often in a negative sense, in the police reform literature. They may also be found in the official pronouncements of the organization through its journals, speeches of its leaders, and official reports. Most importantly, they may be found in the nature of the training that is experienced by new recruits to the organization.

In German police history since 1950, one sees two periods in which democratization of police was a major theme and concern within the organization. The first was the early period, from 1950 to 1960, when new norms and new approaches to police work were being fostered by a police leadership just recently disengaged from close supervision by occupation authorities. The second was in the early 1970's, when a chastened and anxious police, prodded by a new regime in Bonn, attempted to respond to challenges to its authority as well as major challenges to public order represented by terrorism and social unrest.

The earlier period, in many ways the more crucial one because it set the tone for the new police, was a period in which much rhetoric and some of the training effort was directed toward greater democratization. The reality was rather less benign, however, with a continuance of the practice of harsh discipline and a military-like atmosphere. "At the time I entered police work in 1958," said one Kripo officer, "the Bepo was a very militaristic institution. The old sergeants only knew how to give orders, make sure that shoes were shined. The facilities were poor—we met in an old prison in Biberach . . . . (After 1968) an entire rethinking of the police took place. Money was put into facilities—this is important for pride—There is a different style of leadership. The Bepo is now more of a training institution."

The continuance of a military atmosphere can be attributed to three factors. First, despite the increasing prosperity and the period of good will in Germany, and the campaign to have the police be seen as "friend and helper" of the people, the police actually were agents in the cold war. As described in Chapter Three, the police organization was built up as a strategic force that would help to guard Germany against external threat. It was about this time also that the Communist Party was outlawed by the Federal Constitutional Court, and fears for internal security relative to communist power were at their peak. Second, the personnel of the new police were chiefly ex-soldiers, many of whom, in the haste to build up a new police in the late 1940's, had had little of the elaborate training that was later developed. The leadership were also trained either as military or as part of the old police of the Weimar Republic, itself with a strongly hierarchical and disciplined atmosphere. Third, the familiar traditions of the Germany bureaucracy—rule-bound, and with emphasis on hard work and correct behavior rather than on cooperation and free exchange—provided a kind of security in an organization that had been shattered, whose legitimacy was destroyed, and whose recent history could not be discussed very well, especially as individuals involved in that history were not likely to boast or tell stories about their adventures.

To try to develop democratic norms and a democratic culture within such an organization was bound to be a difficult task and one in which not all organizational adherents participated whole-heartedly. Nevertheless, a sincere effort to do so can be seen in various aspects of police organization. The unions were important in this effort. The Gewerkschaft der Polizei, in a position paper entitled "Indifference: a Sign of our Times or a German Characteristic?" called on police to get involved rather than to be comfortably disengaged (Gerwerkschaft, 1953). Even Bepo leaders were involved, as one of them described the characteristics of a good police officer: courtesy, tact, moderation, patience, calmness, learning, openness, responsibility, dependability, independence, understanding, intelligence, verbal ability, and perspective (Weimer, 1963: 63). "We must develop a police that has the patience and social consciousness to be a democratic force," said another Bepo commander (Sambuch, 1951: 10).

In the literature on police education and training we can see the zeal and idealism as well as the desire to reform the image of the police that characterized some of the leadership. Again and again there is discussion about ways to educate the police recruits, about how to instill a certain "Zivilcourage," or moral courage in them, how to move them from blind obedience to "innere Führung," or responsibility for one's actions (Harms, 1970). Our work, said Police Institute Director Kalicinski in 1950 (Kalicinski, 1950) "is to create a police personality that thinks and acts independently, and to give police officers the confidence that a thorough schooling in practical matters as well as in general knowledge and understanding can bring. Only in this way will a police officer be able to help with our great goal, namely the development of a democratic police in the true sense of the word . . . ." It will be difficult, he continued, and will take a great deal of work to get away from the habit of thinking that police must blindly obey their leaders, but we need to make them realize that law and responsible individual action should be their guiding principles." "Our highest and ultimate goal . . . is to make the police leadership truly committed carriers of our new democratic governmental ideal."

Special seminars on teaching citizenship and democracy to police officers were held at the Police Institute. The importance of understanding the perversities of the totalitarian state and the realities of a democratic order, as well as of a good understanding of contemporary

politics were included (see, e.g., Mitteilungen, 1954; OTV, 1955; Rossman, 1965). The importance of a good general education so that officers
would be willing to voice their opinions and would be respected by the
people was also stressed. Topics like "The History of Human Rights Philosophy" and "The United Nations" were part of the training of police
leaders (Rossman, 1965: 215).

Teaching police to think in terms of politics and political responsibility was not an easy task. Many officers, even in the leadership training
courses, claimed that they were nonpolitical and were unwilling to get
involved in "political" matters. "The fear of getting involved in politics,
which was a legacy of the National Socialist dictatorship, is still too
deep, the knowledge that the future is still so uncertain, that people are
afraid to commit themselves" (Brill, 1950, quoted in Rossman, 1965:
215). This apoliticism was particularly unwelcome in the eyes of Kalicinski, who gave the example of the police of the Weimar Republic, who
"claimed to be nonpolitical, but who were quick to wave the flag as soon
as the 'big drummer' came on the scene" (Kalicinski, 1955: 47).

Individual dignity was also stressed. The more the police recruit
learned practical matters, the more it was also necessary to inculcate respect for human beings, according to the author of a twenty-year retro-
spect on citizenship training for police. "In the midst of performing this
job—this hard and serious job—with its contacts with deviants and people who have gone wrong—to continue to respect each individual as a
person" (Rossman, 1965: 216).

Between 1948 and 1968 the Police Institute (later Police Leadership
Academy) conducted eighteen one-day seminars on citizenship training for
police, with 782 police leaders in attendance. A general curriculum for citizenship training was developed for leadership candidates, with major sections on history (French Revolution to 1945), government (including
political theories), and constitutional law (with concentration on questions
related to the peculiarities of German geography after 1945), sociology (including German social history since the Industrial Revolution), and international affairs (including sections on Europe, USA, USSR, history of
human rights law, and international organizations) (Ibid.: 217).

This ambitious program of study, to be sure, was only one part of the
three-months training that aspiring police leaders of that time under-
went at the Police Institute. It consumed about 45 hours in a total course
of study of 340 hours, i.e., 13 percent. The rest dealt with matters such
as law, police practice, criminology, pedagogics, police history, and psychology (Lehrplan, 1956).

In effect, the early years, starting around 1950, saw an effort on the part of the highest leadership to create a culture of democracy within the police. At the same time there was strong emphasis on good community relations. Gradually the German police developed a reputation for being a thoroughly professional and "citizen-friendly" organization.

A new wave of reforms took place in the early 1970's. These reforms can be attributed to several causes. With the retirement of a large percentage of the post-war police in the mid-1960's, a new generation of leadership and of police personnel in general took over. Most of these new police personnel had few individual memories of experiences of the Nazi period, had grown up in a competitive democratic atmosphere, and were eager to bring about change. In Bonn, the newly-empowered liberal Social Democratic Party sought to foster democratization of the German bureaucracy, including the police. Furthermore, the bad press received by the police after the demonstrations of the mid and later Sixties, and the serious increase in crime at that time fostered an intra-organizational reappraisal of police tactics and capacities. Terrorism, as exemplified by the Baader-Meinhof group and the murder of eleven Israeli athletes at the Munich Olympic Games in 1972 also served to mobilize organizational self-doubts and reform. The reform efforts were concentrated on both greater democratization within the organization and greater technical capabilities.

It would be impossible to describe all the dimensions of this change in atmosphere. For the first time the police allowed themselves to be researched in depth by academic sociologists. An outpouring of books, articles, and tracts followed, some highly critical and ideologically-inspired (see, e.g., Siebecke, 1972; Roth, 1972; Bolle et al., 1977; Humanistische Union Berlin, 1975), some serious works of scholarship (see, e.g., Murck, 1976; Feest and Blankenburg, 1972; Spiegelberg, 1977), some general appeals for reform (see, e.g., Harms, 1970; Stelter et al., 1968; Paschner, 1970). Among the earliest advocates of reform were police and police union leaders (Kuhlmann, 1969; Hunold, 1968). The Interior Ministers themselves commissioned a group of sociologists at the University of the Saarland to do a comprehensive study of police function and attitude (Helfer and Siebel, 1975). This massive work, reported on in seven volumes, surveyed a sample of 6630 police officers from all over Germany.

Tolerance of alternate lifestyles and changes in societal norms was urged (Niedermeyer, 1980). However, the influence of the new atmosphere was most evident in the training progams. In response to union and outside criticisms that the border police was actually a military organization, BGS training was made identical with Bepo training. Human relations management theories, including "management by cooperation," became part of the curriculum at the Police Leadership Academy. Training in psychology and sociology became more sophisticated. More education prior to police service as well as improved education in the Bereitschaftspolizei was urged and new curricula were developed.

Some police perceived problems associated with the increase in training and education. "Those with better preentry education show more individualism," said one report (Schlussbericht, 1971). " . . . trainers complain about the lack of self-discipline, the lack of care in handling equipment, and the lack of understanding about the problems that arise when a recruit neglects his outward appearance." Although the recruits have become more liberal and democratic, like other young people, " . . . their youth makes them very much subject to peer pressure, and not so ready for the insight and compromise that grows with the years."

The essential parochialism of German police training with the recruit, starting at age 16 or 17, trained exclusively in police installations, and almost exclusively by people who are themselves part of the police organization has persisted in most cases despite criticisms both within and outside the police organization. According to the report of the Saarbrücken University consultants: "In all aspects of police education, it is noteworthy that the instructional personnel come overwhelmingly from within the organization and they have inadequate preparation for their teaching responsibilities" (Helfer and Siebel, 1975: 1183). Even at the Police Leadership Academy, where official policy is now to encourage the use of outsiders as instructors there were, in 1982, only five "outsiders" out of a total of 29 major instructors. Of these two were ministers (teaching ethics), two were psychologists, and one was a judge. The common practice in lower-level police schools is to have police-trained personnel teach all subjects except those, like English and German, that complete the general high school education of the young recruits. Other subjects, even some specialized ones such as psychology, are taught by people who have been educated in their subject fields after first being trained as police officers.

To the extent that a degree of openness has entered into the training of police officers, it seems to have occurred chiefly in the training for the Kommissar rank, or first line of leadership. Instead of continuing with the former practice of providing two years of training in a police school for these leadership candidates, most of them now are trained in colleges (Fachhochschule) of public administration that also train other civil servants in areas such as finance and general administration. This kind of education, which was pioneered in the city-states of Hamburg and Bremen (Tantorat, 1980; Frolich, 1980), has now been adopted in the other states. Within these colleges, however, police are educated separately from the other students and have instructors who are chosen by the police. In some cases they have even been required to wear uniforms to class (Busch et al., 1985).

Even this amount of "outside" schooling has caused some anxiety. In Baden-Württemberg, for example, one officer described his comrades' reservations about his education when he returned to his police duties after the long period of study: "one was waiting to see if the 'Herr Student' would have as much real value as expected from the education he received" (*Die Polizei-Zeitung Baden-Württemberg,* March 29, 1982: 6). In general, according to this account, students who had gone through the Hochschul were well accepted by superiors and colleagues.

In Hamburg, the group of dissident police officers known as the "Working Group of Critical Police" is composed almost exclusively of individuals who have received the Fachhochschul education. Members of the group, who meet every two weeks to discuss their problems and who claim to be attemping to develop tactics for making the Hamburg police more responsive to the public, attribute their interest in reform in part to the fact that they received their leadership education in a nonpolice environment (Arbeitsgemeinschaft kritischer Polizisten, 1986).

Criminal justice college programs, such as have become common in the United States since the early 1970's, do not exist in Germany. An experimental program devoted to such studies was started at the University of Ulm, but was abandoned for lack of students. The fact that graduates of such a program had to start at the same level of introductory Bepo training as the majority of 16-year-old recruits was the major reason for this demise, according to an official at the Police Leadership Academy.

The chief difference between the early years of trying to establish a democratic police culture and the reform efforts of the 1970's is that the latter era was one of greater self-assurance, clearer goals, and generally less strained atmosphere. Most important no doubt was the fact that the police personnel had grown up in a different kind of state, one in which self-expression and concepts of human worth were fostered rather than denigrated. Also important was the fact that, by 1970, the German police had established a world-wide reputation for effectiveness and good citizen relations, and was able to attract people of high caliber into its ranks.

According to one police leader, a case that illustrates this international recognition is that of the Tunisian police. Tunisia, with strong ties to its former colonial power, France, used to send its top leadership candidates for one year of training to St. Cyr, the elite French police leadership academy. Although receiving the same education as the French officers, the Tunisians were kept strictly segregated in terms of living arrangements and social relations. Today, Tunisian officers are sent for one year's training to the Police Leadership Academy in Germany, where, this official claims, they can mingle freely with the German students, are treated with respect, and are initiated into the respected German police technology and operations.

In terms of developing an ethos of democracy, the most troubling aspect of German police culture continues to be the Bereitschaftspolizei and the Bundesgrenzshutz, with their closed atmosphere and paramilitary training, and their use in public order control emergencies. The fact is that the recruits are taken in at an immature age and are brought up to be police officers, with all the implications of solidarity, social ingroupism, and organizational defensiveness that go with this profession in the best of cases. According to the police-sponsored Saarbrücken study: "The intermingling of training and crisis deployment and the paramilitary conception of the Bereitschaftspolizei, according to psychologists, influences the later attitude of the officers, since the police, most of whom go through the Bereitschaftspolizei on their way to street duty, tend to have their attitude toward their later tasks concretized at this point" (Helfer and Siebel, 1975: 326).

For the Germans, deployment of the immature Bepo troops has obviously been of concern, especially in some of the extremely stressful situations that police have been called upon to handle. Media reports that some of the young recruits have been reduced to crying fits during particularly difficult assignments were affirmed to me by one high police official, who felt that the use of 16-year-old troops, even in emergencies when there were no others available, was not wise. "When demonstrators started throwing stones," he said, "some of these boys were crying for their mothers." The policy, developed in the past few years, of keeping personnel in the Bepo for an additional year after the normal Bepo training and using these more seasoned troops as the first ones to respond in social order crises serves the double purpose of allowing for a larger police force, since these troops delay their entry into conventional police work, and having more experienced personnel handle confrontations with citizens.

Although lateral mobility among police forces is one of the organizational facts of German policing that is often contrasted favorably with American practice, moving into middle-level police positions from the outside has become more difficult than before as the number of Schupo officers who are in line for promotion and who have more educational background than the norm, has increased. The exception is the top civilian leadership, who generally, however, do not interfere in the technical side of police practice. The reaffirmed policy of the einheitliches Laufbahn, or single career track for police officers, has strengthened the impression of a rather monolithic organization whose practices and development largely depend on the capacity, vision, and political understanding of a leadership who have themselves grown up within the organization.

LEADERSHIP

Tonis Hunold, in his book on police reform (Hunold, 1970) discusses the problems of leadership: "Today personnel policy has to be oriented toward principles of democracy. The development of the individual from subject to articulate citizen . . . (has) a strong influence on modern leadership style (Ibid.: 271). Unfortunately, says Hunold, in most German bureaucracies, including police, there is confusion about what kind of leadership can be effective in these times. Hunold talks about the concept of "innere Führung," or self-leadership, a concept that is frequently employed in Germany as counter to the "führer-prinzip" with its connotations of absolute obedience to a leader. He goes on to describe a style of leadership that he believes should be practiced in the police: cooperative interchanges, shared responsibility, fostering of a work climate that deemphasizes cleavages by rank and civil service status. He prescribes multiple steps that can be taken to achieve this style of leadership (Ibid.: Ch. 15). Among these are: fair treatment of all, clear explanation of reasons for particular policies, general concern for the welfare of all employees, development of a spirit of community, fostering of the creativity of individuals, willingness to encourage constructive criticism, fostering of individualism and "civil courage" in organizational adherents, emphasis on personal authority rather than authority based on position, and concern for constitutional and legal requirements with respect to employee involvement in governance. The difficulties of achieving all this, especially in a police organization, are great, he says, but reactionary elements within the police should not be allowed to prevail (Ibid.: 281). Nor does this kind of leadership denote weakness — indeed, slackness and weakness should be avoided; rather it is the most appropriate kind of leadership for our times (Ibid.: 298).

In subsequent years other police leaders have reinforced Hunold's statements of values through analysis of the literature on organizational theories that suggests that effectiveness and production are enhanced by a cooperative style of leadership. Maslow is invoked, and opportunities for self-actualization ("Selbstverwirklichung") are furthered as ways to improve police performance (Grommeck and Neumann, 1975; Berndt, 1985). The contrast between authority based on merit and the ability to convince ("persönlichkeitsautorität") rather than on position within a organization ("amtsautorität") is stressed, with the former seen as more appropriate to these times. One author calls for a cooperative leading style to deal with the "burnout-syndrome" among police officers, especially those urban officers who are frequently called on to deal with major social order confrontations (Fullgrabe, 1982).

These rather diffuse efforts to inspire greater participation and better human relations within the police run into a modern counter-trend, which fosters more specialized leadership training and an early determination of leadership potential. This latter trend is justified, say its adherents, by the increased technical knowledge required of police today, by the need for highly-trained leaders for social order confrontations, and by the need to inspire more confidence in the police by the public (Stumper, 1980).

What has all this meant in practice? German leadership training is undoubtedly among the most thorough and well-developed of that of any country in the world. Although police leaders are now routinely trained in human relations approaches to management (Berndt, 1985), the reality hardly seems any different than that in the average police department in the United States: a fairly straightforward paramilitary, command-centered structure, with clear lines of authority, a large group of "street cops," and a small group of "management cops." The "street cops" in general do not have the same personal or career aspirations as the managers, and there is little in the way of consultation or cooperative decision-making that occurs. The exception is the Kriminalpolizei, most of whom are in any case in the leadership grades, and who work in a more informal, team-oriented, cooperative atmosphere. Thus the real distinguishing characteristic that sets the German police apparatus apart from that of most other countries is that of *professionalism*. In terms of training, pride, incorruptibility, and capacity to do the job assigned to them, the German police are admired in many parts of the world. In terms of internal democracy, there is rather a morality of aspiration that prevails.

The principal contrast in the German police, a substantial one, is with its own past rather than with an abstract ideal. Compared to the rigid, militaristic, harsh environment characteristic of past German police organizations, the present arrangement represents a major change in the direction of more openness, more concern for the individual, and more tolerance.

CHAPTER SIX

POLICING A DEMOCRATIC SOCIAL ORDER

BROCKDORF II

IN MARCH, 1983, the Evangelical Academy of Bad Boll had a three-day conference for police leaders in the middle grades. The topic of this conference was "Law Enforcement and Public Consent: Police Behavior in Actual Conflict Situations" (Evangelische Akademie Bad Boll, 1983). Each of the three days of discussions was highlighted by a speech on some aspect of the topic. The speakers were a Kripo agent, a theologian, and a judge. The conference started with the presumption that police behavior, especially in demonstrations, had become a matter of public concern. A further presumption was that police were beginning to feel that they were being treated unfairly by the media and by the public. Some of the problems had to do with the self-image that was being furthered among police. "It makes a difference whether police see themselves as a positive force for good or as a last line of defense against chaos," said Dr. Christian Frey, a minister from Bochum (Ibid.: 22). Common sense on both sides was called for.

The participants at the conference came up with several recommendations under the general title of "To see a human being in the disrupter:"

1. Anonymity in police-demonstrator confrontations should be diminished. This means that demonstrators should not wear masks and that police should not lower the visors on their helmets unless in actual danger of being stoned or otherwise hurt,
2. To the extent possible, demonstrators should be kept informed about what is going on and about what police are planning to do,
3. Police should let people know that they do not support any particular political group, but are operating to enforce particular laws,

159

4. Cases of negative impressions left by police should be openly discussed with outsiders and within the organization,
5. Human problems of police officers should be discussed and explained to the public,
6. The police should strive for continually better contacts with the public,
7. With respect to unusual measures and actions taken, the police should constantly make efforts to explain the legal basis for their actions, and their concern for equal treatment.

In the light of these recommendations, it is interesting to read the official account (Heinson, 1986) of the anti-nuclear power demonstration known as Brockdorf II (to distinguish it from Brockdorf I, the major demonstration described in Chapter Three that took place in 1981 at the same place). The demonstration was scheduled for June 7, 1986, and was to take place near the Brockdorf nuclear power reactor in Schleswig-Holstein. The planned demonstration was advertised all over Germany, and one of the organizers, Representative Hemmings of the Green Party (Green Alternative List, or GAL, an environmentally-oriented political party), met with authorities to discuss the forthcoming demonstration. He estimated that 100,000 people would attend (in fact there were 35,000-40,000, according to police count). Hemmings explained the proposed marching patterns of the demonstrators. He was told that certain areas around the reactor had to be kept free of vehicle traffic, and he agreed to these conditions. The plan was for a march to the reactor area and a rally at 1:00 P.M. on June 7.

Police authorities then "pleaded" (Ibid.: 175) with the authorities of Kreis Steinburg (the local county) to allow this demonstration to take place, reminding them of the legal situation with respect to such demonstrations. Five years previously, prior to Brockdorf I, the local authorities had prohibited a proposed demonstration at the reactor. This ban was ignored and violent confrontations with police took place. Since that time the Federal Constitutional Court had reiterated the constitutional right to peaceful demonstrations and had said, specifically with reference to Brockdorf I, that proposed demonstrations that were expected to be *predominantly* peaceful, also must be allowed to take place.

Prior to the demonstration, police were informed over and over again of plans for violent actions on the part of some demonstrators and plans for transport of armed demonstrators from the Hamburg area, not far from Brockdorf. The Hamburg police was requested to monitor the roads leading to Brockdorf. This the head of the Hamburg police said he could not do, unless his own Bereitschaft troops, that had been sent to Brockdorf, were returned to Hamburg. In the end the Hamburg police remained in the Brockdorf area.

The police leader in charge, Hans-Heinrich Heinsen of the Schleswig-Holstein police, made the following plans:

Phase I, 0500-1200. During the gathering of the demonstrators, police would observe and control traffic,

Phase II, 1200-1300. Heavy police troop defenses would be stationed around and within the reactor property,

Phase III, 1300-1500. The rally in front of the reactor would take place,

Phase IV, 1500-1600. After the rally, police would facilitate efforts to get traffic out of the area. The area would be cleared by 1900.

The actual course of the day went somewhat differently. In the morning, some demonstrators abandoned their cars on the Autobahn, causing a traffic jam and leaving many arriving demonstrators in the dark about why they were not able to proceed. In the town of Kleve, near the reactor, masked demonstrators began to assemble. About 250 of them attacked police, using Molotov cocktails, and stealing some police weapons. Police helicopters brought in reserves, consisting of seven Bepo units, known as Hundertschaften, plus two SEK (Special Action Commando) divisions. More violence occurred and twenty trucks brought in by the demonstrators were burned. Demonstrators continued to fight with stones, clubs, metal pieces, fog grenades, Molotov cocktails, and "light munitions." The police had to retreat and more reinforcements were brought in by helicopter. The demonstrators, who meanwhile had built barricades by tearing up seating benches and fences in Kleve, were pushed back. The problem was compounded when "suddenly, about forty peaceful demonstrators also came on the scene" (Ibid.: 277) and the police had to distinguish between them and violent ones.

At other control points there were other conflicts during the morning. Marchers came up through the Wilster Marsh, adjacent to the reactor. The main gate of the reactor was closed. About 100 demonstrators blocked the south gate so that BGS troops could not go in. One Bepo unit was employed to scatter demonstrators. Starting about 1130, police were attacked with stones, as demonstrators tried to get into the reactor area. When police leaders tried to address demonstrators over loudspeakers a chorus of demonstrators chanted anti-police rhymes.

The violence caused the Landrat (Council) of Kreis Steinburg to make a decision at 1314 that major thoroughfares of the area had to be cleared. This announcement was made through loudspeakers, but again was likely not heard by most demonstrators. At 1318 water cannons with tear gas were brought in. The fighting continued. SEK forces, tied up in the marsh area, could not get to the gates of the reactor as planned. At 1418 the police began to clear the thoroughfares as requested by the County.

Meanwhile, the peaceful rally with speeches went on as planned. After the rally, the peacful demonstrators came in a long train to the edges of the police circle around the reactor and stayed there for about 45 minutes. Gradually they were told by police, over loudspeakers, to leave the area.

At the gates of the reactor, the violence continued for hours. The Bepo of North Rhine-Westphalia was particularly involved in this defense, although Bepo troops from all neighboring states took part in the action. Around 1532, after the rally area was cleared, the police began to clear all the streets in the reactor area. In all, 5300 police were deployed, 2200 of whom were moved around by helicopters in the course of the day.

In the aftermath of this demonstration, the demonstrators who were stopped by the police at Kleve returned to Hamburg and had a further violent confrontation with the Hamburg Bepo the following day (LPD Hamburg, 1986). In Hamburg, where the police handles 600-800 demonstrations each year, police formed a circle around a group of demonstrators who had gathered on a city-owned sport field, the *Heiligengeistfeld* ("Field of the Holy Spirit"), after engaging in a disorderly procession through part of the town. Demonstrators were kept enclosed in this circle throughout the afternoon and evening and gradually transported away. This police action was later declared illegal by a Hamburg court and the demonstrators were awarded damages of 200 Marks (about $100) each (*Der Spiegel,* March 9, 1987: 131).

Bepo leader Heinson had several comments about the experience at Brockdorf (Heinson, 1986: 281):

— Violent demonstrators, under clear leadership and with careful preplanning, come as a mass to these demonstrations, but then mingle with peaceful demonstrators in order to cause embarrassment for the police,
— The use of helicopters to transport police where needed is particularly useful,

— Very useful also were the "video troops," stationed on housetops or other elevated places, in order to document the action in demonstrations. In this way accusations of police brutality and over-reaction can be countered by evidence [Heinson does not refer to the Federal Constitutional Court's interdiction against data-gathering about peaceful demonstrators],

— Few arrests were made and police were criticized for this. In the future more thought must be given to "arrest troops" as opposed to "action troops." SEK units are particularly useful in making arrests, but were tied up at Kleve during most of this demonstration.

In response to criticisms of the police actions in Hamburg on the following day, the Hamburg Interior Minister Ralf Lange also had some comments in a report to the Hamburg police (Lange, 1986). He praised the police for having survived three major local demonstrations in three months (Libya bombing protest on April 19, Chernobyl protest on May 13, and the post-Brockdorf demonstration on June 8) as well as the Brockdorf demonstration on June 7, in all of which police officers had been attacked by demonstrators. He went on to say that a rising cycle of violence by some demonstrators was occurring. Members of the Green Alternative List, despite their claims to a policy of nonviolence, were involved in planning for the Brockdorf demonstration along with "Autonomen" and anarchists. In reference to the GAL's accusation that the police had acted illegally at the Heiligengeistfeld encounter, Lang said, "Could anybody outside of the GAL image that the police could have let such a parade go freely through the streets?" (Ibid.: 290).

Several things are noteworthy in these accounts of police-demonstrator encounters. First is the extensiveness of the police response. In Brockdorf, Bepo troops from all neighboring states were employed. BGS troops were also brought in, as were SEK units. Helicopters, water cannons, tear gas—in other words a sophisticated technology of unruly crowd control—were employed. Further, military phraseology (video troops, action troops, arrest troops) dominated the police account of the encounters.

Second, it is clear that a core of masked, helmeted, and otherwise disguised (e.g., raincoats and umbrellas in good weather) individuals were prepared, for whatever reasons, to provoke a violent encounter with the police. The call for a lessening of mutual anonymity that was voiced at Bad Boll presumes a certain goodwill on each side, which is obviously missing here. The same can be said about the Bad Boll recommendations about maintaining communications between police and demonstrators during an encounter. A certain fear on the part of the police is also detectable in these accounts. Fear leading to excessive violence, in fact, is one of the most serious dangers in deploying the young recruits in social order control situations.

Third, a certain political note has been entered into the equation of police-demonstrator confrontations. The GAL is a legitimate political party which, under Germany's system of proportional representation, commands about 10 percent of the seats in the Bundestag, the German parliament. Police accusations against the GAL are a departure from the usual stance of strict political neutrality and of simple adherence to the police mandate to guarantee law and order. Lange himself, as Interior Senator for Hamburg, is a partisan politician and can be expected to engage in some partisan debate. The nature of his report to the Hamburg officers, however, suggests that the police themselves must consider the GAL to be an outlaw group. To be sure the Hamburg GAL, four years earlier, itself had published a book about the Hamburg police (GAL, 1982) that was essentially an attack on police methods and personnel, but again, this attack was by a nongovernmental group and did not constitute any kind of bureaucratic position-taking.

Finally, there is the difficulty of preserving an image of conventional and professional police work in a situation where police are called upon again and again simply to maintain order. Formal rationality and law enforcement—i.e., deviance control—do not provide the public drama that major police-citizen confrontations or instances of police brutality do. Those individuals who claim that the police is a force whose conventional work has become that of keeping citizens under control (Werkentin, 1984) use these situations as evidence for their claims.

Maintaining a police force that is appropriate for a democratic society in the face of such obstacles is a difficult problem. Indeed, one of the measures of a democracy is the ability to attain peaceful solutions to political disputes. As the German police leaders are very much aware, governmental force pitted against citizen force can lead in extreme cases to the kind of political breakdown, what Dahrendorf calls wholesale anomie, that occurred in Germany in the early 1930's (Dahrendorf, 1985).

Bayley (1985) says that in countries with high collective violence, police are perceived by the public as political, and they lose public confidence. "Police forces preoccupied with collective violence tend to stress authoritative command rather than delegating responsibility to individual officers. They also usually act in groups and mistrust community input. Professionalization occurs along a military model, if it occurs at all" (Ibid.: 223).

Germany today could hardly be characterized as a nation with high collective violence. Furthermore, despite injuries on both sides, no one has been killed by police during demonstrations since the death of a Berlin student, Benno Ohnesorg, in the late 1960's, a death that had major repercussions both within the police establishment and in the public. Nevertheless the need to keep order has naturally become the highest priority in the increasing number of situations where order is threatened. What has happened, however, is that each time, in the 1950's and again in the 1970's, that the police organization itself has embarked on an ambitious campaign to democratize the police, outside pressures have created distractions that have mitigated against successful accomplishment of these goals. In the 1950's fear of communism inspired the re-creation of the Bereitschaftspolizei and the establishment of the Bundesgrenzschutz as part of the police apparatus. In the 1970's and 1980's, new problems have arisen. A compound of general malaise, rising crime, terrorist attacks, environmental concerns, and fear that Germany most likely will be the staging ground for a military confrontation between East and West have created tensions in Germany society that are reflected in police-citizen encounters. There is a marked difference between the two eras, however. In the earlier one the build-up of a security force within the police was directed, in effect, against external threats and was not tested in actual practice. In the latter era, the situation is a more uncomfortable one: police maintaining order in often difficult and volatile internal circumstances.

The problems are exacerbated by the fact that when German police forces become engaged in nonpeaceful encounters with citizens, emotion-laden feelings about, and references to, the police of the Nazi period are brought to the surface. "Nazi Schwein" is one of the most provocative, infuriating, and yet often-used epithets against police by the more radical dissidents in German society (Paschner, 1970: Ch. 1). From the police side, the memory of police inability to deal with the violent youthful bands that roamed the city streets in the Weimar Republic is a disturbing memory that clouds relations with youthful gangs and demonstrators today.

In times of crisis, preservation of order becomes a higher priority than formal rationality, i.e., order takes precedence over law. It is a truism of government that no state, no matter how democratic, will willingly participate in its own overthrowal through nonformal channels.

Even peaceful and legal direct action, as opposed to conventional political processes, is basically threatening as a form of political behavior. This is because, except in minor cases, its course is unpredictable and its containment problematical. Police, as guardians of order, are usually drawn into this arena of confrontation on the side of the governing forces. Thus they become political actors in a political conflict. The real problem becomes one of preserving the integrity of the organization and its ideals and values in the face of such unfavorable outside conditions.

A period of collective violence followed by a period of relative calm can lead to reform efforts, however. In the aftermath of the 1960's in the United States, massive amounts of energy and money went into rethinking and improving police processes. Similar reform efforts have occurred in Italy, England, and France following riots and police-citizen clashes (Roach and Thomanek, 1985). In all of these cases of political and social tension the police themselves, as tends to happen, became a major target of public opprobium, and the reform efforts came in the aftermath of commission inquiries, political promises, and new legislation. Likewise the German police, shaken by the mutual hostility that developed between police and demonstrators in the latter 1960's, embarked on a period of reflection and reform. Today in Germany, however, a certain hardening of attitude is evident. The Parliament, after strengthening the laws regarding demonstrations by outlawing certain types of masking, is now again considering the possibility of stricter control. The police also, judging from its own publications, is becoming more and more concerned with the problem of order control.

The problems are serious. Nevertheless it is important to step back from the obvious drama of direct confrontations between police and citizens in order to understand the true dimensions of the relations between police and community in Germany. These dimensions may be analyzed in terms of attitudes toward and of police, police policy, and police processes, or means by which organization goals with respect to citizen relations are approached and achieved.

POLICE AND CITIZENS: MUTUAL PERCEPTIONS

Based on the rather unsatisfactory data that is available, one finds that citizen opinion about police, has undergone some changes in the past fifteen years. A 1974 survey found that, for 88 percent of the population, police had a positive reputation (Wickert Institut, 1974). In another survey (Kaupen, 1973) asking respondents to classify thirteen types of people according to how sympathetic they were, police were at the top of the list for both Christian Democratic Party respondents and Social Democratic Party respondents. After them came prosecutors, general justice administrators, politicians, union members (for SPD respondents), and on down, with the least sympathetic, for both parties, being guest workers, communists, and "hippies" (in descending order).

There were some differences among respondents: generally police had a more positive image among married than among single citizens, among middle-income as opposed to higher income individuals, among those with less education than those with more, among older rather than younger people. Students and intellectuals in general had a lower opinion of police than other citizens.

A 1980 survey in the heavily industrial state of North Rhine-Westphalia (Naether, 1980) shows some change in position. This survey was commissioned by the state police leadership in order to provide baseline information for a general public relations campaign. A random sample of the population answered questions concerned with attitudes toward police (i.e., sympathy, feelings of closeness, satisfaction), trust in police and willingness to consider policing as a career.

With respect to personal attitudes, the respondents tended to cluster around the middle of the positive-negative scale, i.e., their attitudes tended toward indifference. Some differences within the respondent group existed, however. Women tended to be more positive than men, rural and small-town residents more positive than big-city residents, and younger people distinctively more negative than older ones. Although 41 percent of the population fell into the category of "very sympathetic" or at least "sympathetic," only 24 percent of those between fourteen and twenty-nine years of age fell into these categories. With regard to perception of being well-protected by the police and of feeling personally close or distanced from the police as an institution and police officers as individuals, while there were ranges within the various population groups, the average again was toward the middle of the scales that were employed.

More recently the Police Leadership Academy contracted with the major German public opinion research organization, EMNID-Bielefeld, to do an assessment of public perception of the police (Meier-Weiser, 1984). Nine hundred ninety-one individuals aged fourteen and up in all states were surveyed. On a list of twenty-eight professions, general police were rated sixteenth and criminal police agents were rated eleventh (see Table 3). Highest ratings on this list were given to doctors, veterinarians, lawyers, academic high school teachers, crafts-men, and prosecutors. Lowest ratings (in descending order) were given to private detectives, real estate agents, and professional soccer players. As in the earlier surveys there were differences among respondents, with police rated higher by women than men, by older than by younger people, by less educated than by more educated, and by CDU/CSU party adherents than by GAL adherents. In the city-states of Berlin, Hamburg, and Bremen, where there had been major recent clashes between police and demonstrators, police were rated significantly lower than in the other states.

Table 3

RANK ORDERING OF A SELECTED GROUP OF PROFESSIONS[1]

1.	Physician	5.98
2.	Veterinarian	5.57
3.	Attorney	5.28
4.	High School Teacher	5.26
5.	Manual Laborer	5.08
6.	Prosecutor	5.08
7.	Pastor	5.06
8.	Middle School Teacher	5.04
9.	Architect	5.02
10.	Housewife/Househusband	4.97
11.	Criminal Investigator	4.88
12.	Farmer	4.84
13.	Kindergarten Teacher	4.83
14.	Parliamentary Representative	4.78
15.	Social Worker	4.75
16.	Police Officer	4.71
17.	EDV-Programmer	4.60
18.	TV Journalist	4.60
19.	Newspaper Reporter	4.51
20.	Steward/Stewardess	4.49
21.	Mailman	4.44
22.	Customs Officer	4.15
23.	Professional Soldier	4.05
24.	Financial Analyst	4.01
25.	Court Administrator	3.65
26.	Private Detective	3.65
27.	Real Estate Agent	3.63
28.	Professional Soccer Player	3.48

1. 1 = particularly low; 7 = particularly high

(Source: Meier-Weiser, 1984)

Respondents were also given a list of eighteen characteristics, both positive and negative, and asked to list those that pertained to police officers (Ibid.: 200). The highest percentage (50%) of the respondents found police to be "helpful" and "correct," whereas the lowest proportion found them to be "corrupt" (7%), "violence-prone" (11%), and "inconsiderate" (12%). However only 15 percent of the respondents found police to be "tolerant," and only 17 percent would characterize them as "intelligent."

With respect to how they performed their duties, on a scale of five (one as best, five as worst) police were judged best on dealing with traffic offenses (2.3), insuring smooth flow of traffic (2.37), and providing traffic safety education (2.41). On conventional crime prevention and detection, police were rated from 2.6 to 2.87. Police were least effective, according to this survey, in providing service to old, sick, and lonely people (3.0), in battling white collar crime (3.10), and in dealing with environmental crimes (3.19) (Ibid.: 202).

Because of the differences in the survey instruments themselves, it is not possible to make absolute comparisons between public perceptions of police in the different periods. Nevertheless, there does appear to have been some decline in police status in the past ten years. These data are confirmed by my own impressions from conversations with numerous Germans. Considering the social order problems that Germany has experienced, such a decline in status is not surprising and may have been inevitable.

In addition to public order problems, the very fact of increasing "professionalization" of police has been a cause of increased distance between police and citizen. This is a familiar story in the United States and also in Britain: police have become more mechanized, more specialized, more legalistic in their behaivor. Small local stations have been shut down. The result, according to some researchers (Endruweit, 1985) has been alienation from the public, with less opportunity for direct and friendly interchanges. The leadership has taken stock of this development and begun to experiment with more foot patrols, team policing, and other experimental programs to help bridge the gap between police and public.

As in the United States, police in Germany tend to consider themselves to be lower in public approval than measures of public opinion show them to be. They also often conclude that their hopes for a better social position through police work are disappointed (Endruweit, 1984). The Saarbrücken study (Helfer and Siebel, 1975: 1022) found that only

2 percent of police saw their public image as being "very good." Fifty-three percent found it to be "rather good," 42 percent "rather poor," and 3 percent "very poor." These results, obtained in 1973-1975, showed a sharp contrast between public approval at that time (88%) and police perception of that approval (55%). Whether police perceptions have decreased proportionately to public perceptions in the past ten years is an open question.

An interesting aspect of police perception of public approval is the Saarbrücken study's analysis of correlates of police satisfaction with their own work. Satisfaction or dissatisfaction with police work was related more strongly with pay and benefits than with actual tasks performed. In fact, the only police divisions in which there was strong satisfaction with the actual work itself were the police schools and the Bereitschafts-polizei. The researchers conclude that improvement in police-citizen-ship relations or even reform of internal organizational arrangements will not be as effective in improving police satisfaction as better practical remuneration (Ibid.: 788-797).

POLICE AS AGENTS OF JUSTICE

In the most fundamental sense, police encounters with citizens have to do with their role as enforcers of the formal legal order. As gate-keepers of the justice system police are invested with the whole complex of constitutional and legislative law that defines and controls this power to draw people into the system. Police discretion to invoke or not to invoke this law is a crucial aspect of police-citizen relations.

Three basic principles of German law govern the behavior of police with respect to law enforcement. These are the principles of legality (Legalitätsprinzip), opportunity or discretion (Opportunitätsprinzip), and proportionality of means (Verhältnismässigkeit des Mittelns). These principles are universally invoked in discussions of the behavior of agents of justice. Explanation of their signficance gives a good deal of insight into the peculiarities of German law and police power (see Langbein, 1977, for an extensive English-language analysis of these terms).

The principle of legality is defined as "the professional duty of agents of justice to take formal action on crimes that become known to them" (Creifeld, 1976: 698). The purpose, which is central to the concept of a Rechtsstaat, is to insure equality before the law. Theoretically, both prosecutors and police are guilty themselves of breaking the law if they do not adhere to the principle of legality. The principle suggests that police and prosecutors have no discretion in dealing with offenders. In fact, as German scholars have shown (Feest and Blankenburg, 1972; Weigand, 1978) the impressions of those Americans like Davis (1975), who claim that German prosecutors and police have very limited discretion, is based on a simplistic understanding of the actual practices of police and prosecutors.

The principle of legality, however, should not be confused with the concept of "full enforcement of the law" as it is understood in some American police departments. Here the principle of discretion comes into play. For a prosecutor this latter principle means that, in minor crimes and in other types of cases as specified by law (e.g., juvenile crimes, cases of undue influence), exceptions from the principle of legality are permissible (Creifeld, 1976: 812). For police, although the principle of discretion is not supposed to be employed in criminal matters, it also is used for minor crimes, and is extended very largely for administrative offenses (Schmatz, 1966; Schirrmacher, 1986). Organizational norms are an important aspect of the definition of this principle (Schmatz, 1966: 36). The limits of discretionary behavior that is sanctioned under this principle have actually been substantially narrowed in this century, especially as courts have become involved in defining constitutional rights of accused or suspected individuals.

The idea that discretion, by definition involving choice, can be clearly circumscribed by a "principle of discretion" is intriguing. Empirical studies of both police and prosecutorial behavior, however, have shown that unregulated discretionary behavior is in fact very prevalent in the German justice system (Feest and Blankenburg, 1972; Murck, 1976; Blankenburg, Sessar, and Steffan, 1978). There is a fine legal distinction here, however, that is important in the German context. When police are acting as agents of law—i.e., as prosecutors' helpers in investigating crimes—they are bound by the legality principle. When they are acting as independent agents of order, they are bound by the discretion principle.

The principle of proportionality of means, which is constitutionally mandated, means that police are bound, in all their actions, to use the least intrusive and least harsh methods to achieve the purpose of crime prevention and preservation of order (Schmatz, 1966: 46). The principle is further broken down into elements of suitability, necessity, and proportionality. One author describes it this way: "The basic concept of proportionality of means is a well-known and, for the police, binding principle. An incorrect estimation of a situation that results in insufficient action by the police not only can endanger the possibility of success in a particular case, but also, because the offender senses the weakness and indecisiveness of the police, can lead to a worsening of the problem. This in turn would lead to the necessity to employ a harshness of action that would not originally have been called for. On the other hand, if the police overreact from the beginning of their engagement in a situation, the results can be catastrophic . . . . It is truly not easy for the leader of a police action always to come to the correct decision . . . " (Otto, 1965).

The principle of proportionality is often invoked in cases involving civil order control actions of police. Because of its vagueness it can be used rather freely by courts to justify or disallow particular police behavior. In general, however, consideration of this principle serves to control clear abuses of official power by police authorities.

Because they are legally binding and not goals of the justice system, defining the borders of behavior encompassed by these principles of legality, discretion, and proportionality becomes a matter of seemingly endless debate and legal analysis by jurists as well as practical concern for police. Thus, for example, in 1980 *Die Polizei* carried an article entitled "Professional duties as a risk in police work" (Tetzlaff, 1980). The author explained the risks of acting illegally that are faced by police officers. Adherence to both the legality principle and the discretion principle are professional and legal responsibilities of police officers, says the author. "Police may not make unwarranted, unnecessary, or disproportionate encroachments upon the rights of others," (Ibid.: 284). However, he continues, in most police encounters quick decisions are needed, and the officer risks violating either one or the other principle. The possibility of acting illegally is great and is one of the problems involved in being a police officer.

The principle of legality, being somewhat more concrete than the other two principles, has assumed increasing importance in controlling police behavior since 1945. Constitutional law and statutory law, especially police laws, account for much of this control. In addition, despite the fact that in Germany, with its predominantly Roman law system, case decisions do not have the force of law that they do in the United States or England, a certain body of case law principles ("richterlichengewohnheitsrecht") defining citizen rights in encounters with the police has developed gradually. This case law is generally honored by courts in further decisions (Gude, 1961).

The law in most countries is rife with rather vague guidelines like "discretionary opportunity," and "proportionality." One has only to consider the term "due process of law" to conjure up a mass of explicatory efforts and case law, sometimes contradictory, that still does not get to the heart of the concept. To an outside observer, however, what seems peculiar in the German situation is the extent to which these principles are discussed and regarded as relatively clear mandates for behavior. The drive for rationality, for rules that will cover all situations, even if they are rules that allow discretion, the desire to avoid ambiguity: all are evident in these concerns for principles of law.

These constitutional and case-law principles, as well as the advisory body of transnational law developed by the European Court of Human Rights in accordance with the European Convention on Human Rights cover most aspects of police-citizen encounters relating to search and seizure, arrest, and interrogation (see Schoenfelder, 1981, for a description of rights of the accused in Germany). Rights of the accused are not elaborated to the extent that they are in the United States, however. This is natural, in that Germany is a nation that uses an inquisitorial legal process, as opposed to an adversarial one. Inquisitorial systems emphasize cooperation between accused, prosecutor, and magistrate in arriving at the truth involved in a criminal investigation. This is the antithesis of the basis ideal of the adversary system, in which the accused has the right not to cooperate in the process. In practice a great deal of convergence between the two types of legal systems has occurred, especially since the Second World War. In Germany, especially, with its American-inspired constitution, many principles of criminal procedure relating to protection of the accused are similar to those in the United States. Thus, for example, while the exclusionary rule as such does not exist in Germany, evidence or testimony that is obtained through force, intimidation, hypnosis, threatening of sanctions, promising of advantages, or overtiring is excluded from legal proceedings. Search warrants must be obtained from judges in most cases of search and seizure and in all cases involving editorial houses, newspapers, radio, or TV stations (Schoenfelder, 1981: 136a). A police officer has the duty to warn suspects (when they are charged, not when arrested as in the United States) of their right to a state-appointed attorney. If the officer neglects this duty, however, it does not automatically mean that the evidence obtained will not be used in court. Most courts will allow such evidence in most cases (Schafer, 1976: 276). In general the officer himself is subject to sanctions for not performing his duty.

The German police officer, however, does not face the truly daunting problem of learning a complicated national and state case law of search and seizure that the American officer faces. Because case law as such is not binding, the general practice is to teach only statutory and constitutional criminal procedure in the police schools without much emphasis on interpretation as developed by courts. "We must not allow ourself to be drowned in the flood of decisions that no one can comprehend in their totality, and that no one can distinguish sufficiently from one another . . .", said one judge in a report to police (Gude, 1961: 108). His recommendation was for ". . . thrifty use of decisions in teaching and in advanced training, always trying to develop understanding of a set of large principles of law that are understandable and that can be used easily. In police journals no decisions should be discussed without an explanation that a normal reader could understand . . ." (Ibid.).

The most unusual aspect of German justice, from the point of view of foreigners, is that of administrative offenses, or "Ordnungswidrigkeiten." Ordnungswidrichkeiten must be distinguished from the two levels of German crimes: Verbrechen (major crimes) and Vergehen (minor crimes and misdemeanors). The administrative regulations involved in Ordnungswidrigkeiten are promulgated by various government agencies, and violations result in the leveling of fines—in some cases very large fines, going into the equivalent of hundreds of thousands of dollars. The offenses, however, fall neither in the realm of civil law nor of criminal law, and do not carry the ethical stigma of criminalization.

An example of the difference between Ordnungswidrigkeiten and Strafrecht, or criminal law, in environmentally-conscious Germany is that of cases of environmental pollution. Until recently most such pollution fell into the category of administrative offenses. Now, however, the federal government has added the possibility of criminal charges, with the possibility of prison and public disgrace. In this way, although most polluters would continue to pay a fine, it would be a criminal fine (Strafgeld) as opposed to an administrative fine (Busgeld), and thus the whole procedure would be of a higher order of seriousness.

Police ordinances cover a wide range of activities. Most important are traffic regulations. However, other minor offenses against public order, such as minor domestic disputes, shoplifting, and disorderly conduct may also be covered. If a police officer charges an individual in person with an administrative offense, he can also collect the fine immediately. For those speeding offenses and failures to stop at lights that are detected electronically, as well as for parking offenses, the violator is sent a ticket and has the opportunity to pay by mail. Thus the effect on the individual in terms of time and inconvenience is similar to that in the United States, where the fiction of forfeiting bail is practiced by most traffic offenders. The difference in Germany is the direct involvement of police as both prosecutor and judge at the street level in the case of administrative offenses, and the fact that the perpetrator of these administrative offenses is not involved with the criminal process.

Promulgating ordinances and leveling fines, while apparently giving the German police more street-level power, probably does not have any greater negative effect on police-community relations than occurs in countries without such power. Encounters in which the officer must exact a penalty and the citizen must pay it are not likely to be agreeable in any case. The interesting question is whether or not the officer leveling the fine is tempted to corruption. The easy accessibility to bribes in police work presents a serious challenge to police reformers in the United States and elsewhere. Although, in reading the newspapers, it is possible to pick up accounts of individual officer corruption of one kind or another, the German police in general have the reputation for being remarkably incorruptible. The pervasiveness of corruption in entire departments that has occurred in some American departments does not seem to occur in Germany. The 1984 citizen survey found that only 7 percent of the respondents believed police to be corrupt. The characteristic "corrupt," in fact, was the one that the respondents found least typical of police among the eighteen police characteristics that were included in the survey (Meier-Weiser, 1984).

The lengthy period of formal training and the general tradition of the German civil service were credited by one police leader with the low incidence of corruption among police. Furthermore, careful accounting measures related to the levying of street-level fines was designed to guard against corruption. This leader also believed that overemphasis on "on-the-job" training, such as is practiced in the United States, as opposed to formal training, "tends to teach bad things."

Police-prosecutor interaction is an important aspect of the role of police as agents of the law. This is so especially for the Kriminalpolizei. A peculiar organizational reality is involved in these interactions. In Germany prosecutors are organizationally tied to the various Ministries of Justice in the different states and the federal government. Police are under Ministries of the Interior. Nevertheless, the law prescribes that all police in the middle and higher grades are "helpers" (Hilfsbeamte) of prosecutors. Their general obligation is to bring the prosecutor into the investigation of a case at an early stage.

With the exception of capital crimes, political crimes, and some instances of white collar criminality, the reality is that prosecutors not only do not interfere with the investigatory work of the Kripo, but are generally not aware of the investigations going on until the time is ripe to bring charges against an individual. Police, according to some studies, are actually the prime agents of discretionary justice, making decisions about arrest and investigations before the prosecutor is brought into the process (Steffan, 1976; Stelter and Steinhilper, 1976).

There is some uneasiness in legal circles about the independence of the police in conducting investigations, and some demands for earlier involvement of prosecutors. One account puts it this way: "The prosecutor represents the legal order of the government, whereas the police represent its executive power. The prosecutor must be concerned with protecting the individual as well as investigating him. Therefore it is important to bring the prosecutor in at an early stage of the investigation" (Schabil, 1961: 41; see also, Schäfer, 1980: 155).

There are several reasons for the present arrangement, however. The most obvious one is that of caseload, with prosecutors finding it impossible to try to supervise preliminary investigations, prepare cases for trial, and participate in trials, sentencing decisions, and all the other duties prescribed for them. There is also a certain amount of jealousy and rivalry that develops between the organizations. Kripo agents often feel that prosecutors are getting the credit, whereas police actually do all the work on criminal investigations (Murck, 1976: 36). More importantly, Kripo agents have excellent equipment for crime investigation and are highly trained in criminalistics and other aspects of investigative techniques, whereas prosecutors, trained in the law, would have difficulty in trying to supervise investigations in any direct sense. One Kripo agent even suggested that prosecutors prefer not to be involved at earlier stages of an investigation because the legal safeguards that must be followed once a prosecutor becomes involved would inhibit successful work by the Kripo in clearing up cases.

POLICE INITIATIVES IN IMPROVING COMMUNITY RELATIONS

Should police not only insure the maintenance of law and order, but should they also perform a socialization function for the state? Bayley (1976: 85) tells us that the Japanese police "are preoccupied . . . with the commitment from which compliance flows." Their tasks include the transmission of values, both moral and civic. This socialization commitment has made the Japanese police much admired today by police researchers and also by police reformers.

Such a socialization function carried too far, however, can degenerate into a propaganda effort for those in power. Nevertheless, police are carriers of government power. It is obviously in their interest as an organization to help to legitimate that power.

The situation in the new German democracy in 1949 was one in which the socialization aspect of police function was bound to be an issue, an issue that was tied to the imperative of reestablishing the legitimacy of the police organization itself. The leadership of that time claimed that police, through their behavior and contacts with citizens, should exemplify the new order. "Contact and at the same, education" was the title of one article in the union journal (Kontakt, 1953). There is a new task of the police, says the author ". . . namely to embody in the best sense of the word a democratic governmental force in contacts with citizens" (Ibid.: 37). This is possible, he continued, because police are in contact with the public on a day-to-day basis, and their behavior is being constantly observed. Thus they need to be both helpers and guardians of the people.

A peculiar aspect of police-community relations in Germany, then as now, is the refusal of police to have officers wear name tags or identifying numbers. This refusal is supported by the Gewerkschaft der Polizei (Kuhlmann, 1969) despite its enthusiasm otherwise for improving the image of police. The rationale for this refusal is that random identification of officers could lead to harassment and false accusations against police. An officer does have the duty to identify himself when asked to do so by a citizen, but this may well be a daunting prospect for many of the citizens that police come in contact with.

The intensity of police feeling on this matter seems strange to an American. One explanation offered to me by a scholar of policing is that the general tradition in Germany is for bureaucrats to represent an office of the state, not to be known as individuals, and thus the police are only acting within that tradition. Even the relatively small change represented in the recent attempt by the Berlin Senate to have Berlin's Kontaktbereichbeamte (Area Contact Officers, whose job is to get closer to the people in their community) wear name tags resulted in such massive opposition from the officers and the union, that it had to be abandoned (*Bürggerechte und Polizei*, CILIP 26, 1987, #1: 86). Needless to say, the inability to identify particular officers makes the possibility of legal action against police abuses particularly difficult.

In the essentially optimistic and prosperous decade of the 1950's concern for traffic, furthering the image of police as "your friend and helper," emphasis on politeness, and gradual development of ties with other countries all helped to create a new image for the police, and perhaps also to strengthen the commitment to democracy of the people themselves.

Formal institutions for citizen involvement in police affairs also existed in some states. As a legacy of the British occupation, the states of North Rhine-Westphalia, Schleswig-Holstein, and Lower Saxony had elected police authorities (Beirate), whose job was to help make decisions pertaining to police actions with respect to local community relations. While these authorities were essentially advisory and did not have the kind of appointive, budgetary, and grievance powers that English police authorities do, or that the British occupying forces wanted them to have, they did provide a forum for closer cooperation between police and citizens. This institution was gradually abandoned in Lower Saxony and Schleswig-Holstein; at present only North Rhine-Westphalia continues to have such an authority. A GAL member, recently elected to a police authority in that state, and hoping to use this position for closer surveillance over police, was much disappointed by the lack of power or influence of this body (Kelber, 1983).

Unpaid police auxiliaries were also established in Baden-Württemberg and Berlin. While their primary function was to augment police strength, a secondary benefit was that they served to open up the generally inbred police organization to outsiders. In Baden-Württemberg, by 1970, 4300 auxiliary police officers were enrolled from a wide variety of ages and occupations. These auxiliary forces had contributed over 640,000 hours of work, much of it concerned with weekend and vacation traffic (Reiff and Wohrle, 1971).

As the generally open and friendly relations between police and public in the 1950's and early 1960's gave way to the strains and tensions of more recent years the police leadership has concentrated more and more on self-examination, attempts to restore the atmosphere, and efforts to develop understanding among officers about new societal norms and new ways of thinking (Scherer, 1984; Berndt and Altman, 1985). The importance of keeping order and of channeling conflict into peaceful expressions is stressed (Wasserman, 1985; Maikranz, 1986). Dealing with the stress caused by hostile encounters with the public is emphasized (Rohrig, 1986; Buttner, 1986). The state of North Rhine-Westphalia has developed a system of behavioral training to help officers deal with "stress, anger, and fear-induced resorts to force" (Olsjewski, 1984: 261). This program uses devices like role-playing, brainstorming, cooperative task accomplishment, and general discussions to help officers deal with stress-induced reactions like "anger, insecurity, aggressiveness, stomach problems, fatigue, depression, and tension (Ibid.: 261). Various experiments in crowd dispersal, crowd control, dealing with core antagonists, and use of psychologists to work with police leaders and with rank and file officers were undertaken starting in the late 1960's (Paschner, 1970).

With accumulating problems one can detect a certain defensiveness in tone. The press is blamed for sensationalizing encounters between police and citizens, especially during demonstrations (Murck, 1976: 39; Thoma and Stoffragen-Buller, 1984). Most large departments and agencies now have press officers whose job is to gain the confidence of media representatives and to advertise positive aspects of police work (Ohlsen and Kelling, 1985: 22). The emphasis is on the fact that the police are obligated to protect life and property in the face of unruly and often anarchistic elements in the population.

Whether the German police is doing all it can to alleviate tensions or to maintain legality in the face of increasing pressure is a question that is answered differently by different elements in society. Dissidents who have banded together to publish a journal devoted to "Citizen Rights and the Police" (*Bürgerrechte and Polizei*), as well as some academics (see, e.g., Werkentin, 1984; Busch et al., 1985) see the police as a force for repression. The police, on the other hand, believe themselves to be caught in the front lines of defense against disorder, while the politicians whose order they are defending are not subject to abuse, ridicule, and violence. These sentiments are echoed by many citizens, both conservative and liberal. Despite the major effort to professionalize, modernize, and democratize the police that occurred in the decade of the 1970's the problems seem to have become greater rather than less. That these problems are essentially political is of small comfort to police, who are targeted as the visible agents of the government.

Nevertheless, the 1980's have seen no new or bold reform initiatives related to police structures or operations. Rather it has been a time of reaction, self-doubt, self-criticism, and self-vindication. Although police research has resulted in greater technological capacity in the area of communications, crime detection, and non-lethal weaponry for crowd control, and although tactics, especially with respect to crowd control, are being constantly reevaluated and improved, the optimism and dynamism that followed the public order crises of the late 1960's is not paralleled in the present organization.

This is not to suggest that the only problems of police-community relations have to do with social order control. Just as have Britain and the United States, Germany has experienced alienation between police and public attendant upon increased use of technology, increased specialization, and lack of contact. Thus the very professionalism and technical excellence of the German police have become a problem. Many of the solutions that are being tried in the United States, such as foot patrols and team policing, are also being tried in Germany.

A particular concern is the threat of a technology-driven "Überwachungsstaat," or "big brother state," in which police will have access to large amounts of personal data on all citizens. There has been large resistance to the census that the German goverment has been trying to hold for several years. The first census law passed by the parliament was declared unconstitutional by the German Constitutional Court, with one of the reasons for this action being the projected use of census data for police files. This support from the highest court did not sooth the fears of many Germans that any census is a way to increase state capacity for control. Even the relatively harmless census questions about living space, number of autos, and commuter transportation that were included in the second census attempt of the past few years led to a large boycott movement.

Critics believe that the police, on the pretext of finding terrorists, are building up a formidable capacity to spy on the German people in general. The BKA's strategic placement of videocameras and cables in order to observe traffic and action in the neighborhood of persons who might be subject to terrorist abduction or attack was described at length by *Der Spiegel* in a 1983 article entitled "On the Way to a Big Brother State" (Auf dem Weg zum Überwachungsstaat) (Sternsdorff, 1983). This system was described as "a truly new system of observation, which has no precedent internationally either in police circles or even in intelligence operations" (Ibid.: 47). One of the more disturbing aspects of this system, according to the article, is that the police work more closely with the intelligence services than is constitutionally permissible. Furthermore, ". . . the new video network potentially makes all citizens subject to its oversight. It catches the innocent as well as the guilty, and abuse is inherent in the system . . . . the private sphere of thousands of citizens has already been invaded. Peaceful demonstrators are included as well as members of housing communities and harmless passers-by in railroad passages. Hardly anyone is aware of this, but the video network is constantly being expanded" (Ibid. p. 48).

Procedures of "discovery through default" ("Rasterfandung") have also been critized (Busch et al., 1985). These involve identification of suspicious persons who might be involved in terrorist activities by cross-checking of various points of contact between citizen and state (residence registration, auto registration, tax returns). In one operation, all those who paid their electric bills in cash or through third persons were cross-checked with records on auto licensing, residence registration, and child subsidies. At the end, a "suspicious" group that did not get child subsidies, had no autos, and were not registered with police were left over and targeted for further investigation. "Suspicion has become universalized and abstract," according to one critique (Ibid p. 141).

Even what strikes an American as routine data gathering to aid in crime control, such as centralized computerized criminal history files and computerized message capacity between law enforcement agencies is viewed with suspicion by some citizens. The police, according to one justice system official, hide behind the terrorism problem to keep getting more information on people. In this matter, as in others, police methods of detection and control that were practiced by the totalitarian Nazi state are the prototype that is invoked, and police, who must carry the burden of this past in all their operations, become the target of diffuse and sometimes irrational fears. The already-serious general problem of the citizens of modern technological states, who often do not know or cannot understand what capacities the state has developed for destruction, oversight, or covert policies, become exaggerated in this atmosphere.

The police are aware of the problem related to data. Articles on data protection and especially legal aspects of this protection have appeared with increasing frequency in police journals (see, e.g., *Die Polizei*, 1982, 1985). The entire March, 1985 issue of *Die Polizei* was devoted to articles dealing with this subject. Police have stressed that each citizen is entitled to know what is in his or her file and to challenge this information.

In the face of community unease regarding police actions in confrontations with citizens and police data-gathering technology, the police apparatus has sought to emphasize positive aspects of police-citizen relations. In recent years more and more emphasis and publicity has been placed on the police role in environmental protection, with the hope that this activity, which addresses the intense concerns about the environment that one finds in Germany, will improve the police image. Another example is the program, initiated in Schleswig-Holstein, of having police rather than prosecutors handle minor cases related to juvenile delinquency. Thus contacts between police, parents, and communities, with the purpose of dealing with community problems, are fostered.

One aspect of police relations with the community, relations with the academic community, has been varied. As part of the police reform movement following the disorders of the 1960's some police agencies allowed observational studies by academics of street-level police behavior (e.g., Feest and Blankenburg, 1972; Murck, 1976). The published accounts, although hardly different from those published somewhat earlier in the United States (e.g., Skolnick, 1966; Reiss, 1972) tended to stress the prevalence of discretionary behavior in police operations, never a welcome finding in a system that prizes legality as highly as does the German justice apparatus. At the same time, certain publications accusing the police of overreaction, brutality, and militarism were published by some academics and students (e.g., Roth, 1972; Siebecke, 1972). Again, these reports were not unlike similar ones published in the United States in the early 1970's.

The reaction of the police has been to be extremely cautious about cooperating with researchers. Those who are perceived as hostile or whose orientation is unknown are generally not given much help by local police authorities. Much of the work that has been done has been commissioned by the police themselves under grants of money to particular individuals or agencies. In an article entitled "Withdrawal into the Snailshells" (Steffan, 1984), a researcher concerned with police, and herself attached to the Munich police, has faulted both academics and police for the increasing estrangement. Academic criminologists, she says, look down at doing the kind of practice-related police research that is sponsored by the Police Foundation and the National Institute of Justice in the United States. Their fear is of being compromised or co-opted by the police. In addition, there is little academic status involved in doing such practice-related work. Police, on the other hand, are generally hostile or indifferent to outside research. They suffer from "an excess of touchiness in the face of criticism," criticism that is inevitable if one's organization is open to investigation and experiment (Ibid.: 72). The result is a dearth of vital new research on police operations, and the field is given over to ideologically-inspired hostile critiques by researchers who must work from the outside (e.g., Werkentin, 1984; Busch et al., 1985), and who have little experience of the working problems of police officers.

ORGANIZATIONAL REFORM AND EXTERNAL TENSION

There is something ironic about the development of relations between police and public in post-war Germany. In the 1950's, the organization earned a world-wide reputation as a citizen-friendly police that respected the rights of citizens in a democracy. At the same time the internal organizational processes, with the development of the Bepo and the BGS as strategic forces, and the personnel chiefly ex-military or veterans of previous police forces, could hardly be described as democratic in tone. This was so despite the efforts to inculcate a democratic spirit in the police.

More recently the internal processes can be described as more typical of an organization that is concerned with employee participation and individual rights. A campaign of reform and demilitarization was undertaken in the 1970's and, despite the continued tendency toward a closed organization, the general atmosphere has become more relaxed, the leadership has become more tolerant, the language has changed. Relations with the public have deteriorated, however.

Does this mean that internal organizational democracy and external policing for a democracy have nothing to do with each other? Such a conclusion would be a bleak one for those who believe that organizational democracy and improved achievement go hand in hand, or indeed that working in an atmosphere in which individual right and individual importance are stressed cannot help but have a transforming effect on all aspects of one's relations with others.

This simple conclusion cannot be drawn from an analysis of the German situation, however. Obviously this situation has become increasingly complex, and it would be necessary to sort out and analyze in depth a host of variables other than the historical circumstances leading to tension in Germany society, that have some impact on German police-community relations. To name just a few that have been discussed in this book: the increasing mechanization and professionalization of police operations, the decision to reemphasize the single career ladder for police officers, with all officers starting their careers in the Bepo, the decision to have the Bundesgrenzschutz be a police force, switching to combat status in wartime, the federal nature of the organization, the strength and influence of the unions, and even decisions about basic organizational forms that were made in the early 1950's.

Furthermore, police-community relations cannot be gauged only by a consideration of press notices or occasional public opinion polls. On the one hand, the media is more likely to report on dramatic encounters than on day-to-day operations. On the other hand, even generally favorable public opinion polls do not reflect whether or not police are respecting the rights of individual citizens, particularly minorities or young people. Probably a truer measure of the state of these relations would require massive studies of service delivery and citizen satisfaction related to individual practices in individual geographic locations. Such studies, some of which have been done in the United States (see, e.g., Ostrom, Parks, and Whitaker, 1978), would at least bring us closer to understanding the complex reality that is involved.

CONCLUSION

Individual behavior is often a function of how an individual is regarded within a social group. Systematically labelling a child as "bad," "criminal," or "stupid" is bound to have an effect on how that child reacts to others. Likewise a police organization that has the public image of being friendly, helpful, and effective is going to react more positively in police-citizen encounters than one which believes the public finds it corrupt, brutal, or inefficient. This is the vicious circle of action and reaction that conscientious police officials and police officers are trying to avoid in Germany.

The problem in Germany is intensified by the memory of the twin demons of twentieth century German police history: the inability to keep order in the multitude of armed clashes between Nazis and Communists in the 1920's and the transformation of the police into the atrocious instrument of Nazi policy in the Third Reich. As conflicts arise, police officials are determined not to allow disorder and street fighting to become the norm. At the same time, a sensitive nerve is struck each time police are accused of being fascistic or terroristic. At the lower levels of leadership, according to one respondent, this works out to a certain avoidance of political: i.e., civil unrest control—tasks, or extreme caution and defensiveness. This official says that, in case of a "takeover," these lower level officials, who have no opportunities to advance in the police hierarchy in any case, will not have been implicated in action on the wrong side. Higher officials presume they will be implicated in any case. This general unwillingness to get involved, according to this respondent, results from the experience of the Third Reich.

The contradictory imperatives involved in dealing with both historical traumas have clouded modern German police function to a greater degree than is often realized by police officials from other countries, who see only the well-functioning, efficient, highly-trained German police apparatus, that cooperates fully with international crime control and terrorism control efforts, and that is concerned with maintaining a high profile in international police circles. Without dramatizing the problem to an inordinate extent, it seems fair to say that the German police has not truly come to terms with its own history.

This is a problem that the organization must work out internally, however. Compared to other major European police establishments, the German police does not fare poorly in terms of community relations. In Britain, the so-called "Whig" school of history, which painted a rosy picture of a police officer who truly came out of the people and was just a citizen in uniform, has given way to critical analysis of police problems, behavior, and organization (see, e.g., Holdaway, 1984; Brogden, 1982). The French police, which suffers from perennially poor citizen relations, and which attempted some reforms after the notorious Ben Barka affair of 1965 (in which the police were implicated in the murder of a Moroccan dissident leader) is again under fire (Roach, 1985). Italy does no better, in fact quite a bit worse, in terms of police and community (Collin, 1985). Indeed, in the face of social unrest, the real challenge for a police organization may be to "save its own soul" by trying to preserve its integrity and its faithfulness to law and to correct procedure, rather than hoping to maintain good relations with the public.

The German police organization, however, which has struggled mightily to maintain a good image, is in many ways different from these other European organizations. Corruption has not been a problem, as it is in Italy. Nor is hostility against the police by a suppressed minority the problem that it is in Britain. Furthermore, the German organization operated under a mandate for radical change in the post-war years.

The peculiarity of the German situation is that the nature of most of the police-citizen encounters, especially with respect to social order problems, carries little of the kind of intensity on both sides that has characterized great industrial disputes, minority protests, or other uprisings of the poor and dispossessed. For the most part the conflicts in Germany are not class-based, nor are they based on religion, ethnic, or cultural sectarianism. The issues are general public welfare issues — the environment, disarmament, or general rowdiness at rock concerts or sporting events — rather than bread and butter issues for the participants. Such antagonists actually create a rather different atmosphere than one in which police are clearly suppressing a discontented underclass. Participants come from all ages and walks of life, although most are young and middle-class. A police apparatus facing largely middle-class, well-educated, and often well-positioned individuals does well to cover its tracks in terms of restraint and legality.

In 1970 the Interior Minister of Lower Saxony, Richard Lehners (Lehners, 1970) gave a long speech about problems of a modern police to a group of police leaders. The police, he said, have the job of safeguarding existing order and norms. They do not have the job of carrying through reforms or helping laws to evolve. This upholding of the *status quo* leads to conflict in a time of change. But there is a psychological problem. Why do police react with such aggressiveness to disturbances of the peace? It is because they have become identified with the order they are protecting, said Lehners, and they see the public disturbance as a personal assault. He then went on to call for more openness, the development of better channels of communication, more sport programs, exhibitions, and traffic instruction courses. "We need to develop the underdeveloped sense of civil responsibility of our consumer-oriented society," he explained. Police need to be shown as social helpers and guardians in this process.

At the time of his speech, the German police was about to embark on a program of reform and modernization. Most of this program, however, was directed at internal processes within the organization: training, technology, structural reforms. In the seventeen years since his speech, relations with the public have grow worse rather than better. Although, as has been explained several times, much of this worsening of relations has resulted from tensions in German society rather than police behavior in general, the inherent difficulties that are expressed in Lehners' speech may also inhibit the development of an intensive effort to become more responsive to the public. He calls for an aggressive campaign for establishing better contacts with society and he promotes the role of police as purveyors of civic virtue in a "consumer-oriented society." At the same time he recognizes the deeply conservative nature of police organizations and says that police do not have the task of carrying through reforms and helping laws to evolve. The danger may well be that the German police, in the effort to be nonpolitical, will take refuge in a passive role: angry, defensive, and retreating more and more into its own shell.

CHAPTER SEVEN

CONCLUSION: POLICE POWER AND PUBLIC ACCOUNTABILITY

The internal political development of the Federal Republic suffers to this day from the trauma caused by the legally-maneuvered transition from a democratic state to a totalitarian "fuhrer" regime; to a governmental order, in fact, that could be recognized from the very first day on as a lawless state . . . . No one can free himself from this trauma . . . most certainly not I.

> German social theorist Jürgen Habermas in "Law and Violence—a German Trauma."

WHO CONTROLS THE GERMAN POLICE?

THE CRUCIAL question finally is: to what extent does the German police answer to the German people for its policies and actions? There are no simple answers to this question. The police organization is complex and large. Furthermore, the concept of control itself defies easy description in terms of structural entities, but rather involves careful analysis of organizational dynamics.

Bayley (1985: Ch. 7) presents a typology of control mechanisms for use in analyzing police operations. He distinguishes between internal and external types of control. Internal controls include *explicit* ones (such as hierarchical supervision, disciplinary proceedings, socialization, peer responsibility), and *implicit* ones (such as unions and associations, vocational commitment, rewards, community contact). External controls include *exclusive* ones (such as civilian review boards in the United States and Police Authorities in Great Britain), whose only function is to exercise some measure of control over police, and *inclusive* (such as

187

courts, legislatures, media, political parties), that control police as part of a more comprehensive function, (Ibid.: 170).

Additionally, using examples from such diverse countries as India, Norway, France, and Russia, Bayley makes a point about structure that is relevant to the German situation. Commenting on the American fear that centralized police forces will not be controlled in a representative manner, he says ". . . the fact is that the scale and multiplicity of commands are independent of the nature of control over the police, although one caveat should be added. It is probably true that the larger the scale of the political community directly controlling the police, the more likely it is that supervision will be bureaucratic rather than political. Increasing scale makes supervision more difficult to accomplish without delegating authority to civil servants" (Ibid.: 172).

In Germany, the decentralization of police below the state level in the British and American zones was designed in fact to allow for greater political control by the community. This experiment was abandoned to such a large extent within such a small period of time that its efficacy with respect to control can hardly be judged. Therefore we cannot contrast police accountability to the public under this earlier decentralized system with today's more centralized one. However, we can try to evaluate control over the present police structure, which is strongly bureaucratic.

There are virtually no formal explicit external control mechanisms in Germany. The exception is the Police Authority (Beirat) that continues to exist in North Rhine-Westphalia. Even there, police authorities have only advisory functions. This contrasts with the English police authorities, on which the German ones were modeled, in that the English ones have both financial and administrative functions and in addition also serve as grievance panels for complaints against police.

On a less formal level, one citizen organization, Bürger Beobachten die Polizei (Citizens Observing Police), with the avowed purpose of monitoring police actions and reporting police abuses, exists in several areas. These groups bring various kinds of pressure to bear on police, including publicizing of incidents of illegal police action or excessive use of force. They encourage citizens to report police abuses to them, and counsel victims of alleged police violations of individual rights. Although their complaints against police have met with varying successes at official levels, some police leaders as well as leaders of the citizens groups believe that their existence serves to cut down on police abuse of citizens (*Der Spiegel*, 1983, #24: 63-69).

Among external inclusive control mechanisms, courts and the media are probably the most active agencies. The media generally gives full coverage to demonstrations, police misconduct, and police ineptitude. One quarterly journal, *Bürgerrechte und Polizei (Citizens Rights and Police)* is devoted exclusively to coverage of police and citizen matters.

Cases concerning constitutional rights of accused citizens in their relations with police are heard in the German courts and often appealed to the Federal Constitutional Court. Although case law is not binding in the German legal system, court decisions, especially when they seem to be following a pattern, are influential in affecting police behavior.

In recent years, the courts have heard increasing numbers of cases dealing with police actions during demonstrations. Thus, for example, the Federal Constitutional Court ruled that police had engaged in excessive information gathering about individuals at the first Brockdorf nuclear plant demonstration in 1981. In 1987, the Hamburg state court ruled that police had acted illegally in 1986 by enclosing several hundred demonstrators in a police circle for up to 12 hours without shelter and adequate food (*Der Spiegel,* March 9, 1987: 129). In the latter case, the state of Hamburg was required to pay 200 Marks to each of the complaining demonstrators.

Judicial action against individual officers is hampered by the fact that police officers are not identified by name or number tags. Although it is their duty to give their name when asked, and many carry calling cards, it goes without saying that the necessity for positive action by citizens will have a chilling effect on identification of officers whom they encounter and may even lead to police mistreatment of the asking citizen. A recent effort by CDU and FDP politicians to have the street-level Area Contact Officers in Berlin, whose function it is to develop close contacts with the public, wear name tags was abandoned after encountering a storm of protest from union leaders and the SDP (*Bürgerrechte and Polizei,* CILIP 26, 1987, #1: 86).

Control of police through court actions, although crucial in some instances, is nevertheless a piecemeal and reactive process. More direct is legislative control. Here each state of Germany has both a police organization law, that describes the particular organization of that state, and a police operations law, that defines the obligations and duties of police and the limits on police power. These laws tend to be similar and, as previously explained, go back in large part to earlier police operations laws, and especially the Prussian Police Operations Law of 1931. The laws become controversial when new proposals for police armaments, police use in emergencies, and police use as a strategic force come up. Political and police union opposition can then become so great that the proposed laws are modified or dropped, as was the case with the Model Police Law of 1976.

Police are also regulated to a large degree by federal law. In addition to the criminal law, which is federal for all serious crimes, there is the federal Criminal Procedure Law (Strafprozessordnung). Since most aspects of criminal procedural rights are not constitutionally regulated, this criminal procedure law plays an important part in protecting citizens against police misbehavior. Additional legislation that increases or restricts police power is also occasionally passed. Thus, for example, the Federal Emergency Powers Act (Notstandsgesetz) made possible the greater use of police as security forces in emergencies, while new legislation in 1984 made more explicit the powers of police and restrictions on the rights of citizens during demonstrations. In general German police behavior appears to be controlled considerably more thoroughly in legislation than its American counterpart.

With respect to internal explicit controls the German police generally are conceded to be a well run, highly professional organization that has few rogue officers. Venal corruption as it is known in the United States rarely occurs. Cooperation among states and between states and the federal government is good. A genuine respect seems to exist between rank and file and superior officers.

The major instrument of this control is the training system. At the lowest level, that of the Bereitschaftspolizei, the training is long and, except for its social order components, fairly general. After this training, recruits go through a half year of specific training for street work. By the time an officer takes on the responsibility of conventional street policing he or she has had some of the closest-supervised and thorough police training to be found in the world. Much of the early training has also been of a paramilitary nature, thus emphasizing leadership and hierarchy. Considering the youth of the recruits, this training is a powerful socialization instrument. In such an organization disciplinary problems, corruption, and failure to perform one's duty are not the problems that they are in some police organizations. Despite the fact that younger officers are often in sympathy with the groups that they confront in demonstrations, the rank and file appears to be well in hand.

The vice that accompanies this virtue is that internal explicit control may indeed be so good that the concept of control itself needs to be reexamined. Bayley himself does not put values on the various kinds of control that he describes except to suggest that internal organizational controls seem to work better because external controls are so easy to evade. He says: "Altogether a police force that is willing to make its behavior conform to community standards is much more likely to be effective than an unwilling police force required to conform under threat of external regulation" (Ibid.: 179). The crucial questions are: "What community? Whose standards?". In Germany, with a fairly homogeneous society, these questions may not be as difficult to deal with as in the United States, but in the end the only truly clear standards to which the police can conform are legislative and judicial mandates. This leaves a large area of decision-making and policy that can well be independent of community standards, no matter how well the organization is controlled internally.

This is not to suggest that the German police is not sensitive to community opinion; indeed, reading the police news and journals would suggest the opposite. It means only that a police organization that displays such excellent internal control is not necessarily *being* controlled in the sense that most people would bring to that word. Considering that much of what happens in the German police organization is not transmitted to the media or made easily accessible to the public (even such simple things as number of police personnel are not routinely made public), the matter of control becomes more problematical. The problem is compounded by the awesome technology of oversight and data processing that has been developed, largely in response to the threats of terrorism. What has happened in recent years is that those who probe into police matters, who take pains to unearth the statistics and to criticize police operations often come from an *a priori* hostile and ideologically-charged position. This hostility leads to further defensiveness and secretiveness on the part of police.

Internal implicit controls, in Bayley's typology, are important in introducing a new element—that of officer initiative outside the hierarchy—to the equation of accountability. Here the unions are a force for monitoring police operations. With their concern for individual officer prestige and professionalism leading to better working conditions and remuneration, they provide a tie to community sentiment and community concerns. Likewise the various national and international associations of police leaders provide a kind of internal control based on exchanges of information, technology, and experience. Indeed, the whole apparatus of pluralism, including civilian leadership, described in some depth in Chapter IV, works as a form of internal control to keep the organization from becoming too monolithic.

It is impossible to weigh the degree of control that is being exercised by these various forces. The general picture, however, with respect to internal controls is one of a largely bureaucratic control system, tempered to some extent by the existence of federalism, civilian leadership, and strong worker associations.

POLICE CULTURE IN TWO COUNTRIES: GERMANY AND THE UNITED STATES COMPARED

The concept of control itself suggests a system of supervision, accountability, and power. it suggests that there are two entities: a police that is being controlled and a community or a state (presumably acting for the community) that is controlling. It implies that the "controllee" — i.e., the police as an organization and as individuals — will be directly accountable in some way for its actions to the "controller." It suggests clear ties of accountability and authority between the two.

There is another kind of control over police, however, that might be called "control through powerlessness." In this system police power is so fragmented that the prospect of a powerful police force that could potentially become oppressive to the nation as a whole seems remote. It is in effect a negative system of control. In such a system accountability becomes more of a problem and is exercised in varying degrees and with varying success in different areas. In other words, the scope of any one control mechanism, to the extent that control exists, is greatly diminished.

Such a system of "uncontrolled control" over police is familiar to Americans. It is, in fact, a peculiarly American approach to control, that finds its theoretical roots in the writings of James Madison. The police, that most dangerous of state bureaucracies, partakes of an institutional fragmentation similar to that which was designed to keep the government itself from becoming too powerful.

From a strictly legal standpoint, state governments in the United States could as easily have set up exclusive centralized state police forces as have the Germans. To understand why they did not do so requires an understanding of the difference between American and German police as bureaucratic entities that have peculiarly native cultural properties. Understanding these cultural differences also helps us to understand the reasons why the American structures so hopefully planted in 1945 were not likely to take root in the German soil.

The fact that different organizations have different cultures is by now an accepted idea (see, e.g., Schein, 1984). Comparing organizational cultures across nations, however, involves making one's way through the swampy but fertile ground of "national character" as well as comparative organizational dynamics. The risk of stereotyping is great although, as de Tocqueville's analysis of American democracy has shown, the effort can provide insights that lead to rich further analysis.

There is some research on peculiarities of organizational culture as a national phenomenon. For example, Crozier (1964) characterized French bureaucracies, both private and public, as being hampered by three major dysfunctional characteristics related to French national culture: individual isolation, lack of communication between strata, and avoidance of face-to-face relationships (Ibid.: 223). In such a climate the bureaucracy adapts itself by using impersonal rules and centralization to solve its problems of communication.

More recently Hofstede (1980, 1983) surveyed 1800 employees of one multi-national firm in forty countries. Based on these surveys and other data, he placed these countries on an axis containing four major cultural dimensions: collectivism/individualism, masculinity/femininity, strong uncertainty avoidance/weak uncertainty avoidance, and small power-distance/large power-distance. Hofstede operates from the premise that international business is enhanced if differences in organizational culture across nations are understood.

We must remember, however, that we are comparing, not organizations in general, but police organizations in particular. There are therefore two levels of comparison involved: what makes police organizations different, and what makes them similar across nations. On the one hand, we have the ideas typified by Cozier's statement that "Bureaucratic processes are not uniform from society to society, but are closely linked to basic personality traits, social values, and patterns of social relationships" (Crozier, 1964: 237). For reformers the implications of this statement are that, for cultural reasons, organizational structures that are effective in one nation may not be maintained successfully in another. The Japanese koban, or small neighborhood police station, that some reformers hope to institute in American neighborhoods, may well be an example in point. The close supervision over the public that is exercised by the police through these stations may well be antithetical to the American tradition of suspicion of governmental interference.

On the other hand, there is the countering claim that the peculiar demands of particular occupations—working conditions, technology, client contact, production goals—transcend national boundaries and create a similar organizational culture in different countries. With respect to police organizations, there is much to be said for this claim. The working police culture that Skolnick (1969) described from his work in

California, and that Manning (1977) described with respect to the English police exists also in Germany (Feest and Blankenburg, 1972; Murck, 1976). The elements of danger, conservatism, occupational isolation, and the need to maintain authority are part of a police culture that seems to be determined by the nature of the work. Based on their similarities, and a strong current of occupational empathy, police agencies can trade techniques, information, and innovative organizational experiences across national borders.

The differences in organizational culture, however, are what makes for the peculiarly endemic police system that exists in each country. These differences affect the change process. Comparing American and German police organizational culture leads to insights into why the translation of American institutions to German society was not successful. Structure, as well as other organizational traits related to the ethos of the organization and its operations are important in making such a comparison. In simple terms, then, the German police can be described as a culture of *rationalism*. The American police, on the other hand, can be described as a culture of *empiricism*.

I borrow this terminology from Max Weber (1960) who uses it in comparing Anglo-Saxon and Continental legal systems. This terminology is borrowed primarily because it is relatively neutral in affect and does not connote a value judgment about one system or the other that other possible dichotomies (such as administrative/political or professional/amateur) might have suggested.

The terms "rational" and "empirical," however, do have some intellectual baggage attached since they were used by Weber to describe legal systems. Thus their use can imply that there is some element of continuity in the justice systems of these two countries that carries over from the family of the law itself to the organization that bridges the gap between formal law and pure order in a society, i.e., the police.

I am aware, to be sure, of the fact that Weber probably is best known for his rational/legal model of bureaucracy and that what I will be describing as a particular police culture will parallel in some ways his own ideal of bureaucracy in general. Thus, if it is true that Weber was describing German bureaucracy when he outlined the rational model, it is possible that what can be said about police bureaucracy in Germany may also be said about German organizations in general. This is just the point that people like Crozier and Hofstede are trying to make. On the other hand, the large time lapse and the changed social and political circumstances since Weber's writings on bureaucracy may have brought about many changes in organizational style and culture in Germany. Furthermore, some foreign traditions, such as judicial review, have become firmly institutionalized in post-war Germany. In that case police bureaucracy, conservative and rigid as it normally is, and tied to the whole general structure of German governmental bureaucracy, lacked the institutional capacity to change.

In any case, although some comparisons will be made with Hofstede's findings on German organizations, what I am doing is comparing police bureaucracies in the two countries, rather than bureaucracy in general. At the same time I am suggesting that some elements of similarity may be found between police culture and general legal culture in the two countries.

A final caveat is that term "culture," as used here, encompasses the entire complex of structures, procedures, norms, and traditions that make up what we call an organization. It is my contention that structures and processes are so closely interwoven with less formal aspects of organizational life that they can indeed be considered part of the culture of an organization.

These two police cultures, then, the American one of empiricism and the German one of rationalism, manifest their differences in many subtle ways that can probably only be truly appreciated by one who has experienced both. In addition, we are comparing national police cultures, not local ones, and there are many differences, especially among American police departments, and in lesser degree among German states, that tend to belie any broad generalizations. Nevertheless, there are certain aspects of these police organizations that can be compared in terms of empiricism and rationalism. These will be briefly stated and then compared in some depth.

A Culture of Rationalism: The German Police	**A Culture of Empiricism: The American Police**
1. Structural homogeneity	Structural heterogeneity
2. Structured and compartmentalized public accountability mechanisms	Ad hoc and diffuse public accountability mechanisms
3. Controlled, highly-developed, and internally-administered training	Minimal training plus independently-acquired education
4. Occupational determinism	Aspirational optimism
5. Drive toward certainty	Tolerance of ambiguity

1. Structural Homogeneity vs. Structural Heterogeneity

Despite the differences in organizational structures among the various states of Germany, and between the states and the federal government, the basic organization is a homogeneous one. Similar training, similar divisions between urban and rural areas, similar career paths for Bepo, Schupo, and Kripo, centralized training of top leadership, national policy-making by the Standing Conference of Interior Ministers, centralized decisions about transfer of Bepo troops from one state to another: all of these are elements of a homogeneous structure. A police officer trained and seasoned in North Rhine-Westphalia would not be disoriented if he or she were suddenly transplanted to Schleswig-Holstein or even to Bavaria.

In the United States, by contrast, police structures are disparate and uncoordinated. Sheriff's departments, U. S. Marshals, FBI agents, local police departments, huge urban police departments, state police, various security forces: all are part of the picture. These organizations are independent of each other, and there is no one coordinating agent such as a state Interior Minister, who can control them. Their respective jurisdictions are often not clear and their interrelationships are complex and often informal. Conflict and cooperation are competing norms in such an environment. These structures have evolved gradually in response to historical needs and in terms of historical, chiefly English, traditions. No systematic effort has been made to rationalize them. Even the nationalizing and centralizing tendencies mentioned in Chapter Four must accommodate themselves to this diversity.

2. Structured and Compartmentalized Public Accountability Mechanisms vs. Ad Hoc and Diffuse Public Accountability Mechanisms

This dichotomy is the corollary of the previous one. In Germany, accountability is closely tied to the law and to bureaucratic control. The civilian police leadership, although originally appointed by the political leadership, generally keep their positions until (and if) they themselves opt for a career change. As previously explained, the task definition, obligations and principles under which the German police officer operates are carefully circumscribed by law. Discretion exists, to be sure, but is an unwelcome and little-acknowledged aspect of police work. One senses the comfort of certainty that is tied to the norm of the Rechtsstaat, that is often contrasted by police leaders to the lawless and command-centered Third Reich police. Indeed, the Rechtsstaat itself preceded democracy in Germany by one and one-half centuries and has a grip on German thought that makes it difficult for Germans to distinguish clearly between this concept and the idea of political democracy.

The American situation is again much more complex, ad hoc, and diffuse. Organizational independence and complexity, as passive controls, are in many ways guarantors of, if not accountability in the usual sense, then at least of the improbability of excessive police power. External explicit control mechanisms, such as Civilian Review Boards, have not been effective. Internal explicit controls such as Internal Affairs Units, that exist in many urban departments, serve chiefly to investigate complaints against officers and, in any case, live a rather uneasy existence in most police departments (Goldstein, 1977). Rampant political influence, which has been discredited by reformers (Fogelson, 1977) still exists in some departments. Within departments, the degree of legalism varies greatly. Even the strong general influence of court monitoring of police behavior has not been shown to have major effects on specific operations (see e.g., Milner 1971; Becker & Feeley, 1973; Wasby, 1976). Probably the best way to describe the state of public accountability in American police departments is to say, "It varies," with the degree of accountability dependent on local political norms, police personnel, and some formal controls.

There is, however, one stark contrast in relations between police and public in Germany and the United States. In Germany the fear is real in some quarters that the police apparatus can and will be used to suppress dissidents and, if necessary, to act as a force for repression against the entire population (see, e.g., Werkentin, 1984; *Bürgerrechte u. Polizei*). Historical memory continues to affect relations between police and public. In the United States police of various jurisdictions are often accused of repression of minorities or of general brutality or corruption. Very few Americans, however, see the police apparatus as a danger to American freedom in general. This apparatus is too diffuse, too independent, too vastly different in background, training, and capability to be effectively mobilized. When it comes to major use of public force either to suppress opinion or to keep order, the task falls to the National Guard or the military, neither of which are conventional police, as is the Bepo in Germany.

3. Controlled, Highly-Developed, and Internally-Administered Training vs. Minimal Training Plus Independently-Acquired Education

In contrasting training methods, we are at the soul of the difference between the rational and empirical cultures of police organization. An example that illustrates this difference graphically is the contrast between two programs: one in Germany and one in the United States, both designed to improve police-community contact.

In the United States the San Diego Community Profile Program, financed by the Police Foundation, was an experiment in "beat" policing, started in 1973, that was to emphasize officer responsibility for the beat, officer familiarity with the area under his control, and officer initiative in developing plans for crime control in his area (Boydstun and Sherry, 1975). Twenty-four patrol officers and three patrol supervisors were chosen to take part in this program in the Northern Division of the San Diego Police Department. They were given eight days (sixty hours) of training. Their task was different from that of other street police in that they were to develop a plan of action related to "profiles" of their area. They were to make frequent reports, discuss their plans with other community profile personnel, evaluate progress, and make frequent reports on the relation between goals and achievement. In general the officers were given large responsibility for their beats.

The Community Profile program was highly successful at first, not in terms of crime reduction so much as in terms of community contact and community relations. It was continued at the end of the experimental period. Gradually, however, resentment and lack of appreciation of the program by first-line supervisors as well as officer resentment of the large amount of paper work involved in carrying out the project resulted in modifications leading to a rather more conventional form of team policing in San Diego.

At about the same time, the West Berlin police force developed a cadre of officers known as Kontaktbereichsbeamte, or Area Contact Officers, who were assigned specific districts varying from a few blocks to several square miles (Hubner, 1984). These officers were to become thoroughly familiar with their districts and concern themselves particularly with improved citizen contacts in order to help police become more effective in crime control, environmental protection, and traffic control. Officers chosen for this task worked the usual 40 hours per week, but could choose their own hours according to the needs of their districts.

In order to qualify for this work, an officer had to be at least 40 years old, have high civil service status ("gehobener Dienst"—equivalent to at least a lieutenant in an American urban police department), and have an excellent record. Most important, the nominee had to go through a six-month course of study in order to prepare for the work. According to the Berlin police, this program, now more than ten years old, has been highly successful in terms of community contact and officer satisfaction. Furthermore the crime rate (i.e., most forms of burglary and public vice) went down by 10.9 percent between 1974 and 1983 in West Berlin, a fact that the police attributes in part to the Area Contact Officer Program.

An outsider might be tempted to think that the relatively greater success of the Berlin experience was due to the choice of personnel and the supervisory dynamics involved rather than the much longer period of training for this task. The German answer to such reservations about training in all areas of police work always includes one crucial point: an officer needs to be well-trained in order to be respected by the public. Indeed, one sometimes gets the impression that the whole drawn-out, even over-done emphasis on training serves a legitimization need as much as a training need. The legitimization need is real, however. In Germany even relatively unskilled occupations such as shoe sales are normally entered into only after a lengthy period of training.

The years of training for various levels of police work also serve as a strong socializing force for the police. With few exceptions the education and training of German police officers, starting from their entry into the Bepo as teen-agers, is a highly-controlled, expensive intra-police operation. Even the highest noncivilian leadership, with their years of training and education, receive almost all of it within the police academies at various levels.

Police training in the United States, by contrast, has the appearance of pure anarchy to the Germans. Several German police officers expressed to me their incredulity at the willingness of American police departments to hire officers who had been educated in environments — i.e., universities — over which the police had no control. The recommendations of the President's Commission (1967) that all police officers receive a college education, and the efforts of the federal government's Law Enforcement Education Program to follow through on this suggestion were in large part the American answer to the fact that police were poorly trained and ill-prepared for the kind of work they would be doing. Graduate programs in independent universities have also had increasing numbers of police enrollees, often on their own time and money.

Internal training, on the other hand, varies from virtually nil to the better part of a year in American police departments. State minimum requirements have had some effect on police training in recent years, but again the amount of training that is required is small.

At the leadership level the contrast is enormous. Internal leadership training, when it exists in the United States, is usually of the short-course variety and is not standardized within states. There is no requirement, as there is in Germany, that all of the highest level officers partake of a particular course of training. Although the FBI Academy helps to train police leaders, it does so through short courses and there is obviously no compulsory attendance. The fact that many police chiefs in the United States are college trained is the result of their own initiative, not of job requirements.

In short, as with general structures and accountability, the contrast is between a rational and highly-controlled training apparatus in Germany and an ad hoc, diffuse—i.e., empirical—one in the United States. This difference in preparation and socialization of officers undergirds the whole difference in culture between the two systems.

4. Occupational Determinism vs. Aspirational Optimism

In both the German and American police systems nearly all sworn personnel start at the bottom and work their way up through the ranks to leadership positions. The organization requires large numbers of individuals at the street level, however, and few at the supervisory levels. This presents morale problems for police in the United States, especially as they become more highly educated.

In the Federal Republic, however, as was explained in Chapter Five, upwardly mobile officers are identified through an examination process at a relatively early stage of their career. Despite the organizational equality implied in the policy of the single career track, officers with higher social and educational standing previous to entry into the police tend to do better on these examinations than those of lower preservice status. Acceptance of the role of follower is easier in Germany, however, where a generally stronger class system produces less stigmatization for the lack of advancement than is the case in the United States.

What happens, then, is that there is a certain predictability about promotions, at least to the higher civil service level, that cuts down on competition and anger at the same time that it cuts down on choice and aspirations. The elements of apathy, corruption, and cynicism that can characterize a subculture of "street cops" as opposed to "management cops" (Reuss-Ianni, 1983) is tempered in Germany not only by the greater acceptance of class differences, but also by the long period of training. This period of training legitimizes street work as an acceptable and professionalized occupation.

5. Drive Toward Certainty vs. Tolerance of Ambiguity

Whether a tolerance for ambiguity is the chicken or the egg of American police culture can be debated. This culture, however, with its fragmentation, lack of formal organizational ties between organizations, and variety could not survive without willingness on the part of those involved to operate through informal, temporary, and personalized communications, and to allow many things regarding jurisdiction, power, and administration to remain unclear. Perhaps this is the real point. The organization would not survive if it did not provide a reasonably comfortable framework for action. This is not to imply that efforts to rationalize the structures and operations are not constantly being made. The largely unsuccessful efforts to consolidate small police departments into larger ones is one example of such efforts. Most of these efforts, however, to achieve reforms, such as more standardized training, clearer lines of communication, and better reporting start from the premise of a multiplicity of situations, and are operationalized through methods such as monetary incentives, informal networking, publicity, and professional associations.

Such an organization would not provide a comfortable framework for action for the German police. Although this study is confined to police organizations, it is obvious that we would find similar differences with respect to other governmental and nongovernmental agencies. The roots of this difference lie deep in the history and ideals of the two nations. Germans have often been caricatured as "orderly." This drive for order, a "nostalgia for synthesis" according to Dahrendorf (1965) is based on a certain need to avoid conflict, again according to Dahrendorf (Ibid.: 213).

Hofstede (1983) also finds this tendency in his study of individual values in private industry. Although not found at the extremes on any of his scales, German organizational life was characterized by values of strong uncertainty avoidance, masculinity, low power distance, and high individualism. United States organizations, on the other hand, are characterized, like the Germans, by high individualism, masculinity, and lower power distance. Uncertainty avoidance is weak in American organizations, however. Organizations characterized by strong uncertainty avoidance and relatively small power distance, according to Hofstede, are like "well-oiled machines" (Ibid.: 84). They do not operate under a syndrome of crisis management, and they engage in careful planning. Rules are crucial.

For those who tend to think of Germans as "authoritarian," the scale that measures this trait most closely, power distance (the "degree of centralization of authority and the degree of autocratic leadership" — Ibid.: 81), shows little difference between United States and German organizations, both scoring near the middle, but on the "small power distance" side of the scale. Germany actually has somewhat smaller power distance on this scale than does the United States (Ibid.: 83). This finding, based on private business organizations, would not, in my opinion, hold for police organizations, that continue in the traditional mold of hierarchical distance despite their efforts to improve communications between levels.

With respect to tolerance for ambiguity, we need to take another look at historical tradition, and at Weber's description of the two types of justice: empirical justice in the Anglo-Saxon common law countries, and rational justice in the countries adhering to the Romano-Germanic, or civil law tradition. Empirical justice tolerates case law to a high degree although, as Weber acknowledges (Weber, 1985: 285), a large amount of codification and statutory law also exists in such a system. Furthermore, empirical justice tolerates lay decision-making as exemplified by "lay" (i.e., not trained specifically for the judiciary) judges, jurors, and other personnel, to a high degree (Ibid.: 285-287). Legal education is case-bound, rather than formal (Ibid.: 197-201). The whole cumbersome, diffuse, wide-ranging, and tradition-encrusted individualist, often enigmatic nature of the law in such a system is contrasted to the neat, spare, and above all, logical civil law tradition. In the one, there has to be a large tolerance for ambiguity in order to continue to function while in the other a certain rationality and reliance on expertise is both required and valued.

Several criticisms of this analogy between legal culture and police organization can be advanced. In the first place, police are hierarchically separate (as usual with some exceptions, especially in Great Britain) from the judicial system. In the second place, what we are talking about is a system of organizational values that is deeply imbedded in national culture, not just legal culture. In addition, there has been a large convergence in legal culture between common law and civil law countries, a convergence that does not seem to be rivaled in dimension within police organizations.

Nevertheless, the comparison is a pregnant one and could be carried over into analysis of British police organization as well as of other continental police forces such as those of France and Italy. Such comparisons would highlight the importance of legal-historical as opposed to social-psychological forces at work in influencing contemporary police organizations.

Some critics of German police operations look back to the period of 1945-1949 with a certain nostalgia (Werkentin 1985; *Bürgerrechte und Polizei*, 1986). They believe that the communal police was effective enough in protection of local citizens and that the real reason why the police was reconstituted in the old German tradition was to make it a strong security force that could easily serve the state rather than the citizens.

Without a doubt the German police was built up to serve a strategic security function during the 1950's. This argument, however, by treating as "given" a conflict of interest between state and citizen gives no quarter to the idea of the inseparability of state and citizen in a democratic order. In the final analysis, democratic institutions are the major protection against police excess. With the creation of a German military force in the 1950's, moreover, police function became once again that of providing for law and order in internal matters.

Most important, however, the critique does not consider in enough depth why the old traditions were so strong, but sees their resurrection to be, on the one hand, a function of the desire for strength and, on the other hand, the yearning of those in leadership positions for a familiar bureaucratic climate. While both of these explanations have some validity they do not explore in depth the importance of these bureaucratic traditions as part of the organizational culture of the police.

POLICE AND PUBLIC ORDER: THE GERMAN TRAUMA

The German police today must face serious questions as it performs its order-maintenance duties. Hiring teenagers and keeping them for several years in closed institutions where they learn paramilitary maneuvers is the most problematic aspect of German police organization. Despite sincere efforts in the early 1970's to develop new ways to train officers to deal in an understanding and nonthreatening way with crowd control, and despite continued concern in the police establishment about antagonism between police and citizen in Germany, this antagonism is growing. The rhetoric of police goal-setting has been transformed from that of "friend and helper" to that of "guardian of the society" (von Harach, 1983: 130). Increasingly sophisticated communications technology, motorized equipment, and nonlethal weaponry, pursued in the name of effectiveness and crime control, have increased the fear of police power. The increasing police capacity to gather and retrieve data about the general citizenry worries many Germans. Within the police the idealism of the 1950's has been replaced by emphasis on professionalism, expertise, and manipulation of public opinion. Law, order, and legality need to be sold like soap, said the Polizeipräsident of Munich in 1967 (Ibid.: 127). Since that time, even such a concern for public consent has given way in large measure to determination to prevent chaos and anarchy from taking over. Throughout, a grim appeal to the letter of the law becomes a major self-justifying tactic within the police.

Police power and police action often touch on the painful open wounds of Twentieth Century German history. Police behavior that would be considered at least acceptable in most countries takes on a grotesque dimension in Germany. As long as there were few social order problems and no problem of terrorism, police behavior was not an issue. In more troubled times, however, police efforts to maintain order evoke memories of police performing a strategic, repressive, and blatantly political function. Police efforts to gather information related to crime control bring back the fear of totalitarian control. Indeed, the sharpness of the reaction to police operations may itself be a manifestation of a certain fear of themselves or confusion about the past that possesses the second generation of post-war Germans.

Jürgen Habermas has summed up the problem in his essay "Recht und Gewalt — ein deutsches Trauma" (Law and Violence — a German Trauma) (Habermas, 1985: 105):

> The internal political development of the Federal Republic suffers to this day from the trauma caused by the legally-maneuvered transition from a democratic state to a totalitarian Führer-regime; to a governmental order, in fact, that could be recognized from the very first day as a lawless regime. Trauma, says Freud, is an injury that is so painful that its memory must be suppressed. Therefore it constitutes a lasting injury to the psyche. When symptoms occur to bring this trauma to the surface, it arouses emotional shock and mental confusion. These shocks — including rearmament, the Communist Party ban, the first concentration camp trials in our own territory, relations with countries like Israel, Poland, and the Soviet Union, the question of a statute of limitations, films like *Holocaust,* or the unspeakable life-stories of ministers, judges, professors, and the like, accumulate to create a thickly-woven and vibrating net in which the history of the Federal Republic tosses helplessly. And thus the conflictual climate of mutual suspicion and blame has not yet been dissipated. No one can free himself from this trauma . . . . most certainly not I.

Habermas goes on to say that Germany must try to separate the matter of public protests and civil disobedience related to the peace movement from the "traumatizing happenings fifty years ago" (Ibid.: 106) and to recognize today's protests, when conducted within certain guidelines (nonviolent, relevant to constitutional norms) as a form of creative conflict within the established order. He expresses his disagreement with renowned historian Karl-Dietrich Bracher, who compared the breakdown of order in Weimar with the disorders of today.

Habermas, however, makes an important point relative to his own argument. Germans, he says, are basically Hobbesian in their approach to government. Their fear is that questioning the legitimacy of particular governmental actions puts into question the legitimacy of the entire governmental structure and can lead back to the "state of nature," described by Hobbes, in which no government exists. In other words, conflict and opposition are alarming and threatening because they are destabilizing forces. This attitude must also be overcome, he says. Thus it is not only the German trauma that affects behavior and attitudes: it is also a certain German approach to government—one that emphasizes rational structures that carefully circumscribe conflict.

Habermas' critique and recommendations are particularly relevant to the problems of the police. On the one hand, the inability to keep order that helped to bring about Nazi lawlessness, as well as this lawlessness itself were played out most intensely within the police organization. These wounds, although healed over, have left injuries that continue to cause pain, often very intense pain, when they are touched. On the other hand, the kind of Hobbesianism that he decries—the belief that any order is better than disorder—may be even harder to overcome than the German trauma. Habermas' ideal involves tolerance of a good deal of ambiguity both by state authorities and their opponents, conscious willingness to act symbolically rather than instrumentally, and willingness on the part of the authorities to sacrifice some measure of rationality for a kind of higher legitimacy. As the earlier discussion tried to make clear, however, such uncertainties are particularly antithetical to the culture of the German police, a culture that is tied much more strongly to the ethos of a Rechtsstaat than is American police culture. Thus the advocacy of a more tolerant and legitimizing approach to civil order disturbances, which in any case is not particularly strong even in American police circles, has major impediments to overcome in Germany.

Organizational culture does not imply organizational determinism, however. Change and reform occur frequently in organizational settings, especially in response to crises. Therefore it would be fatalistic and incorrect to assume that the present organization of the German police is cast in stone. Indeed, the two major reform efforts of the post-war period as well as the truly major structural changes of the Weimar Republic suggest that the police is capable of responding to problems with new structures and processes.

The very fact, however, that the German police, at a critical stage in its development — i.e., the early 1950's — chose not to make major structural changes, but rather to resurrect the traditional rational structures based on German ideals of a Rechtsstaat, may actually exacerbate the German trauma for the police. While this regression was perfectly natural considering the intervening shocks and considering the German civil service tradition, it did allow for a certain aura of normalcy to reign at the same time that the period of trauma was in effect being suppressed. Thus the rather hasty reconstruction of the Weimar police apparatus in 1950 may be having some unexpected results in today's Germany.

The general acceptance of the concept embodied by the Bepo and Bundesgrenzschutz evidence the degree to which a strategic military function for police is still part of German culture and thinking. Some reform proposals, however, have called for major modifications of the Bepo structure and functions as well as cutting the BGS out of the police entirely (see, e.g., Werkentin, 1984). The political civil order control function would then be carried by a separate organization, similar to the Bepo, but not tied to police training or to conventional police operations. Freedom from the exercise of this civil order function, at least in its larger dimensions of crowd control during demonstrations, riots, and strikes would then make the promotion of a citizen-friendly police, as well as concentration on crime prevention and control, vastly easier. Furthermore the suspicions of those who believe that the police stand ready to play a strategic military role would be mitigated.

Nor are the Bepo and the BGS old German traditional organizations that go back to the Empire or even before. The Bepo is essentially a creation of the Weimar Republic, whereas the BGS was set up specifically as an ersatz military force in 1950. It is only since the 1960's that the BGS has become more closely integrated with other police in terms of training, personnel, and development. It would be possible to have a rational and well ordered police apparatus without either of them.

What are the alternatives, though? Looking around the world we see that there are no happy solutions to the problem of dealing with civil strife. The hated Republican Security Companies as well as the Gendarmerie

Speciale in France specialize exclusively in crowd control, unlike the Bepo, which incorporates training into its function and uses essentially young unseasoned personnel. As such, the danger of the police in France becoming a repressive force is greatly increased. In the United States the army or the National Guard performs this function, always on an emergency basis, when it is no longer possible to use local police exclusively. For these forces crowd control is an unnatural and uncomfortable duty that detracts from their image as protectors against external enemies (Williams, 1969). Furthermore, civil order control is not a state of war, and the kind of training in criminal law enforcement and procedural justice that police receive is very different from the kind of combat training that military troops receive. The use of military troops diminishes the elements of formal rationality and ties to the legal system that are an integral part of police work.

The law that regulates the Bundesgrenzschutz, as explained in Chapter Three, highlights the comparison between police work and military work. In peacetime the BGS is part of the police and subject to domestic law. When hostilities break out, however, it becomes a military force subject only to the international law of war. While this peculiar arrangement may suggest that use of police for strategic military purposes continues to play an important part in German thinking, a mitigating factor is the fact that BGS training is designed to be similar to that of the Bepo, thus making these troops presumably more highly qualified to handle civil unrest than are purely military personnel.

The British and, in most cases, the American solution to the problems of civil order control—i.e., having local police forces perform these functions as well as deviance control functions—works reasonably well only so long as there are no serious public order problems that tax this police beyond its capacities in terms of manpower and training. The urban riots of the 1980's have shown the weaknesses of the English police system, just as the urban riots of the 1960's showed the weaknesses of the American system. Although some Britons have called for a "third force" similar to the French Republican Security Companies, there is not a large degree of support for this alternative. Indeed, the fact that the police are not strong is seen by some as an advantage, in that the police cannot then provide a kind of shield that protects political leaders from having to come to terms with difficult social problems (Gregory, 1985). Such an argument may be useful to consider in Germany where, probably as a result of the Weimar experience, massive reaction to public order threats seems to be the norm. However, even in Britain the military, though not actually used since the 1920's, remains the essential backup force.

The major problems in Germany are threefold. First is the use of the BGS as a kind of elite federal police force that, despite claims to the contrary, is actually highly militarized. The second is the probable effect of the early years of regimentation in a closed environment on the subsequent thought and actions of the conventional police officer. The third problem is that of maintaining open channels of communication with the public especially with regard to allaying fears of excessive police data-gathering about legitimate political dissent. These problems are not inconsiderable, but they are not insuperable. Their solution requires a great deal of openness, cooperation, and creative endeavor on the part of police, citizens, and policy-makers.

In all systems the military remain the agents of last resource when civil strife becomes excessive and civil order control becomes the only priority, driving out formal legality or institutional integrity of police forces. In these situations, the political nature of the conflict becomes increasingly apparent. Thus, for example, the military takeover of Berlin in 1932 signaled the end of Prussian police efforts to maintain some semblance of law and order. When civil strife becomes excessive, however, we are dealing with a situation that is revolutionary in nature, if not always in final effect. It is in the large area between, when civil strife is a major problem at various times, but does not threaten revolutionary change, that police forces face their greatest challenge. It is then that their claim to legitimacy has to be grounded in painstaking concern for human rights, willingness to refrain from action wherever possible, and scrupulous follow-up in cases of excess by individual officers. Both the appearance and the reality of a maximum of formal rationality are essential. Openness and communication with all sectors of the public need to be pursued vigorously. Most important, the internal dynamics of the organization, through its structures, its leadership, and its value systems should serve to cultivate and maintain the values of a democratic society even in times of crisis.

Democratic values have been recognized and are often emphasized by German police leaders. To the extent that they continue to be part of the organizational life and culture of the various German police organizations, they will serve to help these organizations weather the inevitable and serious crises of the modern technological state.

REFERENCES

Alderson, John C.: Police and the social order. In John Roach and Jurgen Thomaneck: *Police and Public Order in Europe*. London, Croom-Helm, 1985.

Arbeitsgemeinschaft kritischer Polizisten: Hamburger Signal. *Bürgerrechte und Polizei:*
CILIP 25, 1986.

Aufbau: Aufbau der Gemeindepolizei. In *25 Jahre Landespolizei Nordwürttemberg, 1945-
1970, Eine Dokumentation*. 1970.

Balbus, Isaac: *The Dialectics of Legal Repression*. New Brunswick, Transaction Books,
1973.

Banfield, Edward: *The Unheavenly City*. Boston, Little-Brown, 1968.

Bayley, David: *Forces of Order: The Police in Japan*. Berkeley, University of California
Press, 1976.

— — *Patterns of Policing*. New Brunswick, Rutgers University Press, 1985.

Becker, Theodore, and Malcolm Feeley (eds.): *The Impact of Supreme Court Decisions*.
New York, Oxford University Press, 1973.

Bennis, Warren, and Philip Slater: *The Temporary Society*. New York, Harper and Row,
1968.

Berkley, George: *The Democratic Policeman*. Boston, Beacon Press, 1969.

Berndt, Günter: Die Führungslehre. In *Schriftenreihe der Polizei-Führungsakademie:* 3/4,
1985.

— — — and Robert Altman: Wertewandel in der Gesellschaft und die Auswirkungen
in der Polizei. In *Schriftenreihe der Polizei-Führungsakademie:* 138, 1985, #2.

Bibliothek für Zeitgeschichte, Württembergische Landesbibliothek Dokument-
Sammlung D-0551: *Materialen zum einheitlichen Polizeigesetz and zur Praxis und Aufrüs-
tung der Polizei*, 1976.

Bittner, Egon: *The Functions of the Police in Modern Society*. Cambridge, Oelgeschlager,
Gunn, and Hain, 1980.

Blankenburg, Erhard: Recht und Ordnung als Beruf. *Kriminalistik 12:* 529, 1976.

— — —, K. Sessar, and W. Steffan: *Die Staatsanwaltschaft im Prozess Straflicher Sozialkon-
trolle*. Berlin, Dunker and Humblot, 1978.

Bleck, Siegfried: Staatsgewalt und Friedensbewegung. *Die Polizei, 75:*77, 1984.

Blum, Joshua: *Geschlossene Polizeieinheiten im Grossraum Stuttgart*. Stuttgart, Gewerkschaft der Polizei, 1976.

Bolle, B., D. Bruns, G. B. Larking, and F. Schrammer: *Mit Samthandschuh und Eisenfaust, Polizei and Polizisten in der Bundesrepublik.* Hamburg, Verlag Association, 1977.

Booz, H.: Das Gesetz zur Sicherung des Strassenverkehrs. *Deutsche Polizei, 6:* 3/4, 1953.

Borner: 10 Grundsätze für Polizisten im Einsatz. *Die Polizei, 73:*24, 1982.

Bottscher, Karl W. and Rudolf Schafer: Die Polizei in Deutschland: Ihr Aufbau, Ihre Stärke, Ihre Gefahren. *Frankfurter Hefte, 4:*2, 1949.

Boydstun, John and Michael Sherry: *San Diego Community Profile: Final Report.* Washington, D. C., Police Foundation, 1975.

Bracher, Karl Dietrich: *The German Dilemma.* New York: Praeger, 1975.

Bramshill: *Excercise Europa/Atlanta.* Reports of participants in the Bramshill Police Staff College Senior Command Course study of police unions, 1981.

Brill, K.: Politische Bildung and wissenschaftlichen Politik in Deutschland. In *Schriftenreihe für Oberbeamte der Polizei.* Hiltrup, Polizei-Institut, 1950.

Brockdorf. *Bereitschaftspolizei Heute:* March, 1981.

Brogden, Michael: *The Police: Autonomy and Consent.* London, Academic Press, 1982.

Brusten, Manfred: Schichtzugehörigkeit und Aufstiegschancen von Polizeibeamten. *Die Polizei,* 65:185, 1974.

— — —, Johannes Feest, and Rudiger Lautman, (eds.): *Die Polizei-Eine Institution Öffentlichen Gewalt.* Neuwied und Darmstadt, Luchterhand, 1975.

Bundesministerium des Innern: *Innere Sicherheit.* Mannheim, Südwestdeutscher Verlagsanstalt, 1977.

Bundesrepublik Deutschland, Bundeskriminalamt: *Polizeiliche Kriminalstatistik, 1985.* Regensburg, Mittelbayerische Druckerei und Verlagsgesellschaft, 1985.

Bureau of Justice Statistics: *Sourcebook of Criminal Justice Statistics — 1985.* Washington, D. C., U. S. Government Printing Office, 1986.

Bürgerrechte und Polizei (CILIP). Published in Berlin three times yearly by Redaktion CILIP, Berlin.

Bürgerrechte und Polizei: Dem Bürger, nicht dem Staat, dienen-der aufgezwungene Bruch mit deutsche Polizei-tradition, 1945-49, *CILIP* 25:63, 1986.

Busch, Heiner, Albrecht Funk, Udo Kauss, Wolf-Dieter Narr, and Falco Werkentin: *Die Polizei in der Bundesrepublik.* Frankfurt am Main, Campus Verlag, 1985.

Buttner, Christian: *Werte und Entscheidungskonflikte junger Polizisten.* Forschungsbericht des Hessische Stiftung Friedens und Konfliktforschung: Frankfurt am Main, 1986.

Chapman, Brian: *Police State.* New York, Praeger, 1970.

Collin, Richard O.: The Blunt Instruments: Italy and the Police. In John Roach and Jurgen Thomaneck: *Police and Public Order in Europe.* London, Croom-Helm, 1985.

Comfort, Alex: *Authority and Delinquency in the Modern State.* London, Sphere, 1970.

Craig, Gordon: *The Germans,* New York, Putnam, 1982.

Creifeld, Carl: *Rechtswörterbuch.* München, C. H. Beck'she Verlag, 1976.

Crozier, Michel: *The Bureaucratic Phenomenon.* Chicago, University of Chicago Press, 1964.

Dahrendorf, Ralf: *Society and Democracy in Germany.* Garden City, Doubleday, 1967.

— — — *Law and Order.* London, Stevens and Son, 1985.

Davis, Kenneth C.: *Discretionary Justice in Europe and America*. Urbana, University of Illinois Press, 1975.

— — *Police Discretion*. St. Paul, West Publishing Company, 1975a.

Deutsche Polizei: Die Polizei, dein Freund und Helfer. Jan.: 115, 1960.

Deutscher Beamtenbund: *Mitbestimmung und Personalvertretungsrecht*. Geschäftsbericht der Bundesleitung des Deutschen Beamtenbundes, 1979.

Deutscher Polizeibeamte. Amtliches Organ des Kamaradschaftbandes Deutscher Polizeibeamten, Vol. 1, Nr. 1, 1933.

Die Neue Polizei: In Memoriam: Herbert Kalicinski. *Vol. 16*, Nr. 5., 1962.

Die Polizei: Zum Polizeiverwaltungsgesetz. *Vol. 28:*219, 1931.

Dierski, L.: Polizeiliche Zuständigkeiten zu Beginn der Bundesrepublik Deutschland. Pamphlet Nr. PG 6-2-50 in the historical collection of the Polizei-Führungsakademie, Münster-Hiltrup (undated).

Dietel, Alfred: Der Brokdorf-Beschluss des Bundesverfassungsgericht und seine Bedeutung für die polizeiliche Praxis. *Die Polizei, 76:*335. 1985.

— — Neue Ansätze zur weiteren professionalizierung der Polizeiarbeit. *Die Polizei 77:*381, 1986.

Domnik, Otto: 30 Jahre Bereitschaftspolizei. *Bereitschaftspolizei Heute, December:*2, 1981.

Elster, Botho: Hat die deutsche Polizei "militarischen Charakter?" *Zeitschrift für Politik 23:*73, 1933.

Endruweit, Gunther: Ein Neues Polizeiliches Gegenüber. *Schriftenreihe der Polizei-Führungsakademie, 4:*344. 1984.

Englisch et al.: *Die Polizei, Dein Freud, Dein Helfer*. Breslau, Verlag Ferdinand Hirt, 1936.

Erdmann, Karl-Dietrich: *Deutschland unter der Herrschaft des Nationalsozialismus, 1933-1939*. München, Deutscher Taschenbucher Verlag, 1980.

Evangelische Akademie Bad Boll: *Rechtssicherheit und Gesellschaftlichen Konsensus*. Sitzungsbericht über der Tagung von 21-23 Mai, 1984.

Feest, Johannes and Erhard Blankenburg: *Die Definitionsmacht der Polizei*. Düsseldorf, Bertelsmann-Universitätsverlag, 1972.

Fogelson, Robert: *Who Riots? A Study in Participation in the 1967 Riots*. New York, Praeger, 1968.

— — *Big-City Police*. Cambridge, Harvard University Press, 1977.

Fowler, Norman: *After the Riots — the Police in Europe*. London, Davis-Poynter, 1979.

Friedrich, Carl and Zbigniew Brezinski: *Totalitarian Dictatorship and Autocracy*. Cambridge, Harvard University Press, 1956.

Frohlich, Helmut: Leitlinien and Leitsätze anlässlich der Eröffnung der Bremischen Hochschule für Öffentliche Verwaltung. *Die Polizei, 71:*1, 1980.

Fullgrabe, Uwe: Berufsstress und Motivation bei Polizeibeamten: das "Burn-out Syndrom." *Die Polizei 73:*43, 1982.

Fyfe, James Joseph: *Shots Fired: An Examination of New York City Police Firearms Discharges*. Ann Arbor, University Microfilms International, 1978.

GAL: *Ist Hamburg's Polizei Sauber?* Eine Dokumentation der GAL. Hamburg, Hein und Co., 1982.

Gebauer, Hans-Jürgen: Aufbau und Gliederung im Führungsstab des Bundesministers des Innern. *Die Polizei 73:*13, 1982.

Gereke, Heinz: Die Auswerkungen des Polizeigesetzes auf der Organisation der baden-württembergische Polizei. In *10 Jahre Baden-Württembergische Polizei, Ein Dokumentar-bericht.* Stuttgart. Polizei-Verlag Heinz Krause, 1963.

Gewerkschaft: Die Gleichgültigkeit: eine Zeiterscheinigung oder eine deutsche Eigenart? In *Woche der Polizei, 1953.* Stuttgart, OTV, 1953.

– – – Kapitulation vor dem Verbrechen? Eine Untersuchung über die Situation der Kriminalpolizei in der Bundesrepublik Deutschland. Hilden, Gewerkschaft der Polizei, 1968.

Goeschel, Albrecht, Anselm Meyer, und Gertraud Schmidbauer: *Beitrage zu einer Soziologie der Polizei.* Frankfurt am Main, Suhrkamp, 1971.

Goldstein, Herman: *Policing a Free Society.* Cambridge, Ballinger, 1977.

Gregory, Frank: The British police system-with special reference to public order problems. In John Roach and Jurgen Thomaneck: *Police and Public Order in Europe.* London, Croom-Helm, 1985.

Gremmler, Eckhard: Konfliktsregelung als Aufgabe professionalizierter Schutzpolizei. *Die Polizei, 77:*383, 1986.

Grommeck, Siegfried and Günter Neumann: Basisaspekte modernen Führungsverhaltens. *Die Polizei 66:*339, 1975.

Grosser, Alfred: *Germany in Our Time.* New York, Praeger, 1971.

Gude, Max: Polizei und Rechtsprechung. ÖTV Bericht uber der Arbeitstagung *Woche der Polizei:*102, 1961.

Guiesmer, Friedrich: Der Weg zu und mit der GdP. In Gewerkschaft der Polizei: *Die Deutsche Polizei.* Hilden/Berlin, Verlag Deutsche Polizei, 1980.

Gurr, Ted Robert: *Rogues, Rebels, and Reformers.* Beverly Hills, Sage, 1976.

Guyot, Dorothy: The organization of police departments—changing the model from the army to the hospital. *Criminal Justice Abstracts* 9:231, 1977.

Haber, Horst von: Studentendemonstration in Heidelberg. *Die Polizei, 56:*139, 1965.

Habermas, Jürgen: Recht und Gewalt—ein deutsches Trauma. In Jürgen Habermas: *Die Neue Unübersichtlichkeit, Kleine Politische Schriften V.* Frankfurt am Main, Suhrkamp, 1985.

Harms, Klaus: *Mandat der Freiheit.* Berlin, Littner Verlag, 1970.

Heinson, Hans-Heinrich: Der Verlauf der Brockdorf-Demonstration im Juni, 1986 aus polizeilichen Sicht und Wertung. *Die Polizei, 77:*275, 1986.

Helfer, Christian and Wiegand Siebel: *Das Berufsbild des Polizeivollzugsbeamten, Bd. I-VII.* Gutachten im Auftrag der Ständigen Konferenz der Innenminister der Länder. Saarbrücken, Universität des Saarlandes, 1975.

Hepp, Robert: Amtsprestige oder Sozialprestige? Die Polizei zwischen Staat und Gesellschaft. *Zeitschrift für Politik,* 24:122, 1977.

Hermann, Ingo: Darum geht es. *Kriminalist 14,* Nr. 1, 1982a; Nr. 6, 1982b.

Higham, Robin: *Bayonets in the Streets—Use of Troops in Civil Disturbances.* Lawrence, University Press of Kansas, 1969.

Hofstede, Geert: The cultural relativity of organizational practices and theories. *Journal of International Business Studies, Fall:* 75, 1983.

– – – Cultures Consequences. Beverly Hills, Sage, 1980.

Hohn, H.: Gesetzgeberische Probleme auf dem Gebiet der Polizei. *Deutsche Polizei 4,* 9/10, 1951. Continued in *5,* 1/2, 1952.

Holdaway, Simon: *Inside the British Police.* Oxford, Basil Blackwell, 1984.

Hornthal, Steffan: Die Persönlichkeit von Polizeibeamten. *Die Polizei, 66*:334, 1975.

Hubner, Klaus: Ein Jubilaeum seltener Art: 10 Jahre Kontaktsbereichbeamte in Berlin. *Die Polizei 75*:193, 1984.

Humanistische Union Berlin: *Demokratischen Rechtsstaat Zwischen Individuellen Terror und Polizeigewalt.* Berlin, ABC Druckwerkstatt, 1975.

Hunold, Tonis: *Polizei in der Reform.* Dusseldorf, Econ Verlag, 1968.

Innenministerium Hamburg: *Festschrift: 150 Jahre Hamburger Polizei, 1814-1964.* Hamburg, Steintor Verlag, 1964.

Innere Sicherheit: The Internal Security Plan developed by the Standing Conference of Interior Ministers, 1974.

Jacob, Herbert: *German Administration Since Bismarck.* New Haven, Yale Uniersity Press, 1963.

Jesse, Eckhard: *Streitbare Demokratie.* Berlin, Colloquim Verlag, 1980.

Johnson, Chalmers: *Revolutionary Change.* Boston, Little-Brown, 1966.

Kalicinski, Herbert: Aufgaben and Ziele des Polizei Instituts. Speech to police leaders, April 27, printed in *Bericht* über die 3. Arbeitstagung für Polizeichefs, Polizei-Institut Hiltrup, 27-29 April, 1950.

— — — Die Anforderungen an eine modern deutsche Polizei. *Staat und Polizei,* Bericht aus der Mai, 1955, Woche der Polizei. Stuttgart, ÖTV, 1955.

— — — Internationale Zusammenarbeit der Polizei. In *Schriftenreihe der Polizei-Institut Hiltrup.* Hiltrup, Polizei-Institut, 1960.

Kant, Immanuel: *Foundations of the Metaphysics of Morals.* Indianapolis, Bobbs-Merrill, 1959.

Kassem, M. Sami: Introduction: European versus American organization theories. In G. Hofstede and M. Kassem (eds.): *European Contributions to Organization Theory.* Assen, Van Gorcum, 1976.

Kaupen, Wolfgang: Das Verhältnis der Bevölkerung zum Recht in einer demokratischen Gesellschaft. In H. Steinert (ed.) *Die Prozess der Kriminalisierung.* München, Juventa Verlag, 1973.

Kelber, Richard: Polizeibeirate in NRW—Zu Kontrollinsuffizienz eines Kommunales Gremiums. *Bürgerrechte and Polizei (CILIP 26),* 1987, Nr. 1:74.

Kemperer, Robert M.: Police administration. In Edward H. Litchfield (ed.): *Governing Post-war Germany.* Ithaca, Cornell University Press, 1953.

Kiskalt, Hans: *Deutsches Polizeirecht.* Darmstadt, Stoytscheff, 1964.

Klausener, Erich, Christian Kerstens, and Robert Kemperer: *Kommentar zum Polizeiverwaltungsgestz vom 1 Juni, 1931.* Berlin, C. A. Waller Verlag, 1932.

Knocke: Essay upon assuming the position of new Police President in North-Rhine/Westphalia. *Deutsche Polizei, 5*:11/12. p. 103, 1954.

Kohler, Eric: The crisis in the Prussian Schutzpolizei, 1930-1932. In George Mosse (ed.): *Police Forces in History.* Beverly Hills, Sage, 1975.

Kontakt: Kontakt gleich Erziehung. *Deutsche Polizei, 6*:5/6, 37, 1953.

Kosch, Wilhelm (ed.): *Deutsches Literatur-Lexicon, biographisches und bibliographisches Handbuch.* Halle, M. Niemeyer, 1930.

Kosrya, Herbert: *Die Deutsche Kriminalpolizei in den Jahren 1945 bis 1955.* St. Michael, J. G. Blaschke Verlag, 1980.

Kriminalität: Die Kriminalität in der britischen Zone im Jahre 1950. *Deutsche Polizei* 4: 5/6, 1951.

Kuhlmann, Werner: *Moderne Gesellschaft, Moderne Polizei.* Hilden, Verlag Deutsche Polizei, 1969.

– – – Forward. In *Die Gebremste Polizei.* Berlin, Verlag Deutsche Polizei, 1974.

Langbein, John H.: *Comparative Criminal Procedure: Germany.* St. Paul, West Publishing Company, 1977.

Lange, Ralf: Hintergrund zum Verständnis und zur Beurteilung des Polizeieinsatzes in Hamburg am 8 Juni, 1986. *Die Polizei, 77:* 290, 1986.

Lapp, Peter J.: *Frontdienst in Frieden-die Grenztruppen der DDR.* Koblenz, Bernard u. Graefe, 1986.

Lehners, Richard: Gedanken zur aktuellen Probleme einer modernen Polizei. Speech on October 16, 1970 at Polizei-Führungsakademie-Hiltrup.

Lehr, Kurt: Die Zerschlagung der Kriminalpolizei Droht. *Der Kriminalist, 7:* 2, 1975.

Lehrplan: Lehrplan für Polizeibeamte des höheren Dienst. *Schriftenreihe des Polizei-Instituts Hiltrup.* Hiltrup, Polizei-Institut, 1956.

Lenz, Siegfried: *Deutschstunde.* Hamburg, Hoffman und Campe, 1968.

Liang, Hsi-Huey: *The Berlin Police Force in the Weimar Republic.* Berkeley, University of California Press, 1970.

LPD Hamburg: Hamburger Demonstration mit taktischen Einschliessung ist eine Chronologie der Einebung des Unterschiedes zwischen Friedlichkeit und Gewalt. *Die Polizei, 77:* 282, 1986.

Maikranz, Horst: Excessive Handlungen von Polizeibeamten-Ansätze fur ein Verhinderungskonzept. *Die Polizei, 77:*433, 1986.

Manning, Peter: *Police Work.* Cambridge, MIT Press, 1977.

Mather, F. C.: *Public Order in the Age of the Chartists.* New York, Augustus M. Kelley, 1967.

Meier-Weiser, Conrad: Polizei und Bevölkerung, Portrait eines Berufsstandes. *Schriftenreihe der Polizei-Führungsakademie:* 193, 1984, #3.

Michaelis, Karl: *Die Deutschen und ihre Rechtsstaat.* Berlin, De Gruyte, 1980.

Mikutet, Reinhold: Was an der Ausbildung in der Bereitschaftspolizei ist reformbedurftig? *Die Polizei, 61:* 220, 1970.

Milgram, Stanley: *Obedience to Authority.* New York, Harper and Row, 1974.

Militärregieung: *Gesetze und Verordnungen des Obersten Befehlshabers der Miliär-Regierung.* Muhlheim, Hagen & Co., 1945.

Military Government Gazette: Surrender of German police uniforms and equipment. Directive #6 of the Military Government of Germany, British Zone of Control, December 31, 1945.

Milner, Neal: *The Court and Local Law Enforcement.* Beverly Hills, Sage, 1971.

Mitteilungen: *Mitteilungen des Polizei-Institut Hiltrups,* 2 and 3, 1954, 1955.

Mokrusch, Richard: Das Personalvertretungsgesetz. *Der Kriminalist, 7:* 67, 1975.

Muir, William Kerr: *Police, Streetcorner Politicians.* Chicago, University of Chicago Press, 1978.

Muller, Gerhard O. W., and William Kroger: The meeting of two police ideas. *Journal of Criminal Law, Criminology, and Police Science, 51:* 257, 1960.

Müller, Wolfgang: Quo vadis Polizei. *Deutsche Polizei, 4:* 29, 1951.

Munsterman, Jürgen: *Schichtarbeit und Berufsverlauf von Polizeibeamten.* Bonn, Bundes-ministerium für Arbeit und Sozialordnung, 1980.

Murck, Manfred: *Demokratisierung in Organisationen: Soziologische und Kriminalpolitische Probleme einer Reform der Polizei.* München, Verlag für Recht and Sozialordnung, 1976.

Naether, Ernst-Albert: Informations-und Wissenstand der Bevölkerung Nordrhein-Westfalens in Bezug auf die Polizei und den Polizeiberuf. *Schriftenreihe der Polizei-Führungsakademie:*66, 1980, #1.

Niedermeyer, Petrus: Polizeiethisches Verhalten in der Wechselhaftigkeit unserer Zeit. *Die Polizei, 71:* 1, 1980.

Ohlsen, Rainer and Peter Kelling: *Polizei und Medien.* Stuttgart, Richard Boorberg Verlag, 1985.

Olsjewski, Hans: Verhaltenstraining im Polizeidienst. *Schriftenreihe der Polizei-Führungsakademie:* 261, 1985, #3.

Ostrom, Elinor, Roger Parks, and Gordon Whitaker: *Patterns of Metropolitan Policing.* Cambridge, Ballinger, 1978.

Otto, Detlef: Beweissicherung und Dokumentation. *Bereitschaftspolizei Heute:* 6, 1984, December.

Otto, Johannes: Polizeigas-oder Wasserwurfer? *Die Polizei, 56:*113, 1965.

OTV: *Staat und Polizei.* Bericht aus dem Mai, 1955, Woche der Polizei. Stuttgart, OTV, 1955.

Panaat, E. F.: Speech of welcome at opening of German-American Police Con-ference at Heidelberg, June 22, 1960. Document PG 6-20-25 in the Geschich-tliche Sammlung der Polizei-Führungsakademie, Münster-Hiltrup.

Paschner, Gunther: *Was Ist, Was Soll, Was Kann, Was Darf die Polizei?* Boppard am Rhein, Harold Boldt Verlag, 1970.

Pieschi, Gerhard; Einheit von Erziehung und Ausbildung. Speech to leaders of state police academies, October 22, 1980. Reprinted in *Schriftenreihe der Polizei-Führungsakademie:* 1980.

President's Commission: *The Challenge of Crime in a Free Society.* Report of the Presi-dent's Commission on Law Enforcement and Administration of Justice. Washington, D. C., U. S. Government Printing Office, 1967.

Preussisches Staatsministerium: *Preussische Gesetzsammlung Nr. 13604, Poli-zeiverwaltungsgesetz.* Berlin, R. von Decker's Verlag, 1931.

Raible, Eugen: *Geschichte der Polizei: Ihre Entwicklung in den alten Ländern Baden und Würt-temberg und in dem neuen Bundesland Baden-Württemberg.* Stuttgart, Richard Boorberg Verlag, 1963.

Rasch, Ernst: *Polizei und Polizeiorganisation.* Stuttgart, Richart Boorberg Verlag, 1980.

Reiff, Hermann and Gunter Wohrle: *Kommentar zum Polizeigesetz von Baden-Württemberg, 2. Auflag.* Stuttgart, Richard Boorberg Verlag, 1971.

Reiss, Albert: *The Police and the Public.* New Haven, Yale University Press, 1972.

Reuss-Ianni, Elizabeth: *Two Cultures of Policing.* New Brunswick, Transaction Books, 1983.

Riege, Paul: Gedanken über Tradition und Geschichtsforschung in der Polizei. *Der Polizeibeamte, 8:* 1958, #10.

— — — Kleine Polizeigeschichte. Lübeck, Georg Schmidt-Romhild, 1959.

Roach, John: The French police. In John Roach and Jurgen Thomaneck: *Police and Public Order in Europe.* London, Croom-Helm, 1985.

— — — and Jurgen Thomaneck: *Police and Public Order in Europe.* London, Croom-Helm, 1985.

Rohrig, Lothar: Frustrations und Aggressionsursachen für Ausbildenden in der Polizei. *Die Polizei 77*: 369, 1986.

Rossman, Egon: Zwei Jahrzehnte Staatsbürgerliche Bildung. *Die Polizei 56*: 214, 1965.

Roth, Jürgen: *Ist die Bundesrepublik eine Polizeistaat?* Darmstadt, Melzer Verlag 1972.

Rubinstein, Jonathan: *City Police.* New York, Farrar, Strauss, and Giroux, 1973.

Ruckriegel, Werner: Police Operations at Demonstrations. *Police Studies*: 148, 1986 #3.

Ruhmland, Ulrich: NVA, Nationale Volksarmee der DDR in Stichworte-V Auflag. Bonn, Bonner Druck und Verlagsgesellschaft, 1977.

Rupprecht, Reinhard: Zerschlagung der Kriminalpolizei? *Kriminalistik, 29*:170, 1975.

Sambuch, G. K.: Der Polizeibeamte im demokratischen Staat. *Deutsche Polizei, 4*: 11, 1951, Jan./Feb.

Scarman, Lord: Brixton and after. In John Roach and Jurgen Thomaneck: *Police and Public Order in Europe.* London, Croom-Helm, 1985.

Schabil, Robert: Zusammenarbeit vom Staatsanwaltschaft und Polizei. In *Justiz und Polizei*, Bericht über den Vierten Arbeitstagung, Woche der Polizei, Oktober, 1961.

Schafer Carl: *Stafprozessrecht.* Berlin, Walter de Guyter, 1976.

Schafer, Gerhard: *Die Praxis der Strafverfahrens-2 Auflag.* Stuttgart, Kohlhammer Verlag, 1980.

Schein, Edgar: Coming to a new awareness of organizational culture. *Sloan Management Review*: 3, 1984, Winter.

Scheer B. and H. Trubel: *Preussisches Polizeiverwaltungsgesetz vom 1 Januar, 1931.* Hamburg, Verlag Deutsche Polizei, 1961.

Scherer, Hans-Jürgen: Jugendprotest und demokratischen Staat. *Schriftenreihe der Polizei-Führungsakademie*: 76, 1984, #1.

Schirrmacher, Helmut: Die Polizei im Spannungsfeld der Demokratie. Speech to Gewerkschaft der Polizei, 16. Ordentlichen Deligiertenkongress, Hannover, October 17, 1979.

— — — Auswendung des Opportunitätsprinzip in der staatsanwaltlichen und gerichtlichen Praxis. *Die Polizei, 77*:191, 1986.

Schlussbericht: *Schlussbericht über die Arbeitstagung für Leiter und Abteilungsführer der Bereitschaftspolizeien der Länder.* Polizei-Institut Hiltrup, June 28-30, 1971.

Schmatz, Hans-Peter: *Die Grenzen des Opportunitätsprinzip im Heutigen Deutschen Polizeirecht.* Berlin, Duncker und Humboldt, 1966.

Schoenfelder, Heinrich: *Stafprozessordnung.* In *Deutsche Gesetze.* München, C. H. Beck'she Verlag, 1976.

Schorn, Walter: 20 Jahre Polizei-Institut Hiltrup. *Die Polizei, 56*:197, 1965.

Schreiber, Manfred: Die Schwabinger Kravalle. *Die Polizei, 56*:33, 1965.

— — — Anpassung und Weiterentwicklung polizeilichen Methoden. *Kriminalistik, 34*: 462, 1980.

Schriftenreihe: Die Modernisierung des Polizeidienstes. 16. Arbeitstagung für Polizeiverwendung. *Schriftenreihe der Polizei-Institut Hiltrup*: 1957, #4.

— — — Internationales Information. *Schriftenreihe der Polzei-Führungsakademie*: 1980.

Schroeder, Gunter: Allein mit offenem Handkragen und weisser Mütze überzeugen. *Deutsche Polizei 10*: 1982, #8.

Schutzinger: Die Einsatz der Bereitschaftspolizei. *Deutsche Polizei, 4*: 1951, #1.

Schwarze, Johannes: *Die Bayerische Polizei und Ihre Historische Funktion bei der Aufrechterhaltung der Öffentlichen Sicherheit in Bayern von 1919-1933*. München, Neue Schriftenreihe des Stadtsarchivs München, 1977.

Severing, Carl: *Im Wetter und Watterwinkel*. Bielefeld, Buchhandlung Volkswacht, 1927.

— — — *Mein Lebensweg, Bd. I*. Köln, Greven Verlag, 1950.

Siebecke, Horst: *Die Herren der Lage*. Köln, Verlag Wissenschaft und Politik, 1972.

Skolnick, Jerome: *Justice Without Trial*. New York, John Wiley and Sons, 1966.

Sommer, D.: Anzeigepflicht des Polizeibeamten. *Deutsche Polizei, 5*: 1952, July/August.

Sowik, Herbert: Die Persönlichkeit der Polizeibeamten im taglichen Dienst. *Schriftenreihe der Polizei-Führungsakademie*:222, 1980.

Sperrer, D.: Kommunale oder staatlicher Aufbau der Polizei in Nordrhein-Westfalen. *Deutsche Polizei, 4*: 75, 1951, July/August.

Spiegelberg, Rudiger: *Qualifikatorische Aspekte der Sozialisation in den Polizeiberuf*. Frankfurt am Main, Peter Lang, 1977.

Stead, Philip John: *The Police of France*. New York, MacMillan, 1983.

Steffan, Wiebke: Analyse polizeilicher Ermittlungstätigkeiten aus der Sicht der späteren Strafverfahrens. In *Schriftenreihe des Bundeskriminalamt*, Wiesbaden, 1976.

— — — Rückzug in die Schneckenhaüser. *Kriminalistik*, 1984 Nr. 2:70.

Stelter, Bernd: *Die "Explosive" Stimmung in der Polizei*. Lübeck, Georg Schmid-Romhild, 1973.

— — — and Bernhard Doerdelman (eds.): *Die Polizei und die Deutschen*. München, Delp'sche Verlag, 1968.

— — — and Gernot Steinhilper: Die polizeiliche Ermittlungstätigkeit. *Kriminalistik, 30*: 97, 1976, #3.

Sternsdorff, Hans-Wolfgang: Auf dem Weg zum Überwachungsstaat. *Der Spiegel* 1983, Nr. 2:46.

Stumper, Alfred: Föderalismus oder Zentralismus im Bereich der inneren Sicherheit? *Kriminalistik, 5*:193, 1976.

— — — Der Polizeiführer. *Die Polizei, 71*:265, 1980.

Tacke, Walter: Die Beurteilung der Polizei aus der Sichte der Bevölkerung. *Schriftenreihe der Polizei-Führungsakademie*:242, 1982 #3.

Tantorat, Hans-Georg: Fachhochschulstudium für Hamburg's Polizeikommissare. *Die Polizei, 71*:3, 1980.

Tetzlaff, Gerhard: Berufspflicht als Risiko im Polizeidienst. *Die Polizei, 71*:282, 1980.

Thoma, Dieter and Michael Stoffragen-Buller: Polizei in der öffentlichen Meinung. *Schriftenreihe der Polizei-Führungsakademie*: 76, 1984, #1.

Tophoven, Rolf: *GSG-9: German Response to Terrorism*. Koblenz, Bernard und Graefe Verlag, 1984.

Troitzsche, Wilhelm: *Die Polizeipflicht in Politisch Bewegten Zeiten.* Königsberg, Grafe und Unzer Verlag, 1933.

Ule, Carl-Herman and Ernst Rasch: Musterentwurf einer einheitlichen Polizeigesetz, Vorbemerkungen I-XV. In *Allgemeines Polizei und Ordnungsrecht, 2 Auflage.* Köln, Karl Heymans Verlag, 1982.

Ulrich, Speech by Württemberg-Baden's Interior Minister at Polizeicheftagung, Ludwigsburg, March 29, 1951.

van den Bergh, Ernst: Gedanken zur Organisation und Ausbildung der Polizei. Speech to 3. Arbeitstagung für Polizeichefs, Polizei-Institut Hiltrup, April 27-29, 1950.

von Harach, Eva Marie, Gräfin: *Grenzen und Möglichkeiten der Professionalisierung von Polizeiarbeit.* PhD. Dissertation, Westfalischen Wilhelms-Universität Münster, 1983.

Walker, Samuel: *A Critical History of Police Reform.* Lexington, D. C. Heath Lexington Books, 1979.

Walter, Bernd: *BGS-Polizei des Bundes.* Stuttgart, Richard Boorberg Verlag, 1983.

Wasby, Stephen: *Small Town Police and the Supreme Court.* Lexington, D. C. Heath Lexington Books, 1976.

Wasserman, Rudolf: Demokratie und Rechtsstaat-Gefahrdung einer Glückhaften Verbindung. *Schriftenreihe der Polizei-Führungsakademie:* 119, 1985, Nr. 2.

Weber, Max: *Rechtssoziologie.* Neuwied, Hermann Luchterhand Verlag, 1985.

Weigand, Thomas: *Anklagepflicht und Ermessen.* Baden-Baden, Nomos Verlag, 1978.

Weimer, Kilian: Die Bereitschaftspolizei und ihre Aufgaben. In *10 Jahre Baden-Württembergische Polizei: Ein Dokumentar-Bericht.* Stuttgart, Polizei-Verlag Heinz Krause, 1963.

Werkentin, Falco: *Die Restauration der Deutschen Polizei.* Frankfurt, Campus Verlag, 1984.

Wickert Institut, Tübingen: Befragung in Auftrag des Arbeitskreises II . . . . Described in Robert Hepp: Amtsprestige oder Sozialprestige? Die Polizei zwischen Staat und Gesellschaft. *Zeitschrift für Politik, 24*:122, 1974.

Williams, T. Alden: The army in civil disturbances. In Robin Higham (ed.) *Bayonets in the Streets-Use of Troops in Civil Disturbances.* Lawrence, University Press of Kansas, 1969.

Wilson, James Q. *Varieties of Police Behavior.* Cambridge, Harvard University Press, 1969.

ARCHIVAL MATERIAL

1. Hauptstaatsarchiv Stuttgart (HS). The records cited in this book are found in three collections:

        EA 2/11 137. "Entstaatlichung der Polizeiverwaltung."

        EA 2/11 173. "Aufbau, Organisation, Gliederung, Dienstbetrieb, usw. der Landespolizei, 1946-1949."

        EA 2/11 202. "Einstellung in den Polizeidienst, 1946-1953."

2. Geschichtliche Sammlung (Historical Collection), Polizei-Führungsakademie, Münster-Hiltrup. Military government orders and accounts of the rebuilding of the Bereitschaftspolizei may be found in this library.

INDEX

A

Abegg, Walter, 69
Academic community, police and, 182
Accountability
  U.S. and German police compared, 196-197
Adenauer, Konrad, 43, 66, 69
Administrative Police, 98, 101
Alienation
  between police and public, 180
Allied Control Commission, 24
Allied High Command
  and purging of Nazi elements, 88
  1949 orders for police, 103-104
  police requests to, 105-106
Allied High Commission, 43, 66
Allied powers, 4, 23, 76, 119
  plans for German police of, 65, 96, 97, 125, 126
Altman, Robert, 178
Ambiguity, tolerance of
  U.S. and Germany compared, 201
America
  military presence of, 91
  police of, and help for German police, 106
American zone, 43, 120
Anglo-Saxon legal systems, 202
Area Contact Officers (see Kontaktbereichs-beamte)
Arbeitsgemeinschaft kritischer Polizisten, 153
Auxiliary police
  in Baden-Württemberg, 178

B

Baader-Meinhof group, 151

Baden, 65, 106, 108, 178
Baden-Württemberg, 68, 89, 109, 126, 131, 141
  demonstrations in, 74
  police education in, 154
  police law of, 108, 114
  Police Union of, 3
Balbus, Isaac, 11
Banfield, Edward, 8
Basic Law (see Constitution, Federal Republic)
Bavaria, 34, 73, 87, 99, 106, 115, 141, 196
  border police of, 47, 81
  police law of, 108, 109, 113, 114
  Weimer Republic police of, 24, 25, 29
Bayerische Grenzpolizei (see Bavaria, border police of)
Bayley, David, 21, 92, 96, 164, 176, 187, 188, 191
Beamte, status of, 119
Becker, Theodore, 197
Beirat, polizei, 178, 188
Ben Barka, affair of, 185
Bennis, Warren, 127
Bepo (see Bereitschaftspolizei)
Berlin, 76, 106, 113, 168
  Area Contact Officers in, 189, 198
  Auxiliary police in, 178
  police organization in, 47
  Senate of, 77
  Weimar Republic police of, 9
Berlin-Charlottenburg, police academy at, 42
Berndt, Gunter, 156, 178
Bereitschaftspolizei (Bepo), 43, 47, 51, 57, 74, 75, 76, 112, 119, 183
  and demilitarization, 64-66
  and democratization, 154

and structural demilitarization, 77-81
as a back-up force, 92
as a strategic force, 206
federal support for, 46, 113
in demonstrations, 11-12
in Weimar, 24, 25
in Nazi Germany, 35
leadership in, 88
militarism in, 148
re-creation of, 66-72
recruits in, 70
training in, 71, 89, 152, 190
Weimar structure influence on, 130-131
Bereitschaftspolizei, Heute, 73
Berkley, George, 72, 97
Bereitschaftspolizei Zeitungsausschnitte, 67
Berlin, 31
Berufsbereinigungsgesetz, 34
Beuthen, 42
"Big Brother" state (*see* Überwachungsstaat)
Bismarck, Otto Von, 26, 33, 114
Bittner, Egon, 37
Blankenburg, Erhard, 75, 171
Blum, Joshua, 66
Bolle, B., 74, 151
Bonn, 88, 119
Booz, H., 99
Bottscher, Karl, 40, 98
Boydstun, John, 198
Bracher, Karl Dietrich, 22, 205
Bramshill, 85, 121, 141, 143
Bremen, 68, 99
 citizen ratings of police in, 168
 police Employee Committees in, 141
 police law in, 108
 police organization in, 50, 126
 police training in, 153
Brockdorf I (demonstration), 73, 114, 189
Brockdorf II (demonstration), 159-166
Breslau, University of, 42
Brill, K., 150
Britain, 18, 43, 84, 91, 120, 180, 185
Brogden, Michael, 115, 185
Brusten, Manfred, 132, 134
Bund Deutscher Kriminalbeamten, 142
Bundesgerichtshof (*see* Federal Supreme Court)
Bundesgrenzschutz, 43, 46, 72, 73, 74, 75, 93
 and democratization, 154
 as a strategic force, 183, 206

changes in law about, 47
creation of, 67
different functions in war and peace of, 81, 207
Employee Committees in, 142
in Brockdorf II, 161-166
integration into state police of, 113
militarism in, 82, 143-144, 208
Bundesgrenzverein, 143
Bundeskriminalamt, 46, 52, 54, 105, 113, 115, 180
Bundesministerium des Innern, 112
Bundesverfassungsgericht (*see* Federal Constitutional Court)
Bundesverfassungsschutz, 52
Bureau of Justice Statistics, 54
Bürger Beobachten die Polizei, 188
Bürgerkrieg, 121
Bürgerrechte und Polizei, 82, 83, 177, 179, 189, 197, 203
Busch, Heiner, et al., 80, 84, 113, 115, 117, 134, 153, 179, 181, 182
Busgeld, 174

C

California, 194
Carabinieri, 59
Census law, 180
Chapman, Brian, 37, 122
Christian Democratic Union (CDU), 141, 167, 168, 189
Citizenship, training in, 15
Civil order control, 5, 8-17, 66, 78, 115-118, 206-208
Civil order problems, 72-77
Civil unrest, 12
Civilian leadership, 90
Civilian Review Boards, 197
Collin, Richard, 185
Comfort, Alex, 9
Communalization of police, 95-112
 arguments for, 95-97
 the German experience of, 97-103
 decline of, 103-112
Communist Party, 148
Communists, 184
Constitution of the Federal Republic of Germany, 42, 53, 68, 103, 105
 provisions regarding police in, 45-46
Control of police power, 187-192

CS gas, 84
Creifeld, Carl, 170-171
Craig, Gordon, 86
Crime rates, German, 45
Criminal justice programs, 153
Criminal law, 47, 114
Criminal procedure, 173, 190
Crozier, Michel, 194
Culture, police organizational, 192-203

D

Dahrendorf, Ralf, 3, 22, 77, 164, 201
Data gathering, police involvement in, 7, 180-181, 191
Davis, Kenneth Culp, 171
Decentralization of police, 3, 23, 118-121
Delinquency, police, 9
Deutschstunde, 13
Demilitarization, 3
  after World War I, 23-25
  Allied plans for, 61-72
  armaments in, 83-84
  fate of, 77-93
  leadership in, 87-91
  organizational, 58, 60-61
  strategic, 58-59
Democracy
  concept of, 126-127
  in organizations, 127-128
  in police organizations, 128-129
  periods of democratic reforms of police in Germany, 148-154
Democratization, 3, 23
  after World War I, 25-30
  German police and, 125-157
  early post-war efforts at, 129-136
  ethos of, 146-155
  leadership and, 155-157
  personnel and, 131-135
  structural aspects of, 135-146
Demonstrations
  Brockdorf I, 73-74
  Brockdorf II, 160-164
  Frankfurt airport, 73
Denazification of police, 38-42, 87, 125
Denmark, police strength in, 52
Der Spiegel, 76, 77, 82, 142, 144, 162, 180, 188, 189
de Tocqueville, Alexis, 193
Deutsche Polizei, 44, 75, 106, 145

Der Polizeibeamte, 61
Der Württembergischer Landjäger, 58
Deutscher Beamtenbund, 27, 85, 141, 142
Deutscher Gewerkschaftbund, 121
Deviance control, police function of, 5-8
Die Neue Polizei, 42
Die Neue Zeitung, Frankfurt, 68, 69
Die Neue Zeitung, Munchen, 116
Die Polizei, 28, 31, 89, 172, 181
Die Polizei Zeitung Baden Württemberg, 74, 135, 153
Dierski, Paul, 35, 52, 67, 68, 98
Dietel, Alfred, 115, 139
Die Welt, 67, 68, 69, 117
Domnik, Otto, 78, 80
Donner, 39
Dortmund, 113

E

East Europe, 119
East Germany, 67
East Prussia, 42
Education, police
  problems with, 145
  unions and, 144
  United States experience with, 144
Egidi, L., 95
Eichhorn, Emil, 31
"Einheitliches Laufbahn," 120
Einheitliches Polizeigesetz, 113
Einzeldienst, 71
Elbe River, 73
Elster, Botho, 59
EMNID Institute, 115, 167
Empire, German, 30, 83, 85
Empiricism, culture of, 194-203
Endruweit, Gunther, 169
Engelbrecht, Rolf, 106
England, police reform in, 166
Englisch et al., 8
Enlightenment, 122
Environment, 15, 45, 72
Era of Good Feeling, 42-45
Erdmann, Karl-Dietrich, 34, 35
Esslingen, 99
Ethos, organizational, 17-18
Europe, Germany's location in, 91
European Court of Human Rights, 173
European Convention on Human Rights, 173

Evangelische Akademie Bad Boll, 159
Executive police (*see* Vollzugspolizei)
Exhibition, 1926 Great Police, 7

F

Federal Bureau of Investigation (FBI), 18, 19, 115
Federal Constitutional Court (Bundesverfassungsgericht), 47, 77, 114, 115, 148, 160, 180, 189, 190
Federation Supérieure des Chefs Internationales de Police (FSCIP), 44
Feeley, Malcolm, 197
Feest, Johannes, 74, 132, 151, 171, 182, 194
Fogelson, Robert, 61, 197
Formal rationality, 11
Fouché, Joseph, 18
Fowler, Norman, 26
France
  and German demilitarization of police, 58-59
  civil order control in, 60, 207
  control of police power in, 188
  military presence of, 91
  organizational culture in, 193
  police of, 18, 25, 43, 52, 85, 96, 97, 133, 166, 185
  student demonstrations in, 72
  Tunisian police training in, 154
Frankfurt, 73, 77, 113
Free Democratic Party (FDP), 189
Freikorps, 13, 24
Frey, Christian, 159
Friedrich, Carl, 23
"Friend and Helper," police as, 7-8, 31, 44
Frohlich, Helmut, 153
Führung, innere, 15
Fullgrabe, Uwe, 156
Fyfe, James, 84

G

GAL (*see* Green Party)
Gebauer, Hans-Jurgen, 75
Gehobener Dienst, 47, 52
Gendarmerie, 25, 59, 97, 118
Geography, distribution of German police according to, 132
Gerecke, Heinz, 99, 107, 108
German-American Police Conference, 125

German Constitutional Court (*see* Federal Constitutional Court)
German Democratic Republic (*see* East Germany)
German Empire (*see* Empire, German)
German Federation of Unions (Deutscher Gewerkschaftsbund), 143
German Federal Republic, police organization in, 36-45
Germersheim, 101
Gestapo, 7, 36
Gewerkschaft der Polizei (Union of Police), 75, 76, 77, 83, 85, 120, 121, 137, 142, 149
Gleichschaltung, 33
Goebbels, Joseph, 35
Goeschel, Albrecht, 74
Goldstein, Herman, 60, 126, 129, 197
Göring, Hermann, 34
Gottinger Tageblatt, 69
Grassner, Kurt, 57, 69
Great Britain, 110, 115
  civil order control in, 207
  Police Authorities in, 98, 187
  police strength in, 52
Green Alternative list (*see* Green Party)
Green Party, 86, 160, 163, 164, 168, 178
Gregory, Frank, 207
Gremmler, Eckhard, 139
Grommeck, Siegfried, 156
Grosser, Alfred, 15
GSG-9, 90, 146
Gude, Max, 172, 174
Guiesmer, Friedrich, 143
Gurr, Ted Robert, 92
Guest workers, 131
Guyot, Dorothy, 60
Gymnasium, 70

H

Haber, Horst von, 83
Habermas, Jürgen, 187, 204, 205
Hamburg, 24, 39, 68, 113, 141, 168
  police law in, 108
  police of, and Brockdorf II, 160-162
  police training in, 153
  state court decision on, 189
  study of police officers in, 133
Hamburger Abendblatt, 68
Harms, Klaus, 149, 151

Heidelberg, 104, 125
Heidenheim, 39
Heilbronn, 39, 99, 103, 104
Heimannsberg, 41
Heinson, Hans-Heinrich, 160, 161, 162
Helfer, Christian, 80, 132, 139, 151, 152, 154, 169
Hemmings, 160
Hepp, Robert, 139, 145
Hermann, Ingo, 136, 137
Hesse, 76, 99, 101, 106, 108, 126, 141
Higham, Robin, 110
Himmler, Heinrich, 34
Hitler, Adolf, 34, 97
Hobbes, Thomas, 122, 205
Hofstede, Geert, 193, 194, 195, 201
Hohn, H., 71, 107, 116
Holdaway, Simon, 185
Home Office (British), 18
Homogeneity, structural, U.S. and Germany compared, 196
Hoover, J. Edgar, 18
Hornthal, Steffan, 133
House occupation (Hausbesitzung), 72
Hubner, Klaus, 198
Humanistische Union Berlin, 74, 151
Hunold, Tonis, 7, 151, 155, 156

I

Identification and Documentation Troops, 76
India, 188
Inflation, of 1923, 22
Innere Führung, 149, 155
Interior Minister, relation to communal police of, 104, 105, 106, 107
Interior Ministers
  Standing Conference of, 46, 81, 85, 112, 113, 114, 196
  Study of Police commissioned by, 151
Interior Ministry, 46, 90, 97, 118, 175
  and civil order, 75
  in Italy and France, 59
  police leaders in, 121
  Relation of Landespolizei to, 100-103
Internal Affairs Unit, 197
Internal Security Plan, 112, 136, 137
International Association of Chiefs of Police, 95
International Federation of Police Leaders (FSCIP), 44

International Police Association, 42
Interpol, 46
Italy, 59, 60, 85, 97, 166, 185

J

Jacob, Herbert, 23, 24, 33, 83, 114
Japan, 18, 176, 177, 193
Jesse, Eckhardt, 113
Johnson, Chalmers, 9
Justice system, German, and police, 170-176

K

Kalicinski, Herbert, 42, 44, 62, 88, 124, 129, 149, 150
Kant, Immanuel, 13, 31
Kapp Putsch, 14, 26, 29
Karlsruhe, 101, 107
Kassem, M. Sami, 127
Kaupen, Wolfgang, 167
Kelber, Richard, 178
Kemperer, Robert, 28, 36, 125
Kerstens, Christian, 28
Kiskalt, Hans, 11
Klausener, Erich, 28
Kleve, Brockdorf II in, 161-166
Knocke, 90
Koban, Japanese, 18
Kohler, Eric, 16, 19
Kontaktbereichsbeamte (Area Contact Officers), 177, 198-199
Kosch, Wilhelm, 26
Kosyra, Herbert, 36, 46, 101, 136
Kreis Steinburg, 160, 162
Kreuzberg, 76
Kreuzer, General, 69
Kriminalkommissar, 138
Kriminalpolizei, 36, 39, 44, 47, 64, 86, 113, 120, 146
  contentment with police work of, 135
  cooperative decision-making in, 156
  investigation of crimes in, 176
  in Weimar Republic, 137
  relations with prosecutor of, 175, 176
  rivalry with Schupo of, 136-140
  women in, 131
Kriminalpolizei Fachhochschule, 138
Kripo (*see* Kriminalpolizei)
Kuhlmann, Werner, 83, 85, 144, 151, 177

L

Landespolizei, 100, 104
Landespolizeischule, 47
Landjäger, 25, 58, 118
Landrat, 33, 162
Langbein, John, 170
Lange, Ralf, 163
Lapp, Peter, 54
Lateral mobility, German police and, 155
Lautmann, Rudiger, 132
Law Enforcement Education Program, 144, 199
Legal systems, 194
Legitimacy, crisis of, 11
Legalitätsprinzip, 170-172
Lehners, Richard, 186
Lehr, Kurt, 120, 137
Lenz, Siegfried, 13
Liang, Hsi-Huey, 7, 13, 14, 24, 26, 27, 29, 30, 34, 59, 83, 135, 137, 138
Locke, John, 122
Lower Saxony, 47, 49, 68, 108, 178
Ludwigsburg, 39, 105, 106

M

Madison, James, 192
Maier, Reinhold, 104
Maikranz, Horst, 10, 178
Mainz, 113
Mannheim, 68, 101, 107
Mannheimer Morgen, 68
Manning, Peter, 134, 194
Maslow, Abraham, 156
Mather, F.C., 117
McCloy, John, 67
Maier-Weiser, Conrad, 167, 174, 175
Michaelis, Karl, 122
Mikutet, Reinhold, 71, 89
Milgram, Stanley, 15
Military Government of Germany (Militärregierung), 38, 103
Military Government Gazette, 63
Milner, Neal, 197
Ministry of Justice, 119, 175
Minorities, in German police, 131
Missile deployment, American, 72
Mitbestimmung, 141
Mittlerer Dienst, 47, 51, 70
Mobile Action Commando, 90

Mobility, career, 200
Model Police Law, 81, 190
Mokrusch, Richard, 142
Muir, William K., 37
Müller, Wolfgang, 106, 116
Murck Manfred, 10, 74, 132, 134, 151, 171, 175, 179, 194
Munich, 43, 72, 109, 113, 182, 204

N

Naether, Ernst-Albert, 167
Name tags, 83, 189
Napoleon, 18
National Guard, U.S., 53, 79, 110, 197
National Institute of Justice, 182
Nationalization trends in German policing since 1950, 112-115
National Socialist period (Naziism, Third Reich), 8, 15, 22, 23, 25, 41, 42, 44, 55, 74, 78, 83, 87, 97
  data-gathering in, 181
  effect on today's police of, 165, 184, 205
  effect on police political involvement of, 150
  police in, 3, 14, 33-36, 63, 64
  police in exile in, 123-124
  purging of police of, 100
Naziism (*see* National Socialist period)
Neumann, Gunter, 156
Niedermeyer, Petrus, 151
NATO (North Atlantic Treaty Organization), 109, 131
North Rhine-Westphalia, 42, 52, 88, 108, 112, 114, 115, 196
  analysis of police recruits in, 132
  behavioral training for police in, 167
  Bepo of, in Brockdorf II, 162
  citizen attitudes toward police in, 167
  Kripo training in, 138
  Police Authorities in, 178, 188
Norway, 188
Nurnberg, 117

O

Obedience, police obligation to, 13-17
Occupation, Allied, 38-42
Occupational contentment, police, 134-135
Öffentliches Transport und Verkehr (ÖTV), 121, 142, 150
Ohlsen, Rainer, 179

Ohnesorg, Benno, 165
Olsjewski, Hans, 179
Olympic games, 1972, 151
Opportunitätsprinzip, 170, 171
Ordinances, police, 28
Ordnungswidrigkeiten, 174
Oregon State Police, 106
Organizational culture, 4, 192-203
Ostrom, Elinor, 96, 184
Otto, Detlef, 76, 172
ÖTV (*see* Öffentliches Transport and Verkehr)

P

Panaat, E.F., 72, 125
Parks, Roger, 96, 184
Parliament, German, 166
Paschner, Gunther, 85, 151, 165, 179
People's Police (*see* Volkspolizei)
Personalrat, 140, 141, 142
Personalvertretungsgesetze, 141
PFA Schriftenreihe, 53, 71
Pforzheim, 107
Police
  abuse of coercive or manipulative power by, 6
  American, 10, 128
  culture of, 17
  data gathering and dissemination in, 7
  density in FRG, 52
  framework for analysis, 17
  functions of, 37-38
  in dictatorships, 9
  organization of, in Germany, 45-55
  public opinion of, 7
  ratio of personnel to population in German states, 54
  reasons for joining, 16
  recruits, 10
  strength in Germany, 53
  tasks of, 5-17
Police Authorities, British, 98
Police Authorities, German (*see* Beirat, Polizei)
Police-community relations, 23, 159-186
  after World War I, 30-33
  mutual perceptions, 166-170
  improvement of, 176-183
  tensions in, during 1970's and 1980's, 183-184

Police exposition of 1926, 32
Police Foundation, 182, 198
Police Institute at Münster-Hiltrup, 62, 124, 149, 150
Police Leadership Academy (*see* Polizei-Führungsakademie)
Police law of 1921, 97
Police Nationale, 97
Police schools, 47, 51
Police unions, in Weimar Republic, 27
Polizei Behörden (*see* Administrative Police)
Polizei-Führungsakademie, 32, 42, 45, 52, 53, 67, 89, 112, 120, 152, 154, 167
Polizeistaat, 122
President's Commission (U.S.), 144, 199
Pieschi, Gerhard, 71
Press officers, police use of, 179
Preussisches Staatsministerium, 12
Professionalization of police, 119, 157
Progressive Era (U.S.), 61
Prussia, 13, 23, 24, 25, 26, 29, 33, 34, 57, 208
Prussian Comprehensive Police Law of 1891, 28
Prussian Police Administrative Act of 1931, 12, 26, 28, 43, 108, 121, 189
Public education function of police, 5

R

Raible, Eugen, 21, 24, 28, 35, 57, 59, 64, 65, 67, 84, 109, 110, 111
Rasch, Ernst, 81, 126, 181
Rationalism, culture of, 194-203
Readiness Police (*see* Bereitschaftspolizei)
Reagan, Ronald, 75
Rechtmässigkeit, 11
Rechtsstaat, 28, 119, 121-123, 170, 196, 205-206
Refugees (Polish), 102
Reichstag, 33
Reiff, Herman, 178
Reiss, Albert, 126, 128, 182
Republican Security Companies (French), 206, 207
Reuss-Ianni, Elizabeth, 134, 200
Rhineland-Palatinate, 47, 48, 108, 114, 126
Riege, Paul, 21, 34, 35, 59, 61, 62, 107, 108
Roach, John, 166, 185
Rohrig, Lothar, 178
Romano-Germanic legal systems, 202

Rossman, Egon, 150
Rote Hilfe, 113
Roth, Jürgen, 74, 151, 182
Rousseau, Jean-Jacques, 122
Ruckriegel, Werner, 74
Ruhmland, Ulrich, 54
Rundstedt, Gert von, 34
Rupprecht, Reinhard, 140
Russia, 67, 91, 119, 188

S

Saar, University of, 80
Saarland, 108
SA, 35, 36
St. Cyr, 133
Sambuch, G.K., 149
San Diego Community Profile Program, 198
Scarman, Lord., 117
Schabil, Robert, 176
Schafer, Carl, 173
Schafer, Gerhard, 176
Schafer, Rudolf, 40, 98
Schein, Edgar, 192
Scheer, B., 28
Scherer, Hans-Jürgen, 178
Schirrmacher, Helmut, 132, 143, 144, 171
Schleswig-Holstein, 73, 108, 114, 115, 160, 178, 196
Schmatz, Hans-Peter, 171
Schoenfelder, Heinrich, 173
Schools, police 31
Schorn, Walter, 63
Schräder, Ernst, 27
Schräder-Verband, 27
Schreiber, Manfred, 72
Schroeder Gunter, 76
Schupo (*see* Schutzpolizei)
Schutzpolizei, 36, 39, 44, 47, 64, 81, 113, 120, 135
  characteristics and problems of, 132
  demilitarization in, 86
  in Prussia, 19
  rivalry with Kripo of, 136-140
  uniforms in, 82
  upgrading professional status of, 139
Schutzinger, 64
Schutzmann, 59, 119
Schwabinger Kravalle, 72
Schwäbisch-Gmund, 103
Schwarze, Johannes, 13, 29

SEK (*see* Special Action Commandos)
Sessar, K., 171
Severing, Carl, 4, 7, 27, 41, 123, 124
  and demilitarization of police, 57
  and police reforms in the Weimer Republic, 19, 26-27, 29, 31-33
  and military takeover of Prussian police, 29
Selwyn, J.A.S., 63
Sherry, Michael, 198
Sicherheitspolizei (Sipo), 24, 31
Siebecke, Horst, 151, 182
Siebel, Wiegand, 80, 132, 139, 151, 152, 154, 169
Silesia, Upper, 42
Single career track (Einheitliches Laufbahn), 155
Sipo (*see* Sicherheitspolizei)
Skolnick, Jerome, 182, 193
Slater, Philip, 127
Social class, German police and, 132, 133-134
Social Democratic Party (SPD), 4, 22, 23, 26, 27, 29, 30, 33, 41, 123, 167
  influence of police on, 16
  name tags for police and, 189
  police reform and, 151
  re-creation of Bepo and, 68, 69
  Weimar Republic and, 14, 19
Soviets, 43
Sozialistische Monatschefte, 26
Sociological studies, German police as subject of, 132-135
Sommer, D., 83
South Africa, 84
Spartacusbund, 13
Special Action Commandos (SEK), 74, 90, 161
Sperrer, D., 106
Spiegelberg, Rudiger, 132, 151
SS, 15, 36, 69
Stead, Philip John, 52
Steffan, Wiebke, 171, 176, 182
Steinhilper, Gernot, 176
Stelter, Bernd, 135, 151, 176
Sternsdorff, Hans-Wolfgang, 113
Stoffragen-Buller, Michael, 179
Strafgeld, 174
Strafrecht, 174
Structure, police organizational
Structural change, 78-85
Stumper, Alfred, 113, 120, 156

Stuttgart, 39, 40, 99, 102, 104, 107
Süddeutsche Zeitung, 74, 87, 88
Supreme Court of Germany (*see* Federal Constitutional Court)
Swiss, 87

T

Tacke, Walter, 115
Tantorat, Hans-Georg, 153
Terrorism, 72, 75, 180-181
Tetzlaff, Gerhard, 172
Third Reich (*see also* National Socialism), 4, 8, 21, 22, 28, 33, 79, 100, 184, 196
Thirty Years War, 91
Thoma, Dieter, 179
Thomaneck, Jürgen, 166
Tophoven, Rolf, 146
Training, German police, 51, 152, 153, 190, 203-205
    U.S. and German compared, 197-200
Troitzche, Wilhelm, 12
Trubel, H., 28
Tunisia, police of, in Germany, 154

U

Überwachungsstaat (Big Brother State), 180
Ulm, 39, 99
Ulm University, 153
Ulrich, 107
Uniform Police Operations Law, 113
Uniforms, police, 114
Unions, police, 119, 140, 142, 146
United States, 7, 59, 80, 110, 116, 120, 128, 188
    Alienation between police and public in, 180
    civil order control in, 207
    Civilian Review Boards in, 187
    Community organization of police in, 98
    criminal investigation in, 140
    nationalization of police operations in, 115
    police reform in, 166
    police research in, 182
    student demonstrations in, 72

V

van den Berghe, Ernst, 41, 42, 67
Verbrechen, 174

Vergehen, 174
Verhältnismässigkeit, 170-172
Versailles Treaty, 22, 24
Volkspolizei, 67
Volkswacht, 26
Vollmer, August, 61
Vollzugspolizei, 37, 98
von Harach, Eva Marie, 27, 29, 139, 203
von Papen, Franz, 29

W

Walker, Samuel, 61
Walter, Bernd, 81
Wasby, Stephen, 197
Wasserfingen, 101
Wasserman, Rudof, 178
Wasserschutzpolizei, 47
Weber, Max, 194, 202
Wehrmacht, 57, 69, 86, 110
Wendlingen, 102
Weigand, Thomas, 171
Weimar Republic, 4, 7, 12, 21, 22, 25, 26, 27, 29, 30, 41, 44, 45, 64, 78, 79, 83, 93, 118, 119
    civil unrest in, 13
    effect on police operations today, 108-112, 130, 165, 206
    military background of police in, 85
    police history in, 22-33
    police promotions in, 135
    political involvement of police in, 150
    Schutzpolizei in, 19
    Rechtsstaat and, 122, 123
Weiss, 41
Weitmann, Ludwig, 105
Werkentin, Falco, 34, 47, 68, 72, 82, 98, 109, 110, 116, 120, 121, 123, 179, 182, 197, 203, 206
Westfalische Nachrichten, 88, 106
Westfalische Rundschau, 68, 69
Whig school of police history, 185
Whitaker, Gordon, 96, 184
Wickert Institute, 166
Wiesbaden, 46, 113
Williams, T. Alden, 117, 207
Wilson, James Q., 126
Wilson, Orlando, 61
Wilster Marsh, 73
Wohrle, Gunter, 178

World War I, 22
World War II, 10, 12, 21
Württemberg, 25, 58, 101, 102,
    106
Württemberg-Baden, 87, 99, 107,
    108
Württemberg-Hohenzollern, 108
Württembergischer Landjäger, 27

Y

Yalta, 36, 57, 97

Z

Zeitschrift für Politik, 145
Zivilcourage, 149